THE UNOFFICIAL LEGO® TECHNIC
BUILDER'S GUIDE

THE UNOFFICIAL LEGO® TECHNIC BUILDER'S GUIDE

Paweł "Sariel" **Kmieć**

no starch press

Printed in China

First printing

16 15 14 13 12   1 2 3 4 5 6 7 8 9

ISBN-10: 1-59327-434-3
ISBN-13: 978-1-59327-434-4

Publisher: William Pollock
Production Editor: Alison Law
Cover Illustration: Eric "Blakbird" Albrecht
Interior Design: Octopod Studios
Developmental Editor: Tyler Ortman
Technical Reviewer: Eric "Blakbird" Albrecht
Copyeditor: Julianne Jigour
Compositors: Lynn L'Heureux and Riley Hoffman
Proofreader: Paula L. Fleming
Indexer: BIM Indexing & Proofreading Services

Figures 3-17, 3-18, 3-19, 3-20, 3-21, 3-22, 3-23, 3-24, 3-44, 4-5, 6-11, 10-24, 11-29, 11-37, 14-16, 16-4, 19-3, 19-4, 19-8, 19-14, and 19-15 by Eric "Blakbird" Albrecht

Figure 15-13 by Jano Gallo, used under Creative Commons Attribution-ShareAlike 3.0 Unported

Blueprint images (Figures 19-2, 19-5, 19-6, 19-18, 19-19, 19-20, 20-1, 20-6, 20-7, 20-8, and 20-9) are royalty-free images purchased from The-Blueprints.com.

Author's photo by Magda Andrzejewska

The following software has been used for illustrations:
    MLCAD by Michael Lachmann
    LDView by Travis Cobbs and Peter Bartfai
    LPub by Kevin Clague

For information on book distributors or translations, please contact No Starch Press, Inc. directly:
No Starch Press, Inc.
38 Ringold Street, San Francisco, CA 94103
phone: 415.863.9900; fax: 415.863.9950; info@nostarch.com; www.nostarch.com

Library of Congress Cataloging-in-Publication Data
A catalog record of this book is available from the Library of Congress.

about the author

Paweł "Sariel" Kmieć is a LEGO Technic enthusiast based in Warsaw, Poland. A prolific blogger and model builder, Sariel's LEGO creations have been featured in many magazines and the world's most popular LEGO blogs, and have even prompted the LEGO Group to use his help in developing some of its products. Sariel is a guest blogger for the official LEGO Technic website and is a 2012 LEGO Ambassador for Poland. He is YouTube's most viewed LEGO Technic builder. Check out his models and more at *http://sariel.pl/*.

about the tech reviewer

Eric "Blakbird" Albrecht is an aerospace engineer living in the northwest United States. He maintains the globally known Technicopedia, in which he documents the history of every Technic model beginning in 1977, all of which are on display on his shelves. Eric is also an avid user of LEGO CAD tools and has generated over 1,000 photo-realistic renders of official models and MOCs (My Own Creations). He has created dozens of sets of instructions for some of the best Technic MOCs from around the world, averaging 1,500 parts each. Check out his site at *http://www.technicopedia.com*.

brief contents

contents in detail

PART I   BASICS

4
axles, bushes, and joints

PART II   MECHANICS

5
gears and power transmission basics

PART IV   ADVANCED MECHANICS

PART V MODELS

foreword

The LEGO brick was voted "Toy of the Century" by *Fortune* magazine and later by the British Association of Toy Retailers, beating longtime favorites like the Teddy Bear. Why? Playing with LEGO comes with joy and fun but also with real educational values. And more than any other toy, LEGO allows our imagination to take physical form—if you're reading this book, you likely know exactly what I mean.

LEGO Technic expands the traditional LEGO System by providing a challenging building experience. The three core concepts behind LEGO Technic—Authenticity, Functionality, and Challenging building (which the LEGO Group calls its *AFC* strategy)—let you create authentic, real-life models with lots of working functions.

Modern LEGO Technic sets address these principles more effectively than ever, and the challenge is by design. But many builders find freely building their own models difficult in this system, and that's where this book comes in. It is fun to create with Technic, but it can also be quite complex.

Paul has unscrambled the secrets of Technic building in the best way I can imagine, and I'm delighted that his ideas are now available to all LEGO builders and fans. You will find many examples, tricks, and practical advice on assembling sturdy and useful mechanisms. You'll also find detailed information on the history and evolution of LEGO Technic elements, for example, the LEGO pneumatic system's evolution.

The Unofficial LEGO Technic Builder's Guide will certainly help introduce many young builders to the creative possibilities of LEGO Technic. If you're a beginner, you're going to read the introductory chapters and start getting excited. . . . If you're an intermediate practitioner, it will take you to the next level. If you're already an advanced builder, this book has those extra gems and inspiration to push you even higher. Despite my own considerable experience, I still learned quite a bit about Technic from reading the book. I hope that you will too.

I got to know Paul and his work in 2007, not long after I decided to embrace the task of writing a blog devoted to the LEGO Technic theme, called TechnicBRICKs. His ingenious mind revealed itself when he introduced some of his own mechanisms to the fan community, like the pneumatic autovalve, the PF Speed Remote add-on that makes it more intuitive and easier to use, and the gorgeous automated turn signals used in his large trucks, to name just a few.

In this book you'll see building techniques through the eyes of one of the most experienced builders. Although Paul has no formal technical education (he is a linguist by education and an artist in the broadest sense of the word), his interest in mechanics and experience with LEGO bricks shows the unique educational value of the Technic brick. Moreover, he has a constant stream of ideas for new models always flowing from his fingers. All of this makes him one of the most prolific LEGO builders. Paul's models include construction machinery, cars, buggies, bikes, realistic hot rods, large trucks, tanks, and much more. In many of these, he uses a kind of realistic Model Team style taken to the extreme: carefully crafted aesthetics, plenty of internal functions, and infinite details. And this is probably his best ability, to turn the extraordinary into ordinary. I can safely say that Paul stands at the forefront of the LEGO Technic builders.

I hope you find this book valuable in your constructions and an excellent reference in your challenges ahead.

Fernando Correia
Editor in Chief, TechnicBRICKs.com
Lisbon, 2012

preface

The book you're about to read has been created with a simple goal: to teach you everything I've learned about building with LEGO Technic over the last 20 years. Of course, *everything* turned out to be more than a single book can possibly include, and certain omissions were necessary. The book was written with a modern builder in mind—somebody with access to today's LEGO sets—but also includes some material for those who have a history with older sets. If you're an adult rediscovering the joy of building with little plastic pieces, you'll find plenty of help and inspiration in these pages.

I encourage you to explore on your own the topics I had to omit from this book. These primarily consist of various dead ends in the history of LEGO Technic development and some extremely specialized modern elements. LEGO MIND-STORMS and NXT kits are barely mentioned, as there are many other books dedicated to them.

Rather than giving you building instructions for complete LEGO models, this guide attempts to equip you for your own adventure with LEGO Technic. It does so by introducing the principles that make LEGO constructions work, and by showing you component mechanisms, such as transmissions or suspension systems, which you can then incorporate into your own unique creations. LEGO sets usually provide you with complete instructions and no explanation of *how things work*. I decided to take the opposite approach. I strongly believe that playing with LEGO is about unleashing your own creativity, and not about following instructions.

Please do not consider any construction you find in this book to be a final or definitive design. There is always room for tinkering and improvements: As a matter of fact, some of the constructions shown in this guide make deliberate use of basic LEGO pieces, to help those who try to build with limited LEGO resources. If you are lucky enough to have newer, more sophisticated pieces at hand, do not hesitate to experiment with upgrades. If your collection is modest, remember that creative thinking can overcome nearly any limitation.

This guide uses BrickLink's part numbers, part names, and color names. I decided to rely on BrickLink (*http://www.bricklink.com/*) not only because it's the largest and most accurate database of parts but also because its catalog of pieces serves as the de facto marketplace. Any piece or set you find at BrickLink can be purchased with just a few clicks, no matter where you live.

It's my most sincere wish that this book lives up to your expectations. But remember that it only gives you tools to explore—it's up to you to provide the rest. Creating something new and seeing it work the way you intended it to is far more rewarding than building even the coolest LEGO set ever released. Enjoy creating.

Have fun !

Sariel

acknowledgments

While writing this book, I had the privilege of receiving an amazing amount of selfless and unwavering support from the LEGO fan community. I was able to count on a number of prominent creators whose help and expertise improved this book considerably. Most of all, I want to thank Eric "Blakbird" Albrecht for his patience in correcting me, for his insight, and for his discerning remarks, which could easily constitute another book. I also want to thank Philippe "Philo" Hurbain, who came to my rescue repeatedly, and whose enormous (and free) body of work is of immense value to any LEGO Technic builder. And I'm sure I would never have had a chance to write this book without Fernando "Conchas" Correia and his TechnicBRICKs blog, where he featured my creations many times, allowing me to gain recognition and to get in touch with our worldwide community.

I want to thank my parents, who started all of this over 20 years ago by choosing the best toy of all for their kid, without even vaguely suspecting what it would eventually lead to.

Many thanks go to the talented builders who have inspired me, helped me, or contributed to this book in some other way, including Paul "Crowkillers" Boratko, Jetro de Château, Jennifer Clark, Kris Kelvin, Arjan "Konajra" Kotte, Peer "Mahjqa" Kreuger, Erik Leppen, David Luders, Marek "M_Longer" Markiewicz, Emil "Emilus" Okliński, Marcin "Mrutek" Rutkowski, Ingmar Spijkhoven, and Maciej "dmac" Szymański.

I'm also grateful to Poland's LEGO community, the LUGPol, for sticking with me through good and bad; for being home to many awesome and inspiring builders, characters, and creations; for always pushing me to try harder; and for showing me that there is a whole LEGO world beyond the Technic line.

Special thanks go to Monica Pedersen and Gaute Munch from the LEGO Group, who have shown me that even a big company can have a very human face.

I also owe big thanks to Tyler Ortman, Alison Law, and the rest of the No Starch Press crew for putting their faith in an unproven author with a challenging plan.

Last but not least, I want to thank the many people who have been following my work for years, showing their interest through conversation, suggestions and challenges. I hope this book will be as rewarding to you as your support is to me.

PART I

basics

1

basic concepts

This chapter explains the basic concepts we'll be exploring as we build. Note that it aims for strictly practical knowledge. Its goal is to get you acquainted with the laws of physics involved in building working LEGO mechanisms, not to cover everything a practicing engineer or physicist needs to know. So let's get started with the basics.

speed

Speed describes how fast an object moves. When you think of speed, you likely think about the distance a vehicle can travel within a certain unit of time. We call this *linear speed*, and we will be measuring it in kilometers per hour (kph).

But there's another type of speed, called *rotational speed*, which tells us how fast an object rotates. We'll need to understand rotational speed, as most LEGO mechanisms are powered by spinning axles, whose rotary motion is transformed into a vehicle's linear speed using wheels or tank treads. Rotational speed is measured in rotations per minute (RPM). Various types of LEGO motors deliver different RPM, from less than 20 RPM to more than 1,000 RPM.

torque

Torque describes the turning force applied to an object. For example, when a LEGO motor drives an axle, it's applying torque to that axle. The more torque a motor applies, the stronger the rotation and the more resistance it takes to stop the motor. A motor that has enough torque to drive a 1 kg vehicle, for instance, might be stopped when trying to drive a 2 kg vehicle.

In LEGO Technic, the torque of LEGO motors can be measured in units called Newton centimeters (N•cm). The torque available from a motor is constant for a given power source: For example, the weakest LEGO motors provide 0.5 N•cm of torque, while the strongest ones provide 16.7 N•cm. The situation is different when you drive a mechanism manually—the amount of torque is variable and depends on how much physical strength you apply.

Understanding torque is crucial to understanding the capability of motors and the mechanisms they drive, as well as the limits of LEGO pieces. High torque creates stress that can damage and destroy LEGO pieces. We will learn how to prevent such damage in Chapter 11. Even more importantly, we'll explore the relationship between torque and rotational speed.

power

In this book, *power* refers to *mechanical power*, which is the product of torque and rotational speed. So torque multiplied by speed gives mechanical power, which is normally measured in watts (W). LEGO motors provide various degrees of power depending on their type, from 0.021 W to 2.38 W. While the concept of power is fairly complex, we will be using it mainly as a faster way to say "speed and torque together."

The power of a particular LEGO motor is affected by the *voltage* of its power source (that is, its battery). Most modern LEGO motors are meant to be powered at 9V. While they can run at a lower voltage with lower power, higher voltage can damage them.

friction

When two or more surfaces make contact and slide against each other, friction is a force that resists their motion. You'll see friction whenever two LEGO pieces are in contact and moving at different speeds. This, in turn, means that every LEGO mechanism is affected by friction, which we have to overcome when we drive a mechanism. Friction dissipates some of the input force we've applied to the system, thus reducing both torque and speed.

The amount of friction increases as parts press against each other harder, and it also depends on the type of surface: Smooth, firm surfaces generate less friction than rough, soft ones. Friction can be decreased by separating the surfaces with a lubricating medium, such as a grease.

When building LEGO mechanisms, some notable points of friction are between two meshed gears, between a rotating axle and a piece with a pin hole that houses it, and between wheels and a surface they're rolling on. Large amounts of friction, resulting from a large number of moving parts, can render a mechanism useless and wear down or even damage LEGO pieces. (Of course, frictional forces are also present in static, nonmoving connections between LEGO pieces, which is why they stick together.)

traction

Traction, also called grip, describes the maximum frictional force that can be produced between two surfaces before they slip. We will be using the term when discussing tires—tires with good traction don't slip over a surface as easily as tires with poor traction.

Traction depends primarily on the hardness and shape of the tires as well as the type of material that the tires are made of. For example, rubber tires always have better traction than solid plastic wheels because rubber is soft and sticky compared to hard plastic. The differences in shape come down to the profile of the tires and their type of tread. Traction is better when a tire contacts the road's surface over a large area, and a tire's profile and tread determine how much of a given type of surface it contacts. As Figure 1-1 shows, tires that have a flat profile and a small, shallow tread have a larger area of contact on flat, smooth surfaces than tires that have a round profile and a large, deep tread.

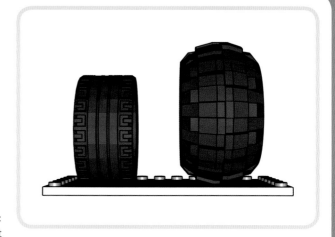

Figure 1-1: A tire with a flat profile and small tread (left) has better contact with a flat surface than a tire with a round profile and large tread (right).

On the other hand, tires with a round profile and a large, deep tread have better contact with irregular, loose, or muddy surfaces. This is why the first type of tire is typical of sports cars designed for roads, while the latter type of tire is typical of off-road cars designed for rough terrain. Finally, the width of the tires also matters simply because wider tires can contact surface over a larger area.

In most cases, you want your tires to provide as much traction as possible. One exception is when you want your tires to slip, for example, to make your vehicle drift. The LEGO 8366 Supersonic RC set comes with two sets of rear tires: one with rubber tires for regular driving and one with solid plastic for drifting.

rolling resistance

Rolling resistance describes the resistance generated by rolling an object on a surface, and it is particularly important for wheels. Solid wheels have similar rolling resistance, but for wheels with tires, it varies a lot depending on the tires' characteristics.

Tires that are soft and wide, such as the one shown in Figure 1-2, generate more rolling resistance than tires that are hard and narrow. The resistance also depends on the vehicle's weight because weight deforms the tires, increasing their rolling resistance. Finally, the type of surface the

Figure 1-2: Typical off-road tires, which are soft and bulging, have particularly high rolling resistance. Apparently, they make up for it with their flavor.

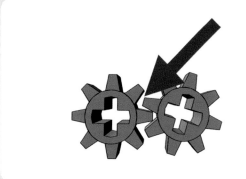

Figure 1-3: Backlash, in the form of a gap between the teeth of two mating gears, is particularly large for 8-tooth gears.

wheels are in contact with affects the resistance. Smooth, flat, firm surfaces—such as asphalt or glass—lower the rolling resistance, while loose, boggy, soft, and sticky surfaces—such as sand, mud, or grass—increase it.

Rolling resistance is an important factor when choosing wheels and tires, but it is usually less important than traction. There are only a few types of LEGO tires whose rolling resistance is a serious concern, so in most cases you will find improved traction worth a little more resistance. Good traction almost always comes at the cost of extra rolling resistance.

backlash

Backlash describes the gaps between mating components, such as two gears, as shown in Figure 1-3. Practically every LEGO Technic connection has some backlash, and too much backlash is highly undesirable. When you start, stop, or reverse a mechanism, backlash will create a delay in the motion between its input and output. High backlash results in a longer delay, making the whole mechanism inaccurate and sluggish.

While building, remember that the backlash of many moving parts sums up, meaning that it accumulates over the entire mechanism. So a mechanism with four gears will have more backlash than a mechanism with two gears. One way to reduce backlash is to make your mechanism as simple as possible, and another is to replace high-backlash components, such as gears, with low-backlash ones, such as pneumatic cylinders (see Chapter 9) or linear actuators (see Chapter 13).

efficiency

Efficiency describes how much of the power we apply to a mechanism is actually used and how much is dissipated to forms of friction. It is usually expressed as a percentage: For example, a 50 percent efficiency means that a mechanism effectively uses half of the power delivered to it and the other half is lost.

In LEGO mechanisms, efficiency is generally low because LEGO pieces are simple and lack sophisticated mechanical solutions designed to lower friction, such as ball bearings. It is difficult to accurately measure the efficiency of any LEGO mechanism. Instead, we should focus simply on keeping the friction as low as possible.

The only way to improve efficiency is to reduce friction in our mechanism, and the simplest way to do reduce friction is to limit the number of moving parts. Weight is also an important factor because heavy moving parts generate more friction than light ones; size is a factor, too, as larger parts are heavier. In general, the simpler and lighter the mechanism, the more efficient it is.

vehicular concepts

At this point, we should have a good understanding of the basic physics and engineering concepts that apply to various constructions. Next we'll focus on issues related to vehicles. Since vehicles form the vast majority of both LEGO Technic sets and custom builds, we will be referring to these concepts throughout this book.

driveshaft

A driveshaft is a mechanical component, usually an axle, that transmits power from the motor to a mechanism. It connects—sometimes not directly—two components: one that *generates* power and a second that *receives* it. A typical car, for example, has a single driveshaft that connects its gearbox to one or both of its axles. In other words, the driveshaft connects the engine indirectly, through a gearbox, to a *receiving mechanism*, which in this case is the wheels.

Driveshafts can also incorporate universal joints or extendable sections, as shown in Figure 1-4. These incorporated pieces allow for variations in the alignment of and distance between the power input and the receiving mechanism.

drivetrain

The drivetrain, also called a powertrain, is a group of components that generate power and deliver it in a vehicle. This group typically includes the motor, transmission (also known as a gearbox), driveshaft, axles, and final drive (the wheels, tracks, or propellers). While components in the middle of a drivetrain may vary—for example, there may be no transmission—the ends of the drivetrain remain the same: One is the propulsion motor (or motors), and the other is the final drive.

driveline

The driveline indicates the three final components: the driveshaft, axle, and final drive. In other words, the driveline is the drivetrain minus the motor and gearbox. If you consider a regular bicycle, the drivetrain would include the bicyclist (acting as a motor), pedals, gears, the chain, and the rear wheel as the final drive. The driveline, on the other hand, would include just the chain and the rear wheel.

steering lock

When we talk about the steering lock in this book, we aren't referring to a physical lock you put on your steering wheel to prevent theft. The steering lock is the maximum steering angle—that is, the maximum angle to which wheels on a steered axle can be turned. Usually the greater the steering lock, the better, as it allows the vehicle to make tighter turns. However, a very large steering lock can be undesirable because it enables the vehicle's direction to change very rapidly, making the vehicle less stable and exerting significant stress on parts of the steering system. See Figure 1-5 for a model with a large steering lock.

turning radius

The turning radius, also called the turning circle, is the radius of the smallest U-turn the vehicle can make. Note that a vehicle's bodywork often overhangs the wheels, and the turning radius can be measured including its frame (a *wall-to-wall* turning radius) or without the frame, taking only the wheels into consideration (a *curb-to-curb* turning radius).

The turning radius is affected by several factors, including the maximum steering angle, the wheelbase, and the number of steered axles. The smaller this radius is, the better for the vehicle, as it can maneuver within tighter spaces. Note that certain vehicles, like tanks and other tracked vehicles, can turn in place, meaning they have a turning radius of zero.

Figure 1-4: An extendable driveshaft section, consisting of two axles with three wedge belt wheels (the thin grey discs) and another three axles inside them. The three axles transmit rotation to all the discs, and these axles are able to slide through the single disc shown on the right, effectively changing the driveshaft's length even as it spins.

Figure 1-5: My reach stacker model had a rear axle (right) with a particularly large steering lock, just like that of a real vehicle. Designed to stack containers in ports' loading areas, reach stackers need to be able to maneuver in limited space.

FWD, RWD, 4×4, 4WD, and AWD

FWD, RWD, 4×4, 4WD, and AWD are abbreviations referring to the arrangement of driven axles in a vehicle. For example, a car with only the front axle driven has *FWD*, or *front-wheel drive*, while a car with only the rear axle driven has *RWD*, or *rear-wheel drive*.

A 4×4 vehicle is an automobile whose four wheels are all driven. With LEGO 4×4 vehicles, we are dealing with a so-called *4WD*, or *four-wheel drive*, where the motor's power is split equally among all wheels. Real 4×4 vehicles can also have something called *AWD*, or *all-wheel drive*, where the power distribution is constantly adjusted to driving conditions by electronic components—something that is extremely difficult to achieve with LEGO pieces.

Note that a third number can be added to the 4×4 description. For example, an SUV or Jeep is 4×4×2, which means four wheels total, four wheels driven, and two wheels steered. Such descriptions are particularly important for multi-axle vehicles, such as mobile cranes and armored personnel carriers, which have many axles driven and steered. For instance, many small armored personnel carriers are 6×6×4, which stands for six wheels, all of which are driven and four of which are steered.

weight distribution

Weight distribution, and in particular whether a vehicle is front heavy or rear heavy, can greatly affect the performance of a vehicle.

Weight distribution primarily affects traction and thus handling. Imagine a car with two axles: one steered in front and one driven in rear. If this car is more front-heavy, it will have better steering traction because its front wheels will have more weight on them. If this car is more rear-heavy, it will have better acceleration because its rear wheels will have better traction with more weight on them.

In four-wheeled vehicles, weight distribution is described as *number:number* or *number/number*. For example, a 40:60 weight distribution means that 40 percent of the vehicle's weight rests on the front axle and 60 percent on the rear one. In off-road cars with 4WD, 50:50 weight distribution is considered ideal, while high-performance race cars with central engines often have more weight in the back.

Weight distribution is also important for tracked vehicles. Since tracks have poor traction on smooth surfaces, weight distribution significantly affects how a tracked vehicle turns and how it climbs obstacles. For example, a front-heavy tracked vehicle won't be able to turn in place because its center of rotation will be moved forward. But this type of vehicle will be good at climbing up hills because its front end will have better traction.

center of gravity

The center of gravity is the central point of an object's weight distribution. It can be located in the actual center of the object—in the case of a solid ball, for example—or elsewhere. The location of the center of gravity determines the object's likelihood of falling over, which is greater for objects with a high center of gravity than for ones with a low center of gravity. In other words, the low center of gravity makes objects more stable.

With LEGO vehicles, the center of gravity is greatly affected by the location of a vehicle's heaviest components, such as battery boxes, and it should always be as low as possible. This is why, for example, builders of off-road vehicles, which need to be very stable, always try to locate battery boxes low in the chassis.

ground clearance

Ground clearance, also called ride height or simply clearance, is the distance between the underside of the chassis and a flat, level surface the vehicle is standing on. It determines the height of obstacles the vehicle can drive over without scraping them with the chassis, as shown in Figure 1-6. Ground clearance depends primarily on the suspension system.

High ground clearance allows a vehicle to negotiate bigger obstacles but makes it taller and less stable due to a higher center of gravity. Low ground clearance improves stability but reduces the ability to drive over rough terrain. High ground clearance is therefore typical of off-road vehicles, whereas low ground clearance is common in sports cars because they are designed for flat roads and benefit from good stability, which allows them to make turns at higher speeds.

Now that you have these basics down, let's start putting them into practice!

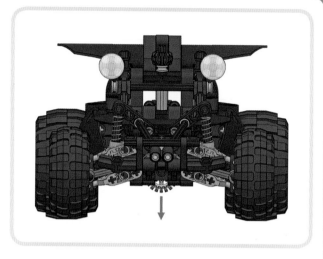

Figure 1-6: The green arrow indicates this simple buggy's ground clearance. Note that the ground clearance is usually measured in the center of the vehicle as seen from front or rear, because this part is most likely to contact obstacles.

2

basic units and pieces

LEGO models and bricks are measured in a fanciful unit called the *stud* rather than in inches or centimeters. One stud equals the width of the smallest brick, which is 8 mm wide. We'll even use the stud to measure LEGO pieces that aren't bricks, like shock absorbers and axles.

When the unit of measurement for a LEGO piece is omitted, you can safely assume that it is the stud—for example, a *1×1 brick*, a *2×2 tile*, and so on. This is how we'll refer to pieces in this book.

NOTE You might also see the stud referred to by other names, such as *module, dot,* or *fundamental LEGO unit (FLU).* The letter *L* is used to indicate length in studs. For example, a 6.5L shock absorber is 6.5 studs long.

LEGO builders generally measure the *height* of their creations, however, in terms of the height of a brick or plate. For example, we say that something is *one brick tall* or *one plate tall.* Note that one brick tall is equal to 9.6 mm, just a bit more than a stud (see Figure 2-1).

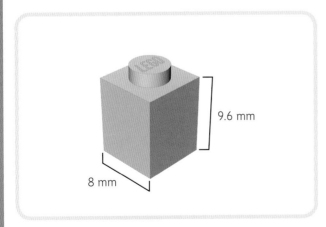

Figure 2-1: A 1×1 brick is 8 mm wide and 9.6 mm tall.

As illustrated in Figure 2-2, LEGO *plates* are only one-third as tall as a brick, meaning that three stacked plates are the same height as one brick.

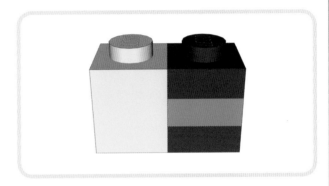

Figure 2-2: A LEGO brick (left) is the same height as three stacked LEGO plates (right).

NOTE The size of the round peg or stud at the top of a brick is not included in its height because the peg is completely hidden inside the brick on top of it. Instead, we measure the height of a brick only from corner to corner.

the Technic brick

As in the classic LEGO system, the basic building block in the Technic system is the *brick*: that easy-to-connect piece that we all know and love. But, as shown in Figure 2-3, Technic bricks are a little different. They have hollow studs, which make them harder to separate and better suited for heavy-duty use. Most Technic bricks also have pin holes centered

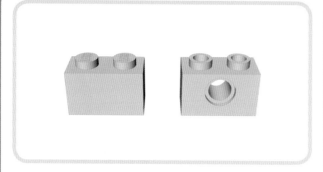

Figure 2-3: A regular 1×2 brick (left) has solid studs and sides, while a Technic 1×2 brick (right) has hollow studs and a center hole.

Figure 2–5: Pin holes (left) allow axles to rotate, while axle holes (right) keep axles from turning.

between the studs: a 1×2 brick has one hole, a 1×4 brick has three holes, and so on. The holes in Technic pieces are vital to the LEGO Technic building system, as they allow you to connect pieces with pins or run axles through them.

Although the holes in most Technic bricks are centered between the studs, you will find variants of 1×1 and 1×2 Technic bricks that have holes aligned with the studs—for example, see Figure 2-4. When the studs are aligned with the holes, the number of holes and studs is equal. Such an arrangement is useful for compact building with densely packed pins and axles, and these pieces can also be used to align pieces by half of a stud.

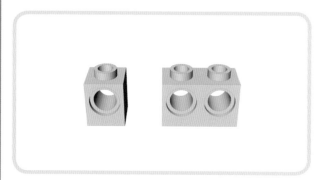

Figure 2-4: Some Technic bricks have holes aligned with the studs.

There are two types of holes in Technic bricks: round *pin holes* and X-shaped *axle holes*. Examine the shape of any LEGO axle, and the purpose of these holes should be obvious: Axles inserted in pin holes can rotate, but axles in axle holes cannot (see Figure 2-5). (Note that only 1×2 Technic bricks have an axle hole.)

pins, for joining and rotating

Pins are critical to building with the Technic system, as they keep bricks and beams together. A pin is a small connector that enters pin holes or axle holes to connect two or more adjacent pieces. As you can see in Figure 2-6, pins vary in length and shape, as well as degree of friction. While simple, pins are indispensable for holding Technic constructions together. The largest Technic sets can include several hundred pins. They're really that important!

Like axles, pins can be used in either pin or axle holes. Unlike axles, each pin has a collar that makes it impossible to push it completely through a hole. For example, the most basic pin is 2 studs long, and each of its ends can be pushed 1 stud deep into a hole but no farther. The long pin, which is 3 studs long, has one end that can be pushed 1 stud deep and another that can be pushed 2 studs deep. The collars on pins keep bricks together, and pin holes are shaped to accommodate them (see Figure 2-7).

Figure 2-6: The most common Technic pins (from left to right: pin, axle pin, long pin, three-quarter pin, and half pin)

collar

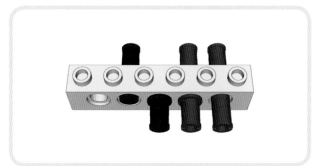

Figure 2-7: Pin holes (from left to right: empty pin hole, two pin holes with pins inserted from opposite sides, and two pin holes with long pins inserted from opposite sides)

Some pins come in two variants: one that can rotate freely inside a pin hole and another that requires some force. The latter type is called a *pin with friction* or a *friction pin*. Different types of pins come in different colors.

You should be able to identify pins with friction by their ridged appearance and behavior, no matter what color they are. Figure 2-8 shows a range of the most common pins in a variety of colors.

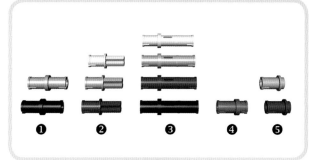

Figure 2-8: A collection of common pins

❶ **pins**   Regular (light grey); friction variant (black).
❷ **axle pins**   Regular (tan, formerly light grey); friction variant (blue).
❸ **long pins**   Regular (tan, formerly light grey); friction variant (blue, formerly black).
❹ **three-quarter pin**   Regular (dark grey); no friction variant available.
❺ **half pins**   Regular (blue, formerly light grey); no friction variant available.

Now that you've been introduced to the most common Technic pins, let's look at some of the less common ones. Figure 2-9 shows a collection of specialized pins. In most cases, they are variations of the basic pins modified to suit specific tasks.

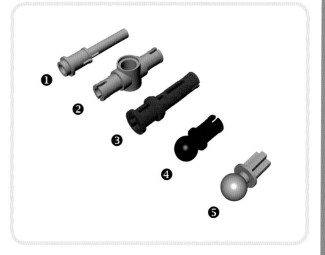

Figure 2-9: A collection of specialized pins

❶ half pin with 2L bar   Regular (light grey); no friction variant available. This pin combines a regular half pin with a 2L shaft, which is of the same thickness as a regular LEGO antenna or bar. As shown in Figure 2-10, a LEGO antenna or bar can fit in the hand of a LEGO minifigure or into the hollow stud on a Technic brick.

Figure 2-10: A LEGO minifigure holds a bar (green) and an antenna (black) in its hands.

❷ long pin with pin hole   Regular (light grey, black, or red); no friction variant available.

❸ long pin with stop bush   Regular variant not available; friction variant exists in a variety of colors. This pin can be used like a regular 2L friction pin, but its bush allows it to be pulled out easily. It is often used in Technic sets to make structural connections that can be removed with ease.

❹ pin with towball   Friction variant (black). This pin usually serves as a mounting point for LEGO links, as shown in Figure 2-11.

Figure 2-11: Two towballs can be linked, for example, to connect suspension parts that move relative to each other.

❺ axle pin with towball   This is a variant of a regular pin with a towball; available in light grey.

beams, the studless alternative

In addition to bricks, the Technic system contains pieces called *beams* or *liftarms*. As shown in Figure 2-12, beams are like bricks reduced to mere pin holes. They come in many sizes and shapes, and some beams even include axle holes.

Figure 2-12: A 1×4 Technic brick (left) and a 1×3 Technic beam (right)

Because they lack regular LEGO studs on top, beams are called *studless*, while bricks and plates are called *studfull* (or *studded*) pieces. The same names—studless and studfull—are also applied to constructions that use mainly one type of piece. For example, you can build a car with a studfull body on a studless chassis. (Chapter 3 describes the differences between studfull and studless pieces in detail; we'll take only a brief look here.)

Many studless pieces come in complex shapes that have no counterpart among the studfull pieces, as you can see in Figure 2-13.

Figure 2-13: Complex studless shapes

While bricks have a 6:5 height-to-width ratio, beams maintain a 7:8 ratio. A simple beam can be up to 15 studs long, but it is always 1 stud (8 mm) wide and 7 mm tall. For example, notice the slight height difference between the 9.6 mm tall brick and the 7 mm tall beam in Figure 2-14.

Figure 2-14: A brick (left) and a beam (right) are not the same height.

Note that the studfull pieces can be connected to the studless ones using pin holes.

Studless pieces are symmetrical: Their tops and bottoms are identical, which makes them much more versatile than bricks, as shown in Figure 2-15. When building with bricks, the orientation of the brick and its studs is important; with beams, it's not.

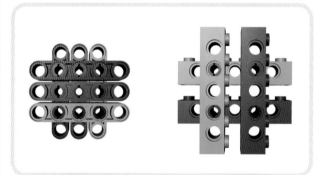

Figure 2-15: A comparison between a construction using beams (left) and one using bricks (right)

Consider that a block of six 1×5 beams connected with pins is symmetrical: It looks the same whether you rotate it 90, 180, or 270 degrees. In comparison, a block of four 1×6 bricks connected with pins is asymmetrical. Rotating it changes the orientation of the bricks and their studs, affecting how you can build onto it.

Studless pieces have nearly ousted studfull ones from LEGO Technic sets, making the use of bricks and plates as measurements of height obsolete. When it comes to measurements, studless pieces offer an advantage because they are orientation independent; therefore, it doesn't matter whether you place them vertically or horizontally.

When speaking in Technic terms, it is common to express height in studs and to measure height using the distance between holes in Technic bricks and beams. Note that these two distances can be aligned using plates. As shown in Figure 2-16, two bricks spaced apart by two plates have exactly 3 studs of distance between their pin holes.

Figure 2-16: The basic rule of alignment for studless and studded pieces: Holes in two bricks separated by two plates are exactly 3 studs apart.

This trick shows how bricks with plates can be repeated at regular intervals to align with beams. For example, in order to have a 5-stud-long space between their pin holes, two bricks need to be spaced apart by seven plates, by a brick and four plates, or by two bricks and one plate, as one brick is three plates tall. Figure 2-17 provides more examples of studless and studfull pieces in alignment.

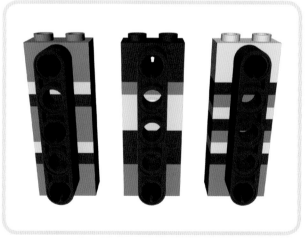

Figure 2-17: More examples of studless and studfull pieces in alignment

The difference between the height of a single stud and the height of a single brick makes 6 stacked bricks exactly 7 studs tall, as shown in Figure 2-18. This relationship is repetitive: 11 stacked bricks are 13 studs tall, and so on.

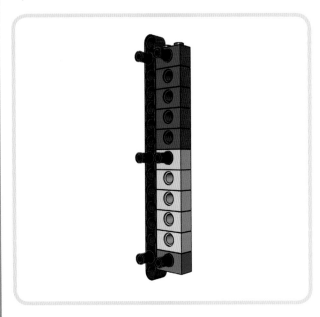

Figure 2-18: Once you connect a brick to a vertical beam, the next connections can be made every 5 stacked bricks.

the half stud as the minimum building unit

While the basic building unit in the world of LEGO is a single stud, some pieces are smaller. For example, plates are one-third of a stud tall, and some beams are one-half of a stud thick. As shown in Figure 2-19, studless pieces that are half a stud thick typically include a lot of axle holes, which makes them useful for creating rigid structures with complex shapes.

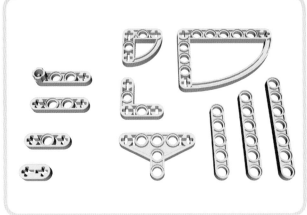

Figure 2-19: Various half-stud-thick pieces

With these pieces, it is possible to use a half stud as the minimum unit, which comes in handy when combining studless structures (normally with odd dimensions) with studfull ones (normally with even dimensions). The pin holes in half-stud-thick pieces won't really fit a regular pin, but a three-quarter pin fits perfectly. Figure 2-20 shows how three-quarter pins can be used to combine half-stud-thick pieces with 1-stud-thick pieces. One end of the three-quarter pin fits perfectly into a half-stud-deep pin hole, while the other end fits perfectly into a 1-stud-deep pin hole.

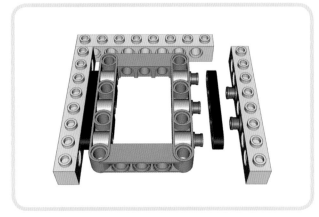

Figure 2-20: Of all Technic pins, the three-quarter pins are best suited to hold half-stud-thick pieces.

Figure 2-21: From left to right: a half pin, a three-quarter pin, and a regular pin used to hold a half-stud-thick beam

Because half pins enter beams only partially, they can easily fall out. On the other hand, three-quarter pins enter the beam completely, securing it firmly in place, and fit inside it entirely with no parts protruding. Regular pins secure beams firmly, too, but they protrude by another half stud, which allows the beam to slide on the protruding part. Figure 2-21 illustrates these three types of pins as they are used to hold a half-stud-thick beam.

two tricks for building with half studs

Figure 2-22: Using a jumper plate to place a brick half a stud off

When building with LEGO bricks, you don't have to use a single stud as your smallest unit: Two techniques allow LEGO bricks to be half a stud off. One technique, shown in Figure 2-22, uses a *jumper plate*, a 1×2 plate with a single centered stud on top, to place a brick half a stud off. Figure 2-23 shows a technique using Technic pins: By inserting one end of a pin into a 1×2 Technic brick with a hole and the other into a 1×1 Technic brick with a hole, you can achieve a half-stud-off alignment.

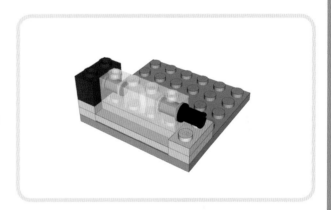

Figure 2-23: Using Technic pins to place a brick half a stud off

3

studless or studfull?

In Chapter 2 we took a peek at the difference between two styles of building with LEGO pieces: studless (using beams) and studfull (using bricks and plates). The two styles are significantly different, and each offers advantages. The styles can also be combined in order to use the best qualities of each technique in a single construction. As a matter of fact, most of today's LEGO Technic sets and *MOCs* (*My Own Creations*, a term builders use for their custom models) use a combination of the two approaches rather than a purely studless or studfull building technique.

The successful builder knows which combination works best for a given construction, which style should serve as its basis, and to what extent the other style should be incorporated. We'll address these issues in this chapter.

First, we'll discuss the pros and cons of each technique and compare one to the other. Then we'll focus on how the two techniques can be combined to bring out the best from both, using official LEGO sets and amateur builders' MOCs (like my Monster Truck, shown in Figure 3-1) as examples.

LEGO evolving

The entire LEGO building system was originally 100 percent studfull. The first studless pieces appeared when the LEGO Technic line was already well developed and initially only complemented the studfull style rather than forming a new one. But as the Technic sets evolved, studless pieces grew very popular, and the studfull pieces were nearly entirely phased out.

Today, most Technic sets are studless, with studfull pieces used to add certain minor details to already mechanically functional and sound constructions. And when you consider the fact that most of the new specialized elements, such as electric motors, pneumatic switches, turntables, and

actuators, are designed specifically to fit the studless style rather than the studfull one, it becomes obvious that studless pieces are of primary importance to Technic today. Learning to build with studless pieces, which is usually more challenging than with studfull ones, is crucial to keeping up with new additions to the Technic system.

But we shouldn't abandon studfull pieces completely. Many amateur Technic builders don't follow the LEGO Group's doctrine, and they continue to publish primarily studfull MOCs that are both very functional and good-looking (like my Kenworth truck, shown in Figure 3-2).

Figure 3-1: My Monster Truck model took the approach of modern LEGO Technic sets: It was almost entirely studless, with studfull pieces used only for minor details, like the grille.

Figure 3-2: My Kenworth Road Train model appeared completely studfull on the outside, despite including an array of Mindstorms NXT elements, which are best suited for studless structures.

studfull building

Technic bricks and regular plates are the basis of the studfull style. Technic bricks differ from regular LEGO bricks (as shown in Figure 3-3) in that they have hollow studs on top and slightly thicker rods inside them.

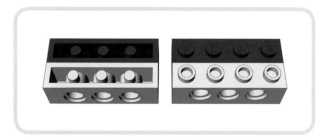

Figure 3-3: Side-by-side comparison of a regular LEGO brick (red) and a LEGO Technic brick (yellow)

Thanks to their altered design, Technic bricks are less likely to come apart when subjected to lateral pressure. (They are still easy to tug apart on purpose.) To make your designs resistant to high torque, you'll need to lock your studfull bricks using pins and other pieces. Studless beams are more space efficient than studfull Technic bricks, as shown in Figure 3-4.

reinforcing studfull constructions

When you add extra pieces to a combination of LEGO pieces to keep them together, you're *reinforcing* them. Technic bricks are usually combined with plates to allow vertical reinforcement. A *brick–two plates–brick* combination is used to ensure proper vertical spacing of the bricks and their pin holes to allow reinforcement with a vertical piece (shown in Figure 3-5). The corner and hinge plates allow for perpendicular connections, as shown in Figure 3-6, or angled connections, as shown in Figure 3-7.

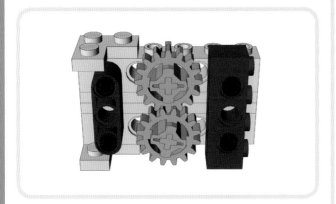

Figure 3-4: Two 1×6 Technic bricks are locked vertically to prevent them from coming apart when high torque is applied to the gears. The little space used by the studless locking piece (left) compared to the studfull one (right) leaves space for plates on the top and bottom of the two bricks and allows the use of bigger gears.

Figure 3-6: Even though the red brick is not reinforced directly, it is kept firmly in place by L-shaped corner plates that are locked with reinforced bricks.

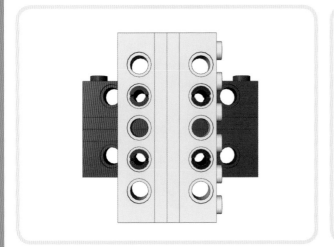

Figure 3-5: The brick–two plates–brick combination makes sure the spacing between bricks allows vertical connection. The addition of plates keeps the pin holes in the bricks exactly 1 stud apart.

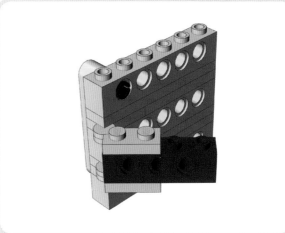

Figure 3-7: Two reinforced hinge plates secure the red Technic brick while allowing it to be set at any angle.

The use of plates as spacers, however, has a disadvantage: It reduces the number of pin holes as compared to an entirely studless structure of the same size, as shown in Figure 3-8. Therefore, studfull structures can house fewer axles and other elements that require pin holes.

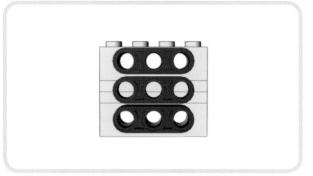

Figure 3-8: As these superimposed images show, the combination of bricks and plates (yellow) not only allows for fewer pin holes than the combination of studless beams (red)—six as compared to nine—but also takes up significantly more space.

In general, studfull constructions are bigger and heavier than studless ones, with a less dense internal structure. They often need to be reinforced, but the resulting structures are very rigid. They are also orientation dependent because of their asymmetry, meaning that the direction their studs face affects the number of possible combinations between pieces.

Additionally, studfull constructions don't work as well with vertical elements; for example, vertical axles are difficult to secure firmly in studfull structures.

studfull advantages

In general, studfull constructions are

* Easy to combine horizontally
* Easy to combine with non-Technic pieces and thus better suited to creative design
* Able to form very rigid constructions with firm horizontal connections
* Able to use a variety of plates for connections at many angles
* Able to create a rigid connection that maintains the relative orientation of the pieces

studfull disadvantages

In general, the disadvantages of studfull connections are that they

* Require reinforcements to prevent vertical separation under torque
* Have pin holes that are distributed less densely, making for bigger constructions
* Are not symmetrical, meaning that their orientation affects how easy they are to combine
* Do not easily fit most of the modern specialized pieces, such as motors and actuators
* Are a poor fit for vertical elements, such as axles and gear wheels
* Are bigger and heavier than studless pieces

studless building

The studless style consists of beams connected with pins, as well as a variety of specialized connectors. Beams are symmetrical, so they can be combined in any orientation, allowing for real three-dimensional building, as shown in Figure 3-9. In most cases, beams are connected with regular Technic pins, but some studless connectors come with integrated pins, as shown in Figure 3-10.

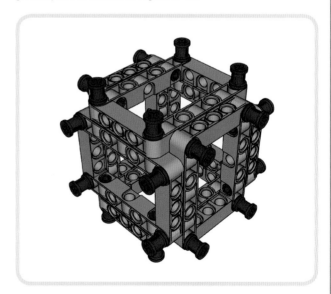

Figure 3-9: This structure, comprised of studless frames connected with pins and bushings, is symmetrical, meaning that it has no definite top or bottom. Unlike studfull structures, it can have axles inserted from any direction.

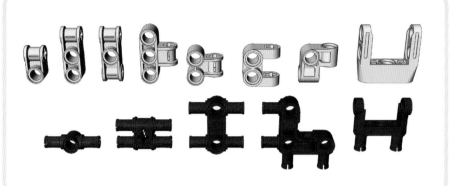

Figure 3-10: While most studless connectors have just pin and axle holes (yellow), some come with integrated pins (red).

creating rigid studless connections

Once connected, studless pieces are much more difficult to separate than bricks and plates, but that doesn't necessarily mean that they are rigid. Since pins are round, any two studless pieces connected with a single pin can oscillate relative to each other. Using pins with friction can make this oscillation a little less likely to occur, but using two or more pins for each connection ensures a truly rigid and static connection.

Figure 3-11 shows the difference between a rigid and nonrigid connection. The advantage of using rigid connections is that a rigid studless structure usually doesn't need additional reinforcement when axles and gears are added, because its pieces remain in place under torque (see Figure 3-12). The axle holes can be used to easily create a rigid connection, as shown in Figure 3-13.

Figure 3-12: Pieces kept together by a rigid connection usually don't need extra reinforcement in order to stay together when torque is applied. These four pieces act as one due to their rigid connections.

Figure 3-11: A comparison of nonrigid (left) and rigid (right) connections between studless pieces. In a nonrigid connection, pieces stay together, but their orientation can change—the yellow beam can be rotated left or right, regardless of the type of pin used for the connection. In a rigid connection, pieces are connected and fixed to each other so that their orientation does not change.

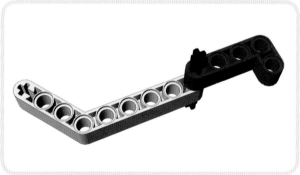

Figure 3-13: When two studless pieces have axle holes, a single axle is enough to create a rigid connection between them. However, such a connection won't be as strong as one made with two or more pins.

Beams are smaller and lighter than bricks, but they are also more elastic. Long beams are therefore more likely to bend or even buckle under a load than long bricks, making it more difficult to create large, rigid studless structures and requiring more complex connections using smaller pieces. Another difficulty comes when you want to create a perpendicular connection between beams without putting one beam on top of the other. It's possible to do so only with a right-angle connector or with a 5×7 studless frame (see Figure 3-14). These frames are quite popular and can also be used as a means of reinforcing builds.

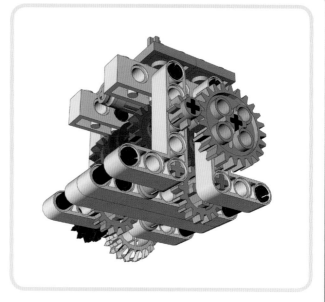

Figure 3-15: I used studless pieces to connect this gearbox. Thus, this build required me to plan which pin holes would be filled with axles and which with pins, to figure out how many connections would be needed to keep the structure rigid, and to carefully select pieces best suited in shape and size.

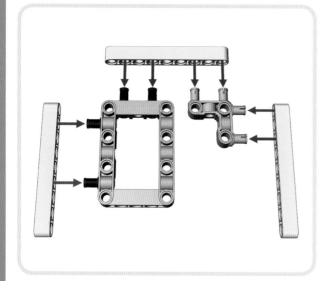

Figure 3-14: Only two types of pieces (light grey) allow you to easily create rigid connections between perpendicular beams on the same level.

The presence of both pin and axle holes means that studless pieces and connectors can also be connected with axles to create bigger, sturdier structures. These sorts of connections require advance planning because of the complexities of the studless technique (see Figure 3-15). When making a structural axle connection, you should have a good idea of the size of your structure and know which pin holes can be used for pins and which have to be reserved for axles. All of these considerations make it more challenging to build with studless pieces. There is even a popular saying that doing so resembles playing chess: The builder needs to plan a couple of steps ahead.

Learning to build primarily with studless pieces allows you to build stronger, sturdier, and more compact structures; hence, studless MOCs are usually more functional, smaller, and lighter than studfull ones. They can give your model a fairly skeletal or "hollow" appearance, though. To avoid this and to create a good-looking studless model (like the Ford GT40 in Figure 3-16), you can add panels and flexible axles, or you can combine a studless interior structure with a studfull body, an idea fully explored later in this chapter.

studless advantages

In general, the advantages of studfull connections are that they

* Are easy to combine in any direction, allowing for three-dimensional building
* Are easy to combine with most modern Technic pieces, such as motors and actuators
* Have more pin holes, making compact construction elements possible
* Rarely need extra reinforcement (if using rigid connections)
* Are smaller and lighter than studfull pieces

Figure 3-16: My Ford GT40 model had a completely studless body. It combined beams, panels, and flexible axles to re-create the flowing lines of the original car. Studless pieces can create shapes that are impossible to model with bricks, at the cost of certain conventions—in this case, panels approximated the shape of the hood in a way not possible with studfull pieces, but there were gaps between them.

studless disadvantages

In general, the disadvantages of studfull connections are that they

* Are less rigid; the largest studless structures have to be complex (or reinforced) to maintain rigidity
* Are harder to combine with non-Technic pieces
* Require at least two pins to create a rigid connection; extra pieces with complex shapes are often needed for rigidity
* Don't always look as good as bricks

combining the styles

Combining the two styles in a clever way can be a key to creating a good-looking, highly functional MOC.

With vehicular models, the chassis and the body are often independent, and we can take advantage of that independence. For example, adding a studless body to a studfull chassis results in a very sturdy but light model, and it's a popular combination when building in large scale, when weight is a serious concern. Adding a studfull body to a studless chassis, on the other hand, results in compact, good-looking models with many functions.

get inspired by Technic sets

Classic LEGO sets ingeniously mixed the two styles before the Technic line evolved into its primarily studless stage. Figures 3-17 through 3-27 provide examples of different styles of building, just to inspire your own creations.

Figure 3-19: The 8448 Super Street Sensation set features a large supercar with a studfull chassis under a studless body. The model combines the rigidity of the studfull pieces, crucial at this size, with the lightness of studless ones.

Figure 3-17: The 8850 Jeep is one of the last completely studfull LEGO Technic sets. Note that while the silhouette of the Jeep is modeled quite well, the bricks facing various directions look somewhat chaotic.

Figure 3-20: The 8466 4×4 Off-Roader set features another large car model, but this time only the center of the chassis remains studfull. This center provides the rigidity needed by the car's impressive suspension system, but the set itself is mainly studless.

Figure 3-18: The 8480 Space Shuttle set does an excellent job modeling the complex shape of the real vessel with bricks and hinge plates. Studless pieces are present, but they don't dominate yet.

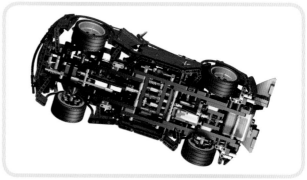

Figure 3-21: The 8070 Super Car set can be considered a direct descendant of the 8448 set. It's completely studless, with a very rigid, although shorter, chassis.

Figure 3-22: The acclaimed 8421 Mobile Crane set is primarily studless, but it uses a combination of bricks and plates for the most heavily loaded part of the boom.

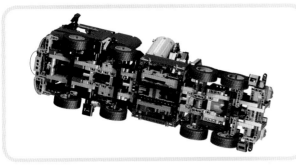

Figure 3-23: The 8285 Crane Truck set is an outstanding achievement in creating a rigid, sturdy studless chassis for a heavy vehicle. Studfull pieces are still there—note the clever use of a Technic brick to attach the license plate under the front bumper.

Figure 3-24: The 8043 Motorized Excavator set has a realistic silhouette created with studless panels, but it also uses studfull ones, mainly tiles and curved slopes, to model its rear end.

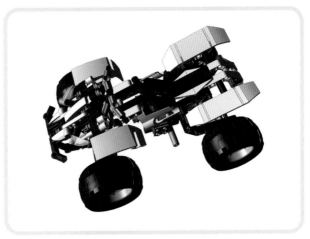

Figure 3-25: Some LEGO panels come in surprising shapes. The 8262 Quad-Bike set proves these panels can be used to excellent aesthetic effect.

Figure 3-26: The 8263 Snow Groomer set uses a number of studfull pieces as cabin details, which are too small to be modeled with studless pieces.

Figure 3-27: The 8048 Buggy set is a great example of creating a small, authentic-looking vehicle using studless pieces only.

While modern LEGO Technic sets use studfull bricks only when necessary, making the distinction between chassis and body quite subtle, MOCs can do something much more dramatic. You can create splendid-looking models by building a studfull body around a studless chassis and then incorporating large numbers of classic LEGO bricks. Many accomplished builders abandon the Technic aesthetic completely and instead aim to make their models look as authentic as possible using any LEGO pieces that suit their needs. This is often called the *Model Team approach*, in reference to the discontinued LEGO Model Team line of large-scale vehicular models. These are Technic models that really "work"—that steer, drive, shift gears, and so on—but don't resemble Technic models. This building technique, possible usually only at medium and large scale, involves covering the Technic structure with bricks and tiles, thus concealing any pin holes, axles, wires, and motors. Figures 3-28 through 3-30 show examples of the Model Team approach, while Figure 3-31 shows a build using studless pieces, panels, and flexible axles as a counterexample.

Figure 3-28: My Humvee model used a studfull body on a mixed chassis. The central bearing structure of the chassis was studfull, and the areas between wheels, where compactness was crucial, were studless. The resulting model was very rigid and compact for its functionality but also very heavy.

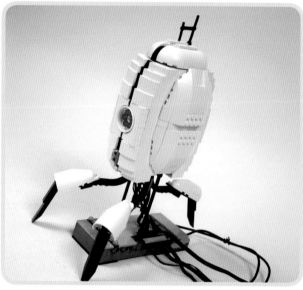

Figure 3-30: My model of a sentry turret from the Portal game used a complex combination of pieces to create an egg-shaped body. The body consisted of five separate studfull parts—front, rear, left, right, and top—attached around a studless skeleton. No existing studless pieces could achieve that body shape.

Figure 3-29: My model of the RG-35 4×4 MRAP vehicle (an armored personnel carrier) combined a completely studless chassis with a fully studfull body. The realistic model was extremely compact, but its densely built body made it top-heavy.

Figure 3-31: My Ford GT40 model used studfull pieces only for minor details of the body and cabin interior. It lacked some rigidity, but it weighed only 2.35 kg while being over 0.5 meter long. It's the counterexample to Model Team builds.

methods for connecting bricks and beams

Now that you've been inspired by models that successfully combine studless and studfull pieces, let's consider the practical aspects of actually connecting the two. In addition to using pins to connect pieces, as shown in Figure 3-32, we can use half pins to work like regular studs, as shown in Figures 3-33 and 3-34.

Some connections are considered incorrect because they align pieces in a manner not equal to a full number of studs, as shown in Figure 3-35. While sturdy, these misaligned pieces will make finishing your model extremely difficult, as the relative spacing of the pieces is no longer 1 full stud.

Electric components are usually designed to fit with either studless or studfull constructions, so incorporating them into mixed models can be challenging. You'll need to think

Figure 3-32: Beams can be easily connected with bricks using pins. Note that we can choose regular Technic bricks (blue) or bricks with centered pin holes (green) to adjust the alignment.

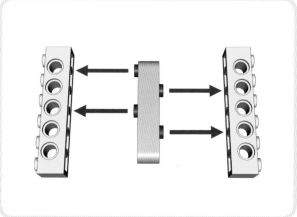

Figure 3-34: The symmetry of the studless pieces allows for complex connections that can grow in several directions.

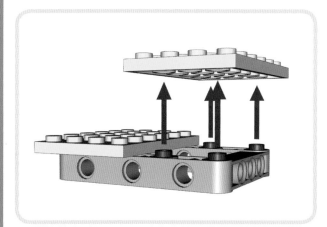

Figure 3-33: When half pins are inserted into pin holes, their tops work just like studs. Bricks or plates can be firmly attached to them, and we can select their exact alignment by carefully choosing the positions of our half pins.

Figure 3-35: This connection, with studs inserted into the beam's pin holes, is sturdy but considered incorrect. This is because—unlike in the previous examples—the spacing between the bricks' pin holes is not equal to a full number of studs. In terms of LEGO units, the bricks are misaligned.

creatively to secure these mismatched elements into your constructions. The Power Functions IR receiver (Figure 3-36), Medium motor (Figure 3-37), and switch (Figure 3-38) are the most common examples. You'll learn more about the Power Functions system in Chapter 13.

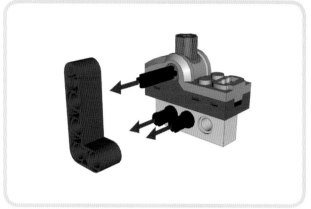

Figure 3-38: The Power Functions switch is easily connected to studfull pieces, but creating a rigid connection with a studless piece is more challenging.

even vs. odd

The final challenge is matching the two styles' widths. Studfull pieces are designed for even-numbered spacings of 2 or 4 or 6 studs, and so on. Studless pieces are designed for odd spacings, 3 or 5 or 7 studs. This difference raises difficulties when combining the two styles—for example, a studless chassis is in most cases an odd width, but a studfull body around it is easier to build at an even width. Of course length and height often also require matching, but in practice width is usually the primary challenge, because the left and right sides of most models are symmetrical. In other words, making a model wider or shorter requires changing its central part, while length and height can be adjusted by adding pieces at the top or back of the model.

A pair of half-stud-wide liftarms (shown in blue in Figure 3-39) are well suited for matching a single stud difference in width. Other pieces and connectors designed to overcome this spacing problem are shown in Figures 3-40 to 3-44.

Figure 3-36: With its plate base, the Power Functions IR receiver is easily connected to studfull pieces. For studless connections, we have the option of using pins or half pins (as studs), shown above.

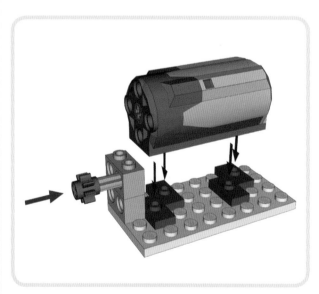

Figure 3-37: Jumper plates (blue) can be used to align the Power Functions Medium motor to studfull pieces.

Figure 3-39: Half-stud-wide beams (blue) and three-quarter pins (dark grey) can be used to create a very firm connection between pieces of even and odd width.

Figure 3-40: Three types of studless connectors created specifically to handle a half-stud difference

Figure 3-42: Connectors (yellow) used to align a 6-stud-long piece (red) to the center of a 5-stud-long structure (blue)

Figure 3-41: Connectors (yellow) used to align a 6-stud-long piece (red) to the center of a 1-stud-long piece (blue)

Figure 3-43: A combination of two connectors (yellow) used to align a 6-stud-long piece (red) to the center of a 7-stud-long structure (blue)

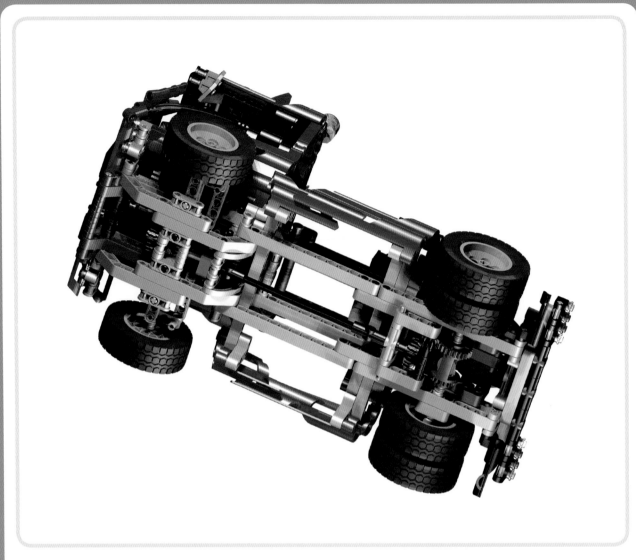

Figure 3-44: The 8436 Truck set, with a studless chassis built around a 4-stud-wide differential, is a great example of combining structures of even and odd width. The use of the adjusting connectors in this set creates a very rigid yet light structure.

Depending on where and when your adventure with LEGO Technic started, you may be unfamiliar with one building style or the other. The best way to understand how an unfamiliar style works is by playing with a LEGO set that uses it extensively. If this proves difficult, remember that there is nothing wrong with sticking to the system you know and like. After all, innovation is quite often driven by our creative constraints!

axles, bushes, and joints

We've already covered most of the basic LEGO Technic pieces. In this chapter, we discuss three other popular pieces: axles, bushes, and universal joints. While all of these elements can be used to transmit drive, they can also be used as structural elements in your builds. Let's take a look.

axles

Axles are one of the most basic and crucial pieces in LEGO Technic. They have a very special property: Depending on the shape of the hole they're put through, axles can either rotate inside other pieces or remain fixed to them (at the same time locking them together), as Figure 4-1 shows.

Axles have two essential tasks: transferring drive and structural reinforcement. The first task requires axles to rotate freely and to be connected to a motor, either directly or through gears, axle joiners, or other pieces.

The task of reinforcing requires axles to remain fixed relative to other pieces, which necessitates an axle hole. It is not uncommon to use an axle exclusively for holding together pieces at fixed angles, as shown in Figure 4-2.

Figure 4-1: A regular axle put through two Technic bricks: The red brick has an X-shaped axle hole that locks the axles, while the green brick has a pin hole that allows the axle to rotate freely.

Figure 4-2: A 5-stud-long axle connecting five other pieces. All the pieces are fixed to the axle, and the axle alone keeps them at fixed angles.

It is also possible to use an axle for both tasks at once—the axle can transfer drive through pieces while at the same time keeping other pieces locked to it. Such a combination is shown in Figure 4-3. Note that any axle that holds pieces together is subjected to structural stress, which adds friction to it. This will matter when you use the axle to transfer drive.

There are three categories of axles, each suitable for a different purpose. They are standard axles, modified axles, and flexible axles.

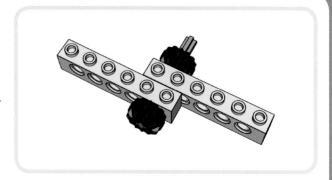

Figure 4-3: A 5-stud-long axle used to keep two bricks (yellow) together between two gears (black). The axle can rotate inside the bricks, and the gears' rotation can be used to transfer drive.

standard axles

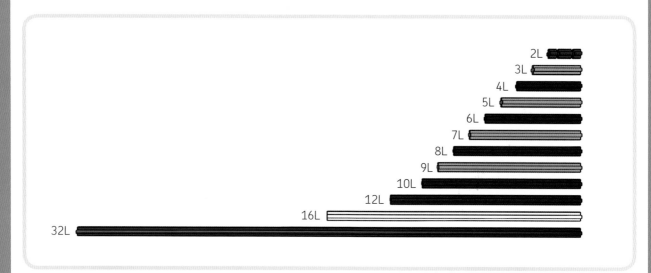

Standard axles come in 12 variants. At first only axles of even length existed, and they were all black. Odd-width axles were later introduced to accommodate the studless system; initially, these axles were also black, but they were later changed to light grey in order to provide a simple distinction between odd and even lengths. Following is a description of various axle lengths and their colors.

2L   Notched to make pulling it out of other pieces easier; primarily red, less often black. There once was a smooth variant of this length.

3L   Primarily light grey, less often black or red.

4L   Primarily black; rare variants in a number of other colors.

5L   Primarily light grey, less often black.

6L   Primarily black, less often light grey; rare variants in a number of other colors.

7L   Primarily light grey.

8L   Primarily black.

9L   Latest variant; available only in light grey.

10L   Primarily black; rare variant in green.

12L   Primarily black, less often red; rare variants in a number of other colors.

16L   Exclusively white. This axle is noticeably more elastic than any other length; it can easily bend and unbend.

32L   Primarily black, less often yellow.

modified axles

Modified axles belong in two groups: threaded axles and axles with stops. Threaded axles are black, come in 4L and 10L variants (top two axles, above), and went out of use in LEGO Technic sets circa 1990. Along with threaded nuts to hold their ends, threaded axles work as bolts to hold parts together. They have a very small cross section and will break if used to transmit torque. Given how rare and expensive they are, builders should be careful not to misuse them.

Axles with stops, on the other hand, are newer and have many practical applications. The stops can't go through a pin hole or an axle hole, so they can be used to prevent undesired sliding of the axle. All four variants of axles with stops used to come in dark grey, but the first variant is now produced in dark tan only.

3L   Has a special kind of stop that ends with a hollow stud, which actually makes the axle a little longer than

3 studs and allows us to connect studded pieces to its end. The end with the stud can also be inserted into a pin hole, which makes the axle rotate with extra friction.

4L   Has a standard, smooth stop that fits entirely inside a pin hole.

5.5L   Has a midpoint stop located 1 stud away from one end (and therefore 4.5 studs away from the other); has a half-stud-long section without grooves adjacent to the stop on the longer side. Although its extra half stud of length often makes it difficult to fit into a structure, it has interesting applications. Figure 4-4 shows one of them: The axle is inserted into a brick so that it protrudes by 1 stud on one side and its stop secures it from sliding through the brick to the other side. This way, the axle won't slide out with the wheel (for example, while making a tight turn), and the wheel can be driven using the gear.

8L   Identical to the 4L variant, only longer.

Figure 4-4: Using the 5.5L axle with stop

flexible axles

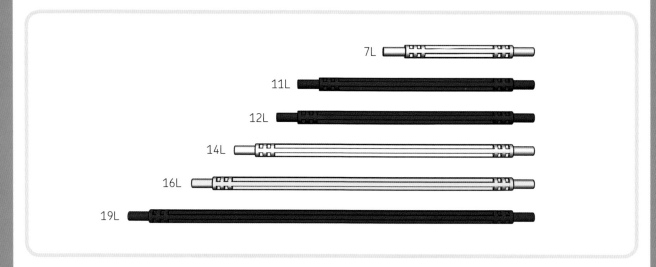

Flexible axles, also called soft axles, are made of soft material and are easily bent without incurring damage. While they can be put through a pin hole, their ends prevent them from being put through an axle hole. Each end has a 1-stud-long protrusion that is less thick than a full stud. The protrusions are most often inserted into half pins, which are then inserted into pin holes to anchor the axle. The axles come in many colors and six variants that vary only by length: 7L, 11L, 12L, 14L, 16L, and 19L.

Flexible axles have few practical or structural uses: It's extremely difficult to use them to transfer drive or to hold anything together. They are also too soft to act as springs, although they can be used instead of shock absorbers to stabilize pendular suspensions. They are most often used as decorative elements, bent to form various arches. Their flexibility makes them popular in LEGO Technic supercars (as Figure 4-5 shows), where they form mudguards, windshield edges, bumpers, hoods, and other curvy elements whose shapes are difficult to model with other LEGO pieces.

Figure 4-5: The LEGO 8070 Super Car set relies on flexible axles to model parts of the body such as the mudguards and the edges of the front bumper.

bushes

LEGO bushes, also called bushings, are small elements put on axles in order to maintain spacing between two or more other elements. They can also prevent pieces from sliding off of axles or keep axles in place. They come in three versions: a half bush (half stud long), a bush (1 stud long), and a bush with a long pin (3 studs long, including a 2-stud-long pin), all of which are shown in Figure 4-6.

Figure 4-6: From left to right: a half bush, a bush, and a bush with a long pin

half bush

The half bush is the only piece from this group that comes in variants (as shown in Figure 4-7). Its variants include a toothed half bush, a toothed half bush with a cut-out axle hole, and the currently produced smooth half bush with a cut-out axle hole.

Figure 4-7: From left to right: a toothed half bush, a toothed half bush with a cut-out axle hole, and a smooth half bush with a cut-out axle hole

toothed half bush

The first variant, the toothed half bush, comes with a complete axle hole and with 16 small teeth on one side. The other side is completely smooth. The rim of the half bush has a groove that allows it to act as a pulley for rubber bands, as shown in Figure 4-8. In fact, all half bushes have the ability to act as a pulley. For more information on pulleys, check out Chapter 6.

Figure 4-8: A half bush and a wedge belt wheel both have grooves for LEGO rubber bands and can be used as pulleys.

The toothed side of the half bush can be meshed with a number of other LEGO pieces: another toothed half bush, a toothed axle connector, or a toothed 16-tooth gear with clutch (as shown in Figure 4-9). It's important to keep in mind that when these pieces are meshed, they come roughly 1 mm closer to each other, which means that there is 1 mm of backlash behind them.

Figure 4-9: Several LEGO pieces can be meshed with a toothed half bush.

It's also useful to remember that the pieces can be meshed at various angles of rotation. Since there are 16 teeth on the side of the half bush, each tooth corresponds to 22.5 degrees; this is the minimum value by which we can change the angle of two meshed pieces. This arrangement creates some useful possibilities. For example, you can use two half bushes to couple two switches in such a way that turning one switch on turns the other one off (see Figure 4-10).

Finally, toothed half bushes can be used as bevel gears (as shown in Figure 4-12), but they must be shifted by a quarter stud each to mesh, and their teeth generate high friction and easily disengage under torque.

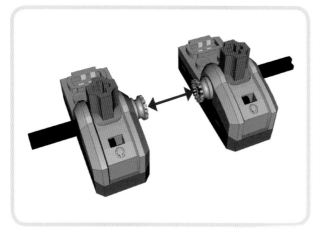

Figure 4-12: Toothed half bushes working as bevel gears. Note the quarter-stud spacings between the half bushes and the adjacent brick. Meshed this way, the half bushes can actually work very smoothly, provided high torque is not applied.

Figure 4-10: By meshing these two half bushes at the same angle, the two switches will be coupled and work as one. But if meshed with one half bush rotated by just one tooth relative to the other one, the two switches will be coupled so that only one of them can be on at a time and turning one off turns the other one on.

toothed half bush with a cutout

The second variant, the toothed half bush with a cutout, is exactly what its name implies: a copy of the previous version with part of the axle hole cut out, which makes the axle hole larger (see Figure 4-13). This modification was introduced to make it easier for children to take half bushes on and off the axles, and that's exactly what makes it much less popular with builders: These bushes are more likely to shift when stressed than the first variant. Other than that, it has every quality of the original toothed half bush except that, having been introduced a few years later, it's newer and thus made of stronger material.

The toothed half bush is still popular today because it takes a lot of force to make it move on the axle. This makes it useful in high-load applications: Two toothed half bushes are preferable to one regular bush because they are less likely to slip along the axle when a load is applied (see Figure 4-11).

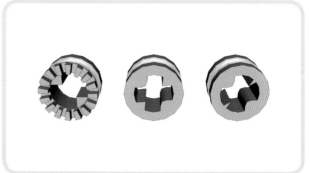

Figure 4-11: Several examples of securing an axle in place using toothed half bushes

Figure 4-13: Half bushes with semireduced axle holes: the toothed half bush and two forms of the smooth half bush

smooth half bush with a cutout

The third and final variant, the smooth half bush with a cutout, is an exact copy of the previous variant minus teeth. More specifically, the teeth haven't been removed but rather have been filled in order to create a smooth side; thus, both sides of this variant are identical. This variant is also identical to the previous variant in terms of how much stress it can take before shifting along the axle. There are two forms of this variant, with the newer piece having a slightly expanded axle hole. The difference is barely noticeable and does not affect the properties of this piece. This half bush variant was introduced 13 years after the first version and is still in use today; therefore, it is always available in better condition than previous variants and is made of stronger material.

regular bush

The regular bush is a far less complex piece, with only one variant available. It can be used for securing axles or maintaining 1-stud spacings. One of its sides is smooth, and the other has four small notches in it. The notches fit LEGO studs and enable the bush to be placed in the middle of 4 studs, as shown in Figure 4-14. That means the bush can be connected to bricks and plates sized 2×2 studs or larger.

Figure 4-15: From left to right: a bush with a long pin, a regular bush, and a regular long pin

This particular combination was developed as a convenience for the official LEGO Technic sets. Large and complex sets are very often divided into several modules that are built separately and then connected. The bush with a long pin is well suited for this task because it can be pushed in and pulled out more easily than regular pins (see Figure 4-16). LEGO uses this piece for temporarily locking some modules together as well: For example, the bush with a

Figure 4-14: A regular bush and two examples of a regular bush connected to studded pieces

bush with a long pin

The bush with a long pin is a combination of two pieces: the long pin and a regular bush. One of its sides is just like a bush, except that its axle hole is only 1 stud deep and it has smooth rims. Its other side is identical to that of a long pin with friction, as shown in Figure 4-15.

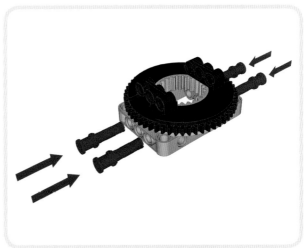

Figure 4-16: An example of the intended use of a bush with a long pin. Let's assume that we want to connect the turntable to a 5×7 frame so that they can be easily disconnected. We can do this by pushing the bushes in to lock the turntable into place and then pulling them out to free the turntable.

long pin enables a truck's cabin to be lifted up, lowered back, and then locked in that position (as shown in Figure 4-17).

Figure 4-17: Another example of the intended use of a bush with a long pin. Let's assume that the 5×7 frame is part of the chassis and the yellow beams are part of the cabin of a truck. We can lower the cabin by rotating the yellow beams and then lock it in that position by pushing the red pieces in. Then we can pull them out and lift the cabin up again.

universal joints

LEGO universal joints, also called u-joints or Cardan joints, are used to transfer rotary motion from one axle to another at an angle. They consist of a central disc with four pegs, located between two hinges with two pegs per hinge, as shown in Figure 4-18.

The main advantage of universal joints is that they can transfer motion along a line, acting like a bent shaft.

Additionally, their angle can be changed at any moment without affecting the speed or torque they are transferring. Their only flaw is that if they are bent at more than 45 degrees, they generate fluctuations in transmitting the motion. These fluctuations increase together with the angle, resulting in vibration, until the joint becomes completely locked at 90 degrees (see Figure 4-19).

Universal joints can be damaged by very high torque in one of two ways: The yoke (the part that embraces the axle) can crack, or the pegs on the cruciform (the disc in the center) can snap. The first type of damage can be prevented by using 2×2 round bricks or round plates, as shown in Figure 4-20. The latter type has no countermeasure beyond building your own style of universal joint (see Chapter 8).

Universal joints were originally 4 studs long. Then in 2008, a new 3-stud-long version was introduced (shown in Figure 4-21). The new version fits well into studless structures thanks to its odd length (shown in Figure 4-22), and it is produced using stronger material than the old one. Additionally, its central disc is solid rather than hollow, and its pegs are less likely to snap; this has made it much more popular and useful than the old version. Like the old version, though, it can be secured with round plates.

When dealing with high amounts of torque, we can also use a ball joint, which combines two studless pieces to create a sturdy, tight housing for the 3-stud-long universal joint (as shown in Figures 4-23 and 4-24). The universal joint can rotate inside the housing without being stressed or pulled. As a result, a ball joint can be used for connecting structures that exert some load on the universal joint between them. This method holds these structures together firmly while allowing a universal joint to pass through, and it also gives these structures a large degree of free movement. The ball joint handles structural loads, leaving the universal joint with only the torsion of its shaft to handle. LEGO first used this method to connect suspended axles to a chassis while transferring drive from the chassis to the axles.

Figure 4-18: A universal joint

Figure 4-19: From left to right: a universal joint when it's straight, a universal joint bent at 45 degrees, and a universal joint bent at 90 degrees (unable to rotate)

Figure 4-20: A universal joint secured against cracking with two round plates

Figure 4-22: A 3-stud-long universal joint used to transfer drive through an articulation point

Figure 4-21: A 4-stud-long universal joint (top) and the newer 3-stud-long variant (bottom)

Figure 4-23: A complete ball joint includes two pieces, one inserted into the other. Note that the light grey part on the left comes with a frame large enough to house a differential; it can therefore be used directly as a basis for an axle.

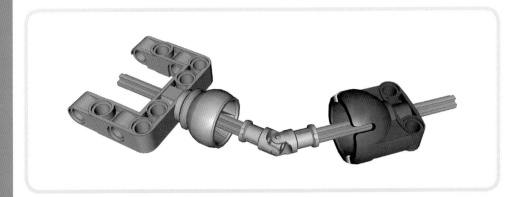

Figure 4-24: An open ball joint with a universal joint visible inside. A universal joint becomes more effective inside a ball joint because it's protected from structural stress; as a result, less friction is generated in it.

PART II

mechanics

5

gears and power transmission basics

Why do we need gears? An intuitive answer is to transfer drive from a motor to a receiving mechanism. While true, this is not the complete picture. The essential purpose of gears is to transform the *properties* of a power input to suit our purposes. Transferring drive is just a side effect of this process.

Gears can be driven by all kinds of inputs, from electric motors and manual cranks to wind turbines and mill wheels. Let's start by considering gears powered by electric motors because unlike other power inputs, motors have constant, measurable properties.

Every motor has a certain mechanical power, consisting of two factors: rotational speed and torque. These are the two properties we can transform using gears. Both speed and torque are explained in detail in Chapter 1.

When do we need speed? When do we need torque? Each mechanism and model you build has unique needs. Some will need more speed and less torque than the motor provides, and for others, the reverse will be true. Using gears, we can transform torque into speed or speed into torque. There are two very important but very simple rules for this relationship:

* Driving a large gear with a small gear increases the torque but decreases the speed. This is called *gearing down* (see Figure 5-1).
* Driving a small gear with a large gear increases the speed but decreases the torque. This is called *gearing up* (see Figure 5-2).

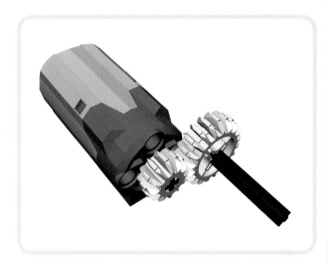

Figure 5-1: Gearing down

Figure 5-2: Gearing up

Speed and torque are *inversely proportional*: If we decrease the speed by a factor of two, the torque is increased by a factor of two. We can't transform one property without affecting the other, unless we modify the power input by exerting more force on a manual crank or by providing an electric motor with a higher voltage.

When propelling a vehicle that is light and needs little torque to move, we can transform the abundant torque into extra speed by gearing up. The amount of torque we can transform depends mainly on the vehicle's weight. Experienced builders can estimate the range of possible transformation knowing just the vehicle's weight and the type of motor used to drive it.

drivers, followers, and idlers

Let's consider a simple example of a geared power transmission, shown in Figure 5-3, in which the grey motor is connected to a wheel via two gears. The green gear that is closest to the power input (the motor) is called a *driver gear*. The red gear that receives the drive from the driver gear is called a *follower gear*.

Figure 5-3: Driver and follower gears. Illustrations in this chapter will use the same color scheme: green for driver gears and red for follower gears.

Whenever there is a pair of meshed gears on separate axles, one of the gears is a driver, and the other is a follower. The driver is the gear the drive is transferred *from*, and the follower is the gear the drive is transferred *to*.

As the gears rotate, so do the axles on which they are mounted. Therefore, a driver axle, called the *input*, and a follower axle, called the *output*, follow the rotation of the gears. Most mechanisms have a single input axle, but the output axles can be numerous. The common differential mechanism is a good example of one input with many outputs (see Figure 5-4).

Figure 5-4: The differential has one green input axle but two red output axles.

In addition to driver and follower gears, we have *idler gears*. If there is a set of gears in a series, the first one is the driver gear and the last one is the follower gear. All the gears in between are called idler gears (see Figure 5-5), because they could just as well not exist. In other words, they don't affect how the torque and speed are transformed.

Figure 5-5: Three gears meshed one by one, with the idler gear in grey. The idler's axle serves only as its mounting point.

Idler gears are typically meshed with two or more gears at the same time, while the driver and follower gears are meshed only with one, as shown in Figure 5-6. Exceptions to this rule are shown in Figure 5-7.

Note that idler gears should be used only when absolutely necessary, as they add friction and need to be properly supported. An excess of idler gears is shown in Figure 5-8.

Figure 5-6: The middle gears in this picture are idler gears. Both are meshed with only one gear, but they are mounted on the same axle and are of exactly the same size, which means that they work just as a single gear would.

Figure 5-8: All the middle gears in this picture are idler gears. They do not affect how torque and speed are transformed between the driver gear and the follower gear.

gear ratios

A *gear ratio* is the relationship between the number of teeth in two interacting gears. *Interacting gears* might refer to two gears that are meshed or otherwise connected, two gears connected by a roller chain, or even two pulleys connected by a drive belt. The gear ratio of two sprockets connected with a chain is exactly the same as the gear ratio of those sprockets directly meshed.

A gear ratio is defined as follows: *number of follower gear's teeth : number of driver gear's teeth*.

For instance, if we drive a 24-tooth gear with an 8-tooth gear, the gear ratio, also known as the *torque ratio*, is 24:8. Know, however, that we should reduce both numbers in a gear ratio until one of them is 1. To do this, we need to find a divisor, usually equal to the smaller number. As you

Figure 5-7: The middle gears in this picture are not idler gears. Both are mounted on the same axle, but they are of different sizes, which means that they affect how torque and speed are transformed. This is because the varying size of the gear affects the torque it transfers.

can see here, if we divide both numbers in a 24:8 gear setup by 8, we will get a 3:1 ratio, which is much more convenient and immediately shows us that three revolutions of a driver gear result in a single revolution of a follower gear.

So what good is this ratio? We can use it to easily calculate how speed and torque are transformed between the two gears. Looking at the 3:1 ratio, we can tell that the speed is reduced by a factor of three, and since the decrease of speed results in an inversely proportional increase of torque, we know that torque is tripled.

Now consider an example where the driver has more teeth than the follower: We have a 20-tooth driver gear and a 12-tooth follower gear. The gear ratio is 12:20, which is equal to 0.6:1. This means that we need 0.6 revolutions of the driver gear to get a single revolution of the follower, so the speed is increased, but at the same time the torque of the follower is 0.6 of the driver's torque, so the torque is decreased.

Our gear ratio also reveals whether we're gearing down or gearing up. If the first number of the gear ratio is greater than the second (as in 3:1), we are gearing down—this is also called *gear reduction*. If the first number of the gear ratio is smaller than the second (as in 0.6:1), we are gearing up—this is also called *gear acceleration* or *overdrive*. If we have a 1:1 gear ratio, speed and torque remain the same.

What if we want to calculate the total gear ratio of a mechanism with many pairs of meshed gears? In this case, we ignore all the idler gears and calculate ratios for all pairs of driver and follower gears. Then, in order to get the final gear ratio of the entire mechanism, we simply multiply these gear ratios. Consider a mechanism with two pairs of 8-tooth drivers and 24-tooth followers. The gear ratio of the first pair is 3:1, and so is the ratio of the second pair. If we multiply these ratios, we get the final ratio of 9:1.

Now that we can calculate gear ratios, let's go back to the previous examples showing idler and non-idler gears.

Consider the first set of gears, shown in Figure 5-6. It consists of two pairs of gears: a 12-tooth driver with a 20-tooth follower and a 20-tooth driver with a 12-tooth follower. The ratio of the first pair is 20:12, and the ratio of second pair is 12:20. If we multiply these, we get the final ratio of 1:1. The idler gears did not change the ratio at all.

Now consider the second set of gears, shown in Figure 5-7. It consists of two identical pairs of gears, which have a 12-tooth driver with a 20-tooth follower. The ratio of each pair is 20:12, and if we multiply these, we get the final ratio of 2.779:1, which is not equal to 1.667:1 (the ratio of the first and the last gear only). Here, the middle gears are not idlers—they affected the final gear ratio of the whole set—and they can't be ignored.

Finally, how do we calculate the ratio if a worm gear is used? Well, that's even simpler: *number of follower gear's teeth : 1*. That's because a single revolution of a worm gear rotates the follower gear by a single tooth. For example, it takes 24 revolutions of the worm gear to rotate a 24-tooth gear fully, and hence, we get the ratio 24:1.

efficiency and gears

Every gear we use has its weight and generates friction that has to be overcome if we want the gear to rotate. Every gear in our mechanism dissipates part of the drive motor's power, and the *efficiency* of the gear tells us how much power is fully transferred and how much is lost. Unfortunately, it's extremely difficult to calculate the individual efficiency of each gear, especially since gears wear over time. We do know, however, how power is lost in mechanical systems, so we can safely assume two basic rules for maximum efficiency:

* The fewer the gears we use, the better.
* The smaller the gears we use, the better.

In practice, low efficiency results in a loss of torque and speed. This loss happens because low efficiency generates resistance—resulting from friction, among other things—that a motor has to overcome. You can see this with motorized vehicles; in most cases their wheels rotate faster when you lift them off the ground. All of this means that the real, functioning mechanism is never as effective as the gear ratio alone indicates, and how much its efficiency is diminished is determined by the efficiency of the gears.

You can see the importance of efficiency in any mechanism that includes a worm gear. A worm gear's extremely high gear reduction comes at the cost of efficiency. Some sources estimate that a worm gear loses almost one third of the motor's power due to high friction and the gear's tendency to slide along its axle. The friction is high enough to make worm gears hot if they handle high torque for a prolonged period of time, and the friction is also the reason why LEGO worm gears can't be follower gears. Worm gears are irreplaceable for some applications, but in general, they should be used in moderation.

backlash and gears

For LEGO gears, we can simply assume that *backlash* is the free space between the meshed teeth of two adjacent gears. In an ideal situation, there would be no free space at all, but in practice, LEGO gears always generate some backlash. The general rules are as follows:

* Old-type gears generate much greater backlash than the new bevel gears.
* The smaller the gear, the greater the backlash.
* The backlashes of any directly meshed gears sum up.

Why is backlash so bad? Consider, for example, any steering mechanism: Any significant backlash between it and the motor that controls it will not only degrade the accuracy of steering but also make the wheels have some margin of freedom so that they may turn a bit when they meet an obstacle. This may cause your vehicle to waver out of a true straight line as it navigates bumps or create a noticeable delay as you steer a vehicle.

Backlash can become troublesome whenever accuracy is needed. Many sorts of cranes, drawbridges, and turntables suffer from backlash. The best way to avoid backlash is to use pneumatics instead of mechanics (see Chapter 9) or to use linear actuators, which currently have the least backlash out of all the mechanical parts produced by LEGO (see Chapter 13).

How does backlash work with a worm gear? Again, this gear proves unique in generating nearly no backlash—except for the fact that it can slide along the axle a bit, being slightly narrower than 2 full studs. Now, that doesn't mean that mechanisms with the worm gear have *zero* backlash—unfortunately, there is still backlash from the follower gear. Therefore, a mechanism with a worm gear and a 16-tooth follower gear will always have greater backlash than one with a worm gear and a 24-tooth follower gear. And again, it is recommended that you use a worm gear with bevel gears due to their relatively insignificant backlash.

controlling rotational direction

When gears are meshed directly, the driver gear affects the follower gear's direction of rotation. Whether the follower rotates in the same or in the opposite direction as the driver depends on the number of gears between them. When gears are in a parallel series, the rule is simple: With an even number of gears (2, 4, 6, and so on), the follower rotates in the opposite direction, and with an odd number of gears (3, 5, 7, and so on), the follower rotates in the same direction (see Figure 5-9). You may find yourself adding or removing idler gears to adjust the follower's direction.

Direct observation may be the quickest means of determining the output rotation of gears that mesh perpendicularly. For example, in a 4×4 vehicle's drivetrain with a longitudinal driveshaft, the front and real differentials must be oriented in opposite directions for the front and rear wheels to rotate in the same direction, as shown in Figure 5-10.

Figure 5-9: An even number of meshed gears (left) and an odd number of meshed gears (right)

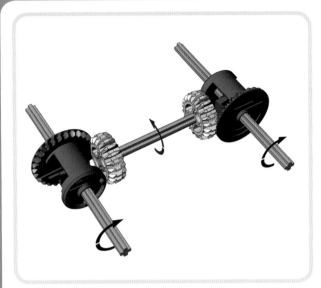

Figure 5-10: The proper orientation of differentials and bevel gears in a 4×4 drivetrain

gears (tan), and nine *old-type* gears (presented in their most common colors). Despite their differences, almost any two of these gears can be meshed together. The unique property of the bevel gears is that they can be meshed in both a parallel and a perpendicular manner. Their size makes them better suited for use in studless constructions, while the shape of their teeth makes it impossible to put LEGO chains on them.

NOTE The names of types of gears, such as *8-tooth gear* and *24-tooth gear*, can be shortened to *g8t* and *g24t*, respectively. These so-called straight-cut gears are also known as spur gears.

worm gear

This special gear has a number of unique properties. First, it is impossible to drive a worm gear with any other gear; a worm gear can be used only as the *driver* gear, never as the follower gear. The worm gear comes in handy for mechanisms that need to lift something up and keep it raised; in this case, a worm gear acts like a lock that, once stopped, keeps its follower gear immobile, resisting any load on it. This is useful in building cranes, forklifts, railroad barriers, drawbridges, winches, and basically any mechanism that needs to keep something steady once the motor stops. Second, the worm gear is extremely useful for gearing down.

an inventory of gears

LEGO has released various types of gears throughout the history of the Technic line. The gears can be divided into a few different groups, and we will discuss them group by group. First, we'll examine the most common and familiar gears.

As you can see in Figure 5-11, the group of common and familiar gears consists of one special gear called a worm gear (first on the left), five gears of a new type called *bevel*

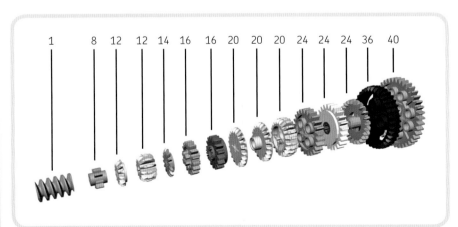

1 8 12 12 14 16 16 20 20 20 24 24 24 36 40

Figure 5-11: LEGO gears and their respective numbers of teeth

Every revolution of the worm gear rotates the follower gear by just a single tooth, reducing speed and increasing torque drastically. Therefore, worm gears are used for gearing down whenever very high torque or low speed is needed and there is little space to use.

Finally, as the worm gear rotates, it has a tendency to push against the follower gear and slide along its own axle. Usually this tendency has to be stopped by placing a strong casing around the worm gear, but there are certain mechanisms that put it to use (see Chapters 8 and 10 for examples).

Despite its unusual appearance, the worm gear can drive any other gear from the group. With proper spacing, it can drive bevel gears, too (see Figure 5-12).

Figure 5-12: A worm gear with single- and double-bevel follower gears

It's even possible to use the worm gear to drive racks, which results in a very compact boom-extending mechanism (see Figure 5-13), which could be useful in a crane or a telescoping forklift, or any other application where space is at a premium.

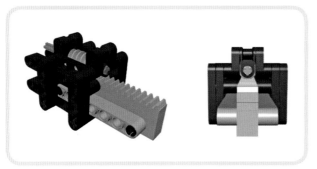

Figure 5-13: A worm gear driving a rack

8-tooth gear

This is the smallest LEGO gear in existence, and it's a fragile one. It's not suited for high torque, but due to its size, it's very popular, especially for gearing down. The 8-tooth gear has the disadvantage, however, of generating extremely significant backlash.

There are at least three variants of this gear coming from three slightly different molds (shown in Figure 5-14). The initial variant of the 8-tooth gear has thin teeth around a thin central ring, which is called *back iron*. The later, middle variant has the same central part, but its teeth are shorter, thicker, and presumably stronger. The third variant is the one most sought after, but it is unclear when it was in production and in which sets it was included. It maintains the shape of the teeth introduced in the middle variant, but its central part has an extra layer of material between the teeth, adding to its thickness. This change is clearly intended to prevent the teeth from bending under torque, thus making the entire piece significantly stronger.

Figure 5-14: Three variants of the 8-tooth gear, from left to right: the initial one, the middle one, and the reinforced one

single-bevel 12-tooth gear

This is the smallest of all bevel gears and the most fragile one. But it's irreplaceable in differential mechanisms, and it's very popular when there is a need to transfer the drive in a perpendicular manner inside a tight space. It's easily broken under high torque, which has led many builders to exclude differentials completely from their off-road vehicles.

double-bevel 12-tooth gear

This gear is much stronger than its single-bevel counterpart, and it's most often used with a double-bevel 20-tooth gear. It doesn't fit inside differentials or in tight spaces, which makes it less popular for perpendicular meshing.

14-tooth gear

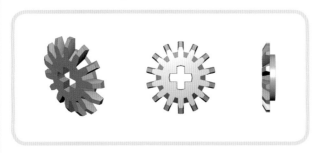

The first gear used inside differentials, this gear proved so fragile that it was later replaced by the 12-tooth version. It is no longer used in the official LEGO models and is unpopular with builders.

16-tooth gear

This is a reasonably strong and useful gear. This is the smallest gear that can be operated with a LEGO chain, and it's a popular one thanks to its convenient size. As of early 2011, it was replaced in LEGO sets by a slightly updated version (see Figure 5-15). The shape of the new version's outer rim is exactly the same, whereas the structure in the middle of it has been reinforced. The new version is generally more massive and therefore more torque resistant.

Figure 5-15: The old version of the 16-tooth gear on the left (#4019) and the new version on the right (#94925)

16-tooth gear with clutch

This gear was designed specifically for gearboxes. It's weaker than the regular version and doesn't work well with a LEGO chain because its shorter teeth make the chain slip. Instead, it has the unique ability to be engaged or disengaged by the transmission driving ring (see Figure 5-16). Without the ring, it remains loose on the axle, but it can be meshed with an old-type half bush (the one with teeth) and thus get fixed to the axle (see Figure 5-17). In 2011, it started being phased out and replaced by a newer version without teeth (see Figure 5-18).

Figure 5-16: A 16-tooth gear with clutch engaged by a transmission driving ring

Figure 5-17: A 16-tooth gear with clutch engaged by an old-type half bush with teeth

Figure 5-18: The toothed (left) and toothless (right) variants of the 16-tooth gear with clutch. Both variants wear the same number, which means that LEGO considers them to be basically the same piece. The most likely reason for the change from toothed to toothless is the fact that all pieces the teeth could be meshed with have been long out of use in LEGO Technic sets.

single-bevel 20-tooth gear

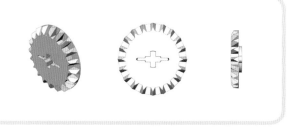

This is a larger version of the single-bevel 12-tooth gear. It is relatively rare and not really popular because of its thin body, which makes it prone to snapping under high torque.

single-bevel 20-tooth gear with pin hole

This modification of the single-bevel 20-tooth gear was intended to offer some new possibilities rather than to replace it. These possibilities include the ability to rotate freely on an axle so that the gear can be used to transfer drive "over" the axle without driving it and without adding the axle's friction to its own. The new gear also has a half-stud-thick collar at its base, which makes it remain on the axle more securely. It is much less likely to snap than the single-bevel 20-tooth gear, but it can act only as an idler gear.

double-bevel 20-tooth gear

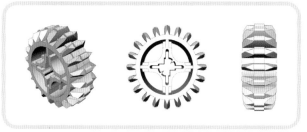

This is a very popular, strong, and reliable gear. It's most commonly used with a single-bevel 12-tooth gear, but it's useful in other setups, too.

24-tooth gear

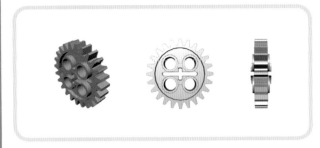

There are at least three variants of this popular, strong, and reliable gear, the newest ones being the strongest ones (see Figure 5-19). The 24-tooth gears are some of the most useful gears available.

Figure 5-19: The two most common variants of the 24-tooth gear: the older, weaker one on the left and the newer, stronger one on the right

24-tooth gear with clutch

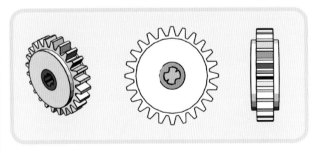

This 24-tooth gear is white with dark grey in the center, and it has the unique ability to harmlessly slip around the axle if a sufficiently high torque is applied. It's most often used for end-to-end applications—that is, applications in which the motor can run only until it reaches a certain point. This includes almost all steering mechanisms, in which the wheels can be turned only within a limited angle, and the railroad barrier mechanism, by which the barrier can be raised or lowered only to a certain degree. In these types of mechanisms, the gear slips when that end point is reached so that the motor can continue to run while the mechanism itself is stopped. This gear is also used for the motorized winches in official LEGO sets, where it ensures that the motor doesn't get damaged when the end of the winch's string is reached. Note that this gear slips under a very specific amount of torque, and in most cases, you will want it to slip only under extremely high torque (in other words, you'll need to make sure that the steering mechanism stops turning when the end point is reached, not merely when a wheel meets an obstacle). This can be achieved by adding some gearing down between it and the mechanism it controls (see Figure 5-20).

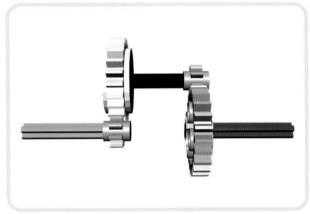

Figure 5-20: An example of the 24-tooth gear with clutch being protected by gearing down (right). The gear ratio is 3:1, which means that the gear is subject to just a third of the overall torque, thus requiring three times the amount of torque to slip.

LEGO builder Jetro de Château discovered that there have been at least three versions of this gear released over the years: one that came with the 8479 set, which has a light grey center and requires more torque to slip; one that is most commonly used, which has a dark grey center; and one that is from an unknown set or sets, which has no inscriptions on its sides.

24-tooth gear with crown

This crowned gear was the first gear among the regular gears that could be meshed in a perpendicular manner. Again, there are at least three variants of this gear, the older and weaker ones having been gradually replaced with newer and stronger versions. The arrival of bevel gears made this gear unpopular: It's weak and inconvenient to use due to its shape and protruding central hub.

36-tooth gear

This is the largest bevel gear and the only one with no single-bevel counterpart. A convenient and surprisingly strong gear, though a rare one, it usually comes in black.

40-tooth gear

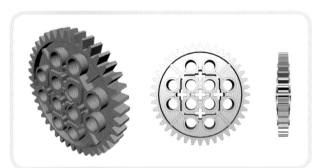

This is the largest gear of all. While rare and rarely used because of its immense size, it is popular in tracked models as a sprocket wheel for the old type of tracks.

differential gears

LEGO has produced three different differential gears. Let's review them starting from the left in the figure above:

old-type 28-tooth differential gear

The oldest differential gear, it's designed for use with 14-tooth gears inside but also compliant with the single-bevel 12-tooth gears. It takes a lot of space and comes with 28 teeth that can be meshed in both a parallel and a perpendicular manner. It always comes in light grey.

16/24-tooth differential gear

The successor of the older differential gear, it is much more universal and can be used in situations where other differential gears cannot be. It includes two gears, one with 16 teeth and one with 24 teeth, both of which can be meshed in a parallel manner only. The 24-tooth gear can be driven with a LEGO chain. Additionally, both ends can be engaged by a transmission driving ring, locking the differential (see Figure 5-21). It comes almost exclusively in dark grey.

Figure 5-21: A 16/24-tooth differential gear locked by a transmission driving ring. Once locked, it works like a solid axle, not like a differential. A lockable differential is useful in many off-road vehicles, which are put at a disadvantage by regular differentials.

new-type 28-tooth differential gear

This variant was introduced with the growing popularity of studless constructions, in which a differential of even width is difficult to incorporate. It has 28 teeth that can be meshed in a perpendicular manner only, and it's just 3 studs wide. Much less massive than the other differentials, it is surprisingly strong, especially when enclosed inside a 5×7 studless frame that was designed specifically for it (see Figure 5-22). Its inside is redesigned to work with the single-bevel 12-tooth gears only, and it includes a special structure that keeps them in place more securely.

Figure 5-22: A new-type 28-tooth differential gear in a common and robust setup: enclosed inside a 5×7 studless frame and driven by a double-bevel 20-tooth gear

turntables

older style   newer style

LEGO Technic turntables come in big and small versions. There are two variants of the big one, with the only real difference being the fact that the older style (left) is suited for studfull constructions, while the newer one (right) is suited for studless ones. Additionally, the older one is 4 studs tall, and the newer one is 3 studs tall. The outer ring of both turntables has 56 teeth. The inner one has 24 teeth and is the exact size of the 24-tooth gear; however, the construction of the studless turntable makes it impossible to put a 24-tooth gear inside it. Still, a turntable can be meshed with smaller gears.

Both variants consist of upper and lower halves, which can get separated if sufficient force is applied. The outer ring is most often driven by an 8-tooth gear or a worm gear. The turntables can be used in a normal or an upside-down position (the studless one is better suited for an upside-down position), depending on whether we want to drive them from above or below.

As of 2012, a small turntable has been introduced. It consists of two halves (see Figure 5-23), each with two pin holes, and it has a ring of 28 teeth attached to one of the halves. One side of the teeth is chamfered, as in bevel gears, and the other one is unaltered, as in straight-cut or spur gears. Therefore, the turntable can be engaged by bevel gears only from the side of the toothless half, as shown in Figure 5-24. The combination of gears that can be used with this turntable is limited, with the single- or double-bevel 12-tooth gear clearly being the best-suited one.

Figure 5-23: A small turntable consists of two halves

The small turntable is 3 studs tall, and its diameter is slightly over 3 studs: exactly 28 mm. The hole in its middle has a shape of 1×1 studs square, which means that we can put the following through it: an axle, even with a bush or an axle joiner on it; a universal joint; the rod of a pneumatic cylinder or of a linear actuator; up to four pneumatic hoses; or even a beam, although the beam's square profile will stop the turntable from rotating. What we can't put through a small turntable are wires—because their plugs are too big—and LEGO LEDs, which are also too big.

Figure 5-24: A small turntable meshed with a double-bevel 12-tooth gear

knob wheel

This is an important and popular piece, even though it's technically not a gear. Knob wheels can mesh only with other knob wheels, in both a perpendicular and a parallel manner. To their advantage, they are much stronger than gears, and they can handle significantly higher torque. They are most commonly used in the perpendicular setup because the regular gears that can transfer the drive in such a setup are much more likely to snap under torque than the knob wheels are. The disadvantage of knob wheels is that the unique shape of their teeth makes them work *unevenly*. This is particularly apparent when a large torque is applied to a perpendicular setup of knob wheels—their speed of rotation starts to fluctuate. Also, because all the torque is applied to so few points, knob wheels are prone to wearing out. It is not

uncommon to see knob wheels rub away at their meshing points, but this happens only with really heavy loads and only after a while.

Hailfire Droid wheel gear

This is a very large and very rare gear. It has an impressive diameter equal to 26 studs, and it has 168 teeth on the inner ring. The whole gear is 3 studs thick, its inner teeth are 1 stud wide, and it has 1-stud-deep troughs on both sides. This makes it relatively easy to drive, either by building some structure inside it or by attaching it to an external structure.

The gear got its name from the only set it appears in: It's the wheels of the 4481 Hailfire Droid. Since the set is no longer produced and there were only two gears of this type included in each set, they have become rare and expensive.

Hailfire Droid wheel gears are highly desired for use as turntables in very large models. With two gears like this, it is possible to put them on top of each other, filling the troughs on their facing sides with up to 41 LEGO balls (see Figure 5-25). The resulting mechanism acts like a ball bearing, which makes it capable of rotating under significant loads; additionally, the sheer size of the gear makes it very stable.

Figure 5-25: It takes 41 standard LEGO balls to fill the Hailfire turntable entirely.

obsolete gears

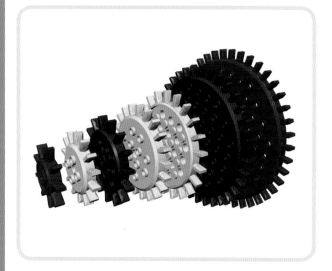

These odd and colorful gears are parts of two early systems of LEGO gears: the Samsonite system introduced in 1965 and the Expert Builder system introduced in 1970. They are predecessors of today's Technic system, which replaced them in 1977. These gears have been absent from LEGO sets since then, but they're still relatively easy to find in secondhand sales. They mesh in both a parallel and a perpendicular manner but only with the gears from their own group. Just like knob wheels, they have teeth that make them work unevenly. Note that they are massive and made from very durable material, and some even have metal centers, which makes the smallest of them popular with builders seeking heavy-duty gears. The larger ones are rarely used because of their enormous size.

6

chains and pulleys

Transferring torque with LEGO pieces is possible not only with gears and axles but also with two additional systems: pulleys and chains. All of these systems work with similar principles.

LEGO pulleys are wheels that can be connected via strings or rubber bands, allowing for the transfer of drive and movement. You've seen similar pulleys in "belt" systems in real life. Pins without friction, bushes, and other circular elements can also be used as LEGO pulleys. A pulley system is particularly useful for lighter loads, transferring drive silently and over a long distance.

LEGO chains work similarly, though they're better suited for higher torque than a pulley. A chain replaces the rubber band of a pulley system, and gears replace the pulleys. The driver gear in a chain is known as a *sprocket*, just as in a tracked vehicle. Instead of being held by the frictional force of a string or rubber band, a chain is held by meshing its links with gears. Figure 6-1 shows the pulley and chain systems side by side.

Since the chain system is less versatile and therefore simpler, we are going to discuss it first. Then we will move to pulley systems and configuration. Keep in mind that the same configurations are possible for chain and pulley systems, though they're often more practical with pulleys.

chains

The LEGO chain system has been present in the Technic line since 1979, and despite its rarity, it's unlikely to go out of use. The chain consists of small, rigid links that can be connected so that every link can be tilted relative to the next one (see Figure 6-2). In this way, we can create a flexible but rigid chain of any length, which can be wrapped around gears. Figure 6-3 shows the size of the LEGO chain compared to a 1×2 brick. You may also recognize the chain link as similar to the LEGO track link (see Figure 6-4), which is used for tracked vehicles.

Figure 6-1: Two pulleys with a rubber band (yellow) and two gears with a chain (black). The two systems share the same working principles.

Figure 6-2: A single chain link and a section of four connected links, shown with slots facing upward and downward. In theory, the chain is less likely to come apart when its slots face the gear, but in practice, the difference is negligible.

Figure 6-3: An individual chain link is very small and practically impossible to combine with any other type of LEGO piece.

| 16-tooth | 16-tooth reinforced | 24-tooth | 24-tooth with clutch | 40-tooth |

Figure 6-5: All the chain-compatible gears

Figure 6-4: The chain link (left) is similar to the LEGO track link (right) and can be combined with it. To learn more about tracks, see Chapter 16.

Figure 6-6: The 8-tooth gear also works with a chain but cannot drive it due to its small size. It can still be used as an idler gear, adapting the shape of the chain to the surrounding structure.

Five different gears work with the chain, as shown in Figure 6-5. While the 8-tooth gear can work with the chain, too, it cannot drive the chain as it's simply too small (see Figure 6-6). Also note that by using the 24-tooth gear with clutch, you can make a chain slide when its output is stopped (for example, under load), meaning that the chain will behave just like a rubber band would over pulleys. Chains can also be wrapped around turntables to drive them, but they are rarely used this way as there are other, much less space-consuming methods of driving a turntable (for example, with a worm gear or an 8-tooth gear).

Even though the chain is rigid, it has a degree of elasticity because the links are made of thin material. This allows us to adjust the *tension* of the chain. In general, the chain should not be very tight, as a tight chain is more likely to come apart under torque. Some *play* in the chain is therefore desired. The section of the chain that makes contact with

the gear has no play; rather, the play of a chain accumulates between the gears, usually in the lowest section of the chain due to gravity (see Figure 6-7). This play allows the system to withstand more force and becomes a problem only when it's large enough to decrease the chain's area of contact with the gears, increasing the risk of links skipping their teeth, or when it's large enough to come in contact with the structure around the chain, where it can catch. When dealing with chains longer than 20 links, it's a good idea to add 1 extra link just to lower the tension. Soft shock absorbers can be used to add a bit of tension.

The chain can be used to change the gear ratio by simply connecting two gears of different sizes. Linking two gears via a chain works exactly like directly meshing them: The gear ratio is equal to the number of follower gear's teeth divided by the number of driver gear's teeth. For instance, by using a chain to drive a 24-tooth gear with a 16-tooth

Figure 6-7: A close-up view of the chain wrapped around a gear shows that each link occupies two teeth. The section of the chain that has contact with the gear has no play in it, and its elasticity is minimized.

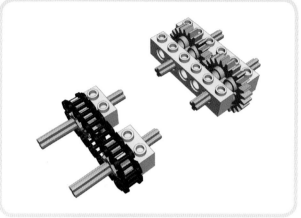

Figure 6-8: One major advantage of a chain (left) is that it does not require reinforced structure around it to handle high torque, unlike gears meshed directly (right).

gear, we obtain a 16:24 ratio, which can be reduced to 1:1.5, just as in a direct connection. And in the same way, the ratio of a chain system is not affected by idler gears. The only difference is that the chain keeps all the gears it's wrapped around rotating in the same direction, with the exception of idler gears that are located outside the chain rather than inside it (see the idler gear in Figure 6-6). Note that you can use one chain to drive several follower gears of various sizes, creating a different ratio for each of them.

The important characteristic of a chain is its behavior under torque. When a high torque is applied to gears meshed directly (shown at left in Figure 6-8), it pushes them apart, which may cause their teeth to skip. But when a high torque is applied to gears connected with a chain, it pulls them together. This means that a chain has an advantage in high-torque applications: Gears connected with a chain don't need a reinforced housing—the chain is something of a structural reinforcement itself.

pulleys

Pulleys are circular LEGO pieces designed to work with rubber bands or strings. They are distinguished by a groove around the rim, and there are only four types, as shown in Figure 6-9. Other LEGO pieces can be used as pulleys, too, but without a groove, they don't hold rubber bands or strings as securely. Note that many wheels without tires can also be used as pulleys.

| half bush | Micromotor pulley | wedge belt wheel | large pulley |

Figure 6-9: All four LEGO pulleys

The two most common pulleys are the regular half bush and the wedge belt wheel (so named because of its resemblance to real-life wheels designed to work with wedge belts, which we replace with rubber bands). The large pulley is less common, and the Micromotor pulley is the rarest, as it was originally meant to appear only with the LEGO Micromotor. When we connect two pulleys with a rubber band or a string, we create a gear ratio between them, just as we do in a chain system. The ratio depends on the proportion of their driver and follower diameters, which are shown in Figure 6-10. By driving a wedge belt wheel with a half bush, for example, we get a 21:5.8 ratio, which is equal to 3.6:1. And by driving a Micromotor pulley with a large pulley, we get a 9:32 ratio, which is equal to 1:3.55.

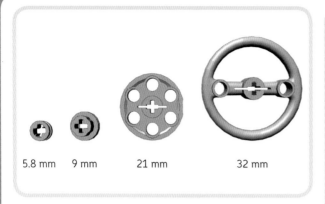

5.8 mm   9 mm   21 mm   32 mm

Figure 6-10: The diameters of the pulleys, which determine their ratios

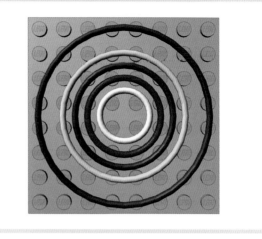

Figure 6-11: LEGO rubber bands come in five sizes, with diameters of 2, 3, 4, 5, and 7 studs. This figure also shows the most common color for each size.

However, ratios between pulleys are less reliable than ratios between gears because there is no solid connection between driver and follower, just an elastic rubber band or a string that can slip, extend, or retract under load, thus altering the ratio. We can actually use this lack of a solid connection to our advantage—for instance, such slippage could prevent a motor from stalling. The diameter-based calculation should, therefore, be considered just an approximate value. The *effective ratio* depends on a number of factors, including the torque transferred and the tension of the element connecting the pulleys, and it varies rather than staying at one fixed value.

Using pulleys with strings is the subject of the next section. For now, we will focus on rubber bands. It's perfectly possible to use any kind of thin rubber band, but LEGO actually has its own rubber bands, which work noticeably better. The rubber bands found in Technic sets are made of a high-quality silicone that rarely breaks and stays elastic for years, and they have a round cross section that fits pulleys' grooves better than the square cross section of ordinary rubber bands.

The pulley-dedicated LEGO rubber bands come in five sizes from a 2×2-stud band to a 7×7-stud band. Other than size and color, the bands are identical, and each of them can be stretched to a larger size, with the bigger bands able to stretch more than the smaller ones. The various bands and their most popular colors are shown in Figure 6-11.

The general behavior of two pulleys connected with a rubber band is very similar to that of two gears connected with a chain: The rubber band acts as a belt, keeping all the pulleys inside it rotating in the same direction. Its shape can be changed with idler pulleys, and it pulls pulleys together when subjected to high torque. One band can also be used

to drive several follower pulleys of various sizes by a single driver pulley, effectively creating a different ratio for each of them.

The main difference between rubber band and chain drive systems is that the rubber band should be as tight as possible because any play can stop it from transferring drive or even make it fall off the pulleys. Slippage in a pulley system isn't entirely negative—the fact that a band can slip when the follower pulley is stopped or blocked eliminates the need for a clutch of any kind. Note that when tight enough, the LEGO rubber bands can transfer surprisingly high torque without slipping, although they are generally considered less reliable than gears in high-torque applications. One problem is that bands are more likely to break, which can be disastrous when dealing with high torque.

Another advantage of pulley systems is their small size and thickness. The two most common pulleys—the half bush and the wedge belt wheel—are only a half stud thick, allowing two pairs of pulleys to fit where only one pair of gears would, as shown in Figure 6-12. That makes them a better choice than gears when space is limited and torque is low. Moreover, as long as the bands don't slip, they create practically no backlash, regardless of their number, which is a huge advantage over gears in mechanisms that need to react quickly and accurately. Finally, they are practically noiseless.

Also note that the band is more flexible than the chain and can be bent in any direction, allowing you to create mechanisms that are just not possible with a chain, such as pulleys that can be driven at an angle (see Figure 6-13).

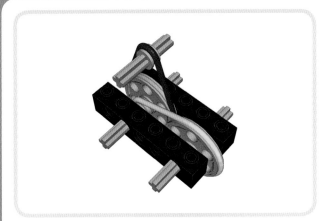

Figure 6-12: Two pairs of pulleys can fit into a 1-stud-wide space, which would be filled entirely by a single pair of gears.

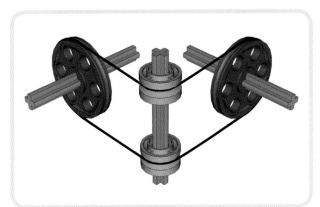

Figure 6-13: Two pulleys are connected by a rubber band at an angle, with two freely rotating rims on a vertical axle used as idlers to guide the band.

string and pulley systems

Using pulleys with strings is different from using pulleys with rubber bands. You can, of course, tie string into a loop and wrap it around two pulleys, but it won't work as well because it won't be as tight as a rubber band—string is simply less elastic and has much less grip. While rubber bands are used to transfer drive between two or more pulleys, string is best used to transfer the actual movement, that is, the displacement itself.

A perfect example of such a system is a winch in a crane, where string is wound on a reel and rotating the reel makes it pull loads up and down through a system of pulleys, as shown in Figure 6-14. In this case, the reel is the driver, and the movement is transferred to the hook at the end of the string. Without pulleys, the reel would have to be located on top of the crane, directly above the load. With pulleys, the string can be guided from the top of the crane to the back of it, where the reel is easily accessible and acts as the crane's counterweight.

There are numerous examples of mechanisms using string to transfer movement, including drawbridges, window blinds, and even cable railcars (where a car literally attaches and detaches to a moving cable to travel). However, pulleys can do more than guide movement.

Pulleys and string can be combined into systems that realize *mechanical advantage*. Mechanical advantage is a measure that shows how much a given mechanism amplifies the force we apply to it. For example, a mechanical advantage of 2 means that the force is amplified twice. This is exactly the kind of speed/torque transformation we have discussed when dealing with gears, and mechanical advantage is simply another way of describing a ratio. So, a mechanical advantage of 2 is simply a ratio of 2:1.

The idea of mechanical advantage is well illustrated by the crane example from Figure 6-14. Let's assume that we have already installed in the crane a system of pulleys that

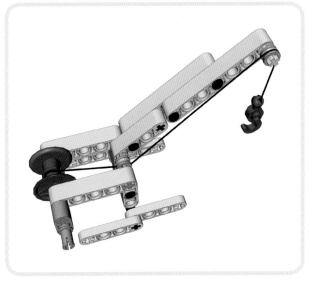

Figure 6-14: A simple crane uses a winch to pull a load on a hook up and down. The movement is transferred through a string, which is guided from the reel to the top of the crane by two half bushes acting as idler pulleys.

grants us a mechanical advantage of 2. This simply means that we have to apply half the force for twice as long—and that's because amplification of the force comes at the cost of the extra length of string to wind up. For example, to lift 100 grams of load 1 meter, we have to rotate the reel long enough to wind up 2 meters of string using only enough force to lift 50 grams. We trade torque for speed, and it works to our advantage because the amount that we can lift is usually more important than how fast we can lift it. With enough mechanical advantage, we can lift or move any load, no matter how heavy—its weight affects only the amount of time it will take. (Obviously, it also requires a structure strong enough to support it.)

Pulley systems that realize mechanical advantage are usually installed just between the top of a crane and its hook. The invention of such pulley systems is attributed to ancient Greeks, and the systems were refined by ancient Romans. It is estimated today that the most advanced Roman cranes allowed a single person to lift up to 3 tons of load, which is quite impressive for simple machines made mostly of wood. This load capacity could be multiplied by using a number of cranes together to handle a single load. Many of the ancient buildings we admire today could not have been created without this invention that allowed human power to move extremely heavy objects.

A pulley system typically consists of at least one pulley that is fixed above the load and stays in place—for example, on the top of our crane—and at least one pulley that moves together with the load—for example, by being attached to the hook of our crane, as shown in Figure 6-15. So, there are two groups of pulleys, one fixed and another moving, and each can consist of many pulleys.

The way the two groups of pulleys are connected with string and how many times they are connected determines the mechanical advantage they provide. There are three categories of pulley systems, each with groups of pulleys connected in different ways, and we will discuss them starting with the simplest one.

simple pulley system

The simplest pulley system consists of two groups that are identical. The upper group is the fixed one. The string goes over the upper group's first pulley and then comes down to the lower group, which is moving, and wraps around the lower group's first pulley. Then it comes back to the upper group and is tied to it, or it can be wrapped around a second pulley and repeat the arrangement between the first two pulleys. This means that the string can't be tied directly to the hook after it comes from the first upper pulley, which

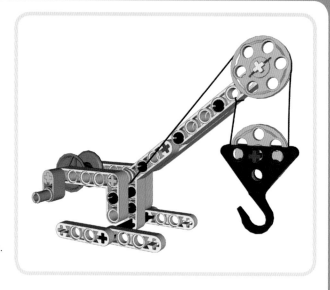

Figure 6-15: Our simple crane equipped with a pulley system. Two groups of pulleys are used, each consisting of a single pulley: The upper one stays on top of the crane, and the lower one moves up and down with the hook. This particular arrangement of string between the pulleys grants a mechanical advantage of 2.

is the main difference between the simplest pulley system and the lack of any such system, as Figures 6-16 and 6-17 show.

As you can see in Figure 6-17, the simplest pulley system has two sections of string connecting the two groups. This means that in order to lift the load, we have to wind up twice as much string as without this system, but using only half the force. The weight of the load is reduced twice at the cost of more string to be wound. There's no free lunch: We are trading time for work, having to do less work but over a longer period of time.

But let's consider what happens if we add another section of string between the two groups. We will need one more pulley to prevent the sections from getting tangled up with one another, as shown in Figure 6-18.

As you see, the string is now tied to the lower group, but only after it goes through three pulleys: two upper ones and one lower one. Three sections of string connect the two groups, granting a mechanical advantage of 3. We need to wind up three times as much string but use only one third of the force. By now you have probably guessed that *the number of sections of string connecting the groups determines the mechanical advantage they realize.*

These simple pulley systems are commonly used in sailboats and have various names depending on how many sections of string connect the two blocks. The system with

Figure 6-16: This arrangement has an upper group with a single pulley and no lower group. The string that comes off the pulley is tied directly to the hook. No pulley system is created, and no mechanical advantage is gained.

Figure 6-18: A pulley system with three sections of string between the groups. The upper group has string coming through it twice and hence two pulleys to prevent the string from getting tangled up. The string is then tied to the red axle in the lower group. This arrangement grants a mechanical advantage of 3.

Figure 6-17: This arrangement has two groups, each with a single pulley. The string comes off the upper pulley and around the lower pulley and is then tied to the element that is part of the upper group and remains fixed to it. It's the simplest pulley system, with a mechanical advantage of 2.

two sections is called a *gun tackle*, and the system with three sections is called a *luff tackle*. Other systems, shown in Figures 6-19 to 6-21, have up to six sections of string. With more sections, the whole system becomes less and less efficient, as each pulley creates additional friction and the significant length of string in the whole system is prone to stretching under load.

differential pulley system

Despite its name, this type of pulley system does not use a differential gear. Instead, it uses an upper group with two independent pulleys that can rotate at various speeds in opposite directions. This is made possible by using two separate axles, one for each pulley, or by replacing one of the pulleys with some circular LEGO piece with a pin hole rather than an axle hole, as shown in Figure 6-22.

As you see, the lower group is fairly simple, while the upper one includes two pulleys of various diameters, one made of a wedge belt wheel and another made of a small rim (#42610). The rim has a pin hole, so it can rotate freely on the axle, regardless of the speed and direction of the other pulley, and it has a deep central groove with an inner diameter of roughly 9 mm. The arrangement of the string is

Figure 6-19: This system, called double tackle, *grants a mechanical advantage of 4.*

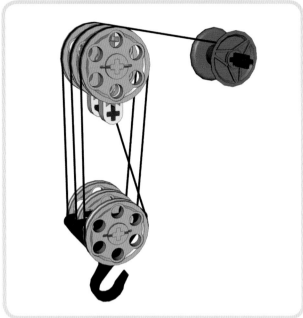

Figure 6-21: This system, called threefold purchase, *grants a mechanical advantage of 6.*

Figure 6-20: This system, called gyn tackle, *grants a mechanical advantage of 5.*

Figure 6-22: Differential block and tackle with two independent pulleys of different diameters in the upper block

no less interesting: It's tied in a loop, first coming off the reel, going over the large upper pulley and the lower pulley, and then coming back to be wrapped around the small upper pulley. Upon coming off, it's tied to the section of string between the reel and the large upper pulley.

When we rotate the reel, it pulls the string on both the large and small upper pulleys, making them rotate in opposite directions at various speeds. The difference in speeds is balanced by the rotations of the lower pulley. The interesting thing is how much mechanical advantage we can gain in this system.

If R is the radius of the large upper pulley and r is the radius of the small upper pulley, then the mechanical advantage of the whole system is equal to

$$\frac{2 \times R}{R - r}$$

In our example, R is 10.5 and r is 4.5, which gives a mechanical advantage equal to 21/6, which is 3.5. As you see from this formula, the mechanical advantage is bigger if the difference in the upper pulleys' sizes is very small. But the pulley sizes cannot be the same because that would stop the lower group from moving up or down.

Let's check the mechanical advantage given by other pulley combinations. For example, with the Micromotor pulley (R = 4.5) and a half bush (r = 2.9), we can get 9/1.6, which is equal to 5.63—quite a result from such small pieces. The combination of another freely rotating rim (#56902), shown in Figure 6-23, with a deep central groove and an inner diameter of 10 mm (R = 5), and the Micromotor pulley (r = 4.5) grants a mechanical advantage of 10/0.5, which is equal to 20.

The differential pulley system allows us to easily obtain a high mechanical advantage. The travel of its lower group, however, is limited by the distance between the point where the string is tied to make a loop and the reel (for lifting) or upper pulleys (for lowering). This means that in order to lift loads very high, a long distance between the reel and the upper pulleys is needed.

power pulley system

The power pulley system is the most complex and most effective of the three systems. It's distinguished by having one upper group and several lower groups that are connected in series, with the hook attached to the last one, as shown in Figure 6-24.

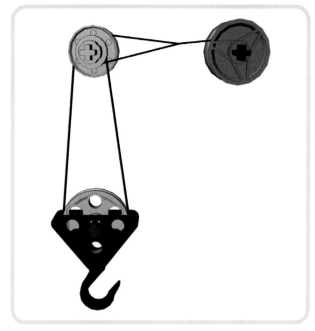

Figure 6-23: A differential pulley system with upper pulleys made of a freely rotating rim and a Micromotor pulley. There is only a 0.5 mm difference in the radius inside the grooves of the pulleys, resulting in a mechanical advantage equal to 20.

As you see, this system starts with one section of the string (black) coming off the reel, going through the upper pulley, going through the pulley of the first lower group, and then being tied to part of the upper group. Then the lower group has another section of string (green) attached to it. This string goes through the pulley of a second lower group and is then tied to part of the upper group, just like the first string's section. This series of repetition can continue until the final lower group, which has a hook attached to it and handles the actual load. In Figure 6-24, the hook is present on the 4th lower group, but it could just as well be present on the 20th one. Note that by moving the points where strings are tied to the upper group away from its pulley (to the left in Figure 6-24), it's possible to make the lower groups travel not only up and down but also forward and backward.

The mechanical advantage of the power pulley system is equal to $2n$, where n is the total number of lower groups. This means that the mechanical advantage increases rapidly with the number of lower groups, starting with 2 for one group, 4 for two groups, 8 for three groups, 16 for four groups, and so on. This may not sound impressive compared

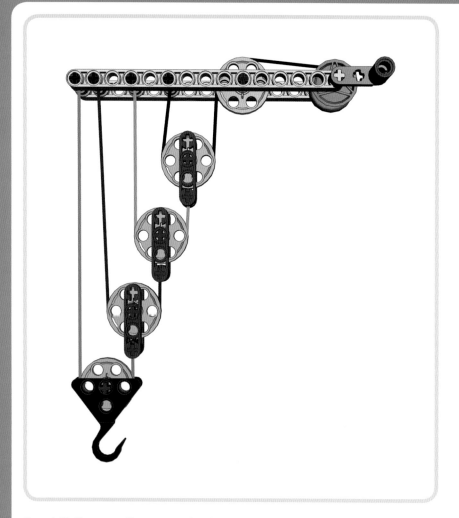

Figure 6-24: The power pulley system consists of one upper group and a number of moving lower groups connected in series. There are four lower groups here, granting a mechanical advantage of 16.

to the 22 we achieved with the differential pulley system, until you realize that the advantage in the power system exceeds 1,000 with 10 lower groups and 1 million with 20. And there is no technical limit to how many lower groups can be used, although just like the other systems, this one becomes inefficient with many pulleys adding friction and a lot of string stretching under load.

7

levers and linkages

Levers and linkages are some of the simplest machines and form the basis for countless more complex mechanisms. While levers are mostly used to provide a mechanical advantage that allows us to move heavy loads, linkages are mostly used to transform one type of a motion into another. Both are common in everyday life: If you have ever played on a seesaw or used pliers, you have relied on levers and linkages.

levers

A basic lever is simply a beam that has one point of support in the form of a hinge or a pivot, as shown in Figure 7-1. We will call this point a *fulcrum*. A lever also has input and output forces. We will call the applied, or input, force the *effort* and the reaction force the *load*. Finally, we will call the sections of the lever between its fulcrum and its ends *arms*.

When a lever provides a mechanical advantage, our input force is amplified. But that increase in force does come at a cost, just as it does with all other simple machines. A lever with a mechanical advantage of 2 allows us to move the load using half the force it would take without the lever but covering only half the distance (traveling at half the speed).

The mechanical advantage of the lever depends on the distances between the fulcrum, the load, and the effort. The so-called *law of the lever* states that the mechanical advantage of a lever is equal to d_e/d_l, where d_e is the distance between the effort and the fulcrum, and d_l is the distance between the load and the fulcrum. For example, for the lever shown in Figure 7-2, d_e (indicated by the blue arrow) is 5 studs long, and d_l (indicated by the red arrow) is 3 studs long. Therefore, the mechanical advantage of this lever is 5/3, or 1.67. This means that in order to lift 1 kg of load 1 meter with this lever, we have to apply the

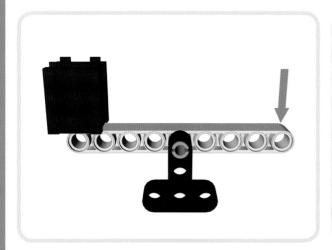

Figure 7-1: A simple lever, consisting of a beam (yellow) supported by the fulcrum (black). The brown crate is the load and the green arrow represents the effort. When effort is applied downward, the load is lifted up.

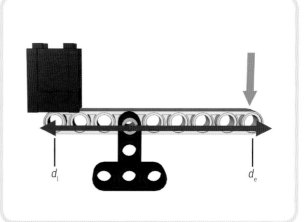

Figure 7-2: This lever has a mechanical advantage of 5/3, or 1.67, because the distance between the fulcrum and the effort is 5 studs and the distance between the fulcrum and the load is 3 studs.

effort needed to lift 0.6 kg and move the end of the lever 1.67 meters. The mechanical advantage still benefits us because we're trading time, which we have plenty of, for force, which is limited.

The law of the lever also means that the force applied to the arm of a lever is *inversely proportional* to the arm's length. Therefore, it takes more force to move a lever with a short arm than it takes to move a lever with a longer arm. A lever with a 3-stud-long arm will take twice the force as a lever with a 6-stud-long arm to move the same load. The lever with the 6-stud-long arm, though, will move the load twice as far because of its longer length.

Figure 7-3 illustrates the distance/force proportion. We have a lever with a 3-stud-long arm and a 7-stud-long arm. If we apply force to the longer arm, the lever offers a mechanical advantage of 2.33 (7/3), and if we apply force to the shorter arm, the lever offers a mechanical advantage of 0.43 (3/7). If we put a 1 kg load on the longer arm and a 2.33 kg load on the shorter arm, the loads will balance each other.

Note that a lever can have equal d_e and d_l distances, resulting in a mechanical advantage of 1. This simply means that there is no mechanical advantage and the distance/force balance remains unaltered. Such a lever can still be useful, as it reverses the direction of movement (that is, by pushing down, you lift a load up).

Finally, note that a lever does not necessarily have to be a straight beam. It can be bent and work just the same. A simple crowbar is a good example of a bent lever (see Figure 7-4): It has a long arm, a short arm, and a central part that we put on the floor, thus creating a fulcrum. By shoving the short arm under the load, we are able to use the long arm to lift that load using less force than without the crowbar.

classes of levers

The positions of the fulcrum, the load, and the effort on a lever can vary. There are three possible combinations, which are called *classes*. Fortunately for us, the law of the lever is exactly the same for each class, meaning that the mechanical advantage is calculated in the same way for all of them.

The lever classes are as follows:

* **Class 1** (see Figure 7-5): The fulcrum is located in the middle of the lever and the load and effort at its ends. This is the only class of lever where effort and load are applied in opposite directions (that is, to lift a load up, you have to apply effort downward). Examples: a seesaw or a crowbar.
* **Class 2** (see Figures 7-6 and 7-7): The load is located in the middle of the lever and the fulcrum and effort at its ends. Example: a wheelbarrow, with the wheel being its fulcrum.
* **Class 3** (see Figures 7-8 and 7-9): The effort is located in the middle of the lever and the load and the fulcrum at its ends. Because of this arrangement, the class 3 levers have a mechanical advantage of less than 1 and are used to trade force for distance rather than the other way around. This makes them useful when there is plenty of force that can be used to move the load over greater distance. Example: a boom of a crane elevated by a pneumatic cylinder attached to its middle.

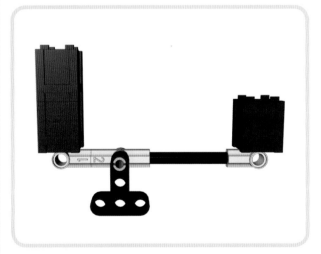

Figure 7-3: This lever has a mechanical advantage of 2.33, meaning that one of its arms is 2.33 times as long as the other one. Therefore, any load put on the longer arm can balance a 2.33 times heavier load on the shorter arm.

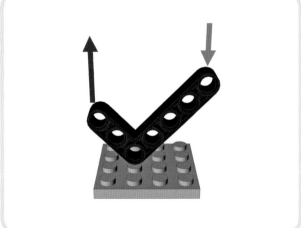

Figure 7-4: The bent 3×5 beam can work just like a crowbar.

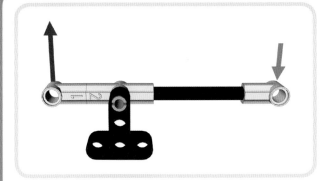

Figure 7-5: Class 1 lever with the fulcrum in the middle and the effort (green) and load (red) at its ends

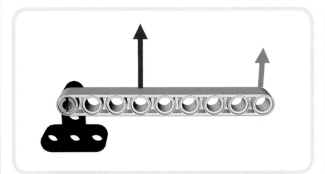

Figure 7-6: Class 2 lever with the load (red) in the middle and the fulcrum and effort (green) at its ends

Figure 7-7: An ordinary wheelbarrow is an example of the class 2 lever, with its wheel being the fulcrum. The load is located in the middle of the wheelbarrow, and the effort is applied to the end of it. Wheelbarrows usually provide a mechanical advantage greater than 1, unless you apply the effort exactly where the load is located.

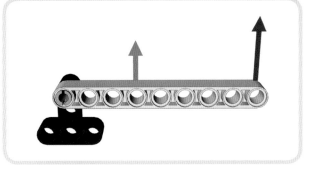

Figure 7-8: Class 3 lever with the effort (green) in the middle and the fulcrum and load (red) at its ends

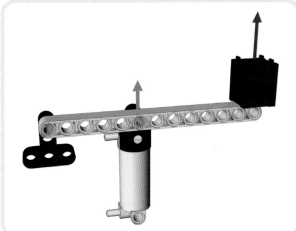

Figure 7-9: A boom of a crane is an example of the class 3 lever, with the load and the fulcrum at its ends and the effort applied to its center (in this case, by a pneumatic cylinder). Class 3 levers have a mechanical advantage less than 1, meaning that they require plenty of effort but can move loads over large distances. This is favorable when it comes to pneumatics, which can exert huge force but have limited reach.

from levers to linkages

An interesting thing happens when you connect ends of two identical levers located one above the other: The elements connecting their ends will maintain the same position as the levers move. This happens at every point in the levers' range of movement, regardless of their length. We can use this system of parallel levers, also known as a 4-bar linkage, to our advantage.

As Figure 7-10 shows, we can expand our crane's boom in Figure 7-9 by adding a parallel lever to it. This addition provides two advantages: First, we can move both levers by applying effort to only one of them because the elements connecting them will transfer the movement from one to the other. Second, and more importantly, the element at the "load" end of the levers will move with the levers while maintaining constant orientation. This means that the load's angle won't change as it moves up and down with the levers, which is useful when moving loads that we don't want to tip over.

Many kinds of machines—front loaders and telescopic forklifts, for example—use parallel levers to handle loads. The LEGO 8265 set, shown in Figure 7-11, is an excellent example of a front loader: Its bucket is connected to arms that form parallel levers. Note that a linear actuator on each side acts as the lower lever, and by extending or retracting, it controls the bucket's height. When it extends or retracts to the point that its length differs from that of the upper levers, an additional linkage between it and the bucket keeps the bucket level. The same additional linkage allows us to tip the bucket with another linear actuator. The bucket's orientation depends entirely on the lengths and locations of the levers.

For the orientation to be maintained, the two levers have to be of identical length, and their ends have to be connected with identical spacing, as shown in Figure 7-12.

Note that the levers connected in this way can't make a full rotation: They limit each other, colliding at a certain point. Therefore, their rotation is limited to a certain range, which can be adjusted by locating the levers not exactly one above the other but with a small displacement, as shown

Figure 7-10: A boom of a crane made of parallel levers. The parallel levers ensure that the element on the end of the levers maintains constant orientation as the levers move it up and down.

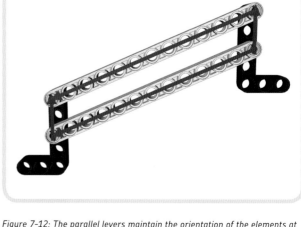

Figure 7-12: The parallel levers maintain the orientation of the elements at their ends only if the levers' length and spacing are identical.

Figure 7-11: The LEGO 8265 set features a complex front loader whose arms (elevating the bucket) form parallel levers.

Figure 7-13: The parallel levers are displaced to adjust their range of movement. By moving the upper lever a little backward (left in the figure), we can increase the maximum reach upward at the cost of maximum reach downward.

in Figure 7-13. Also note that the elements connecting the two ends of the levers don't have to be identical, nor do they need to be set at the same angle—it's only the angle and distance between the points of attachment that matter (see Figure 7-14).

Other variations are possible with a parallel-levers arrangement. For example, the element connecting the levers at the fulcrum can be rotated, making the element at the other end rotate at the same angle, as shown in Figure 7-15. This is one way to tip the bucket of our front loader.

Figure 7-14: The functioning of the parallel levers relies on the positions of their points of attachment. These positions can be made identical on both ends using various elements set at various angles.

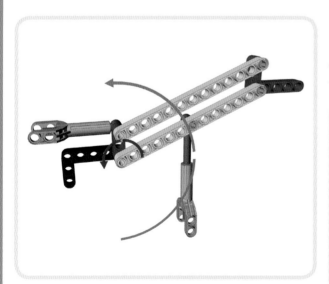

Figure 7-15: This boom variant uses one actuator to lower and raise the parallel levers (green arrow) and another to rotate the element that connects them at the fulcrum (red arrow), thus making the element at their other end rotate.

As Figure 7-16 shows, there is an interesting effect if the levers are not exactly parallel: Rotating the levers makes the element connecting their ends rotate slightly as well. This limits the levers' range of movement but can sometimes be desirable—in particular, when we want the element at the levers' end to be oriented differently in the lowermost and uppermost positions. This is the case with the LEGO 8460 Pneumatic Crane Truck set, where such an arrangement is used to control the stabilizing outriggers. This arrangement makes the outriggers nearly horizontal when lowered and nearly vertical when raised, effectively increasing their reach.

Finally, you can use the fact that the parallel levers rotate relative to the elements that connect them to your advantage. By putting gears on the axles that rotate together with the levers, we can transfer that rotation through these elements (for example, to another pair of parallel levers connected to it).

Figure 7-17 shows two pairs of parallel levers connected in such fashion—gears that transfer the rotation of one pair (left) to another (right). All the levers are identical and the gears maintain a 1:1 ratio, the result being that the element at the end of the series moves along a horizontal line. There is technically no limit to how many pairs of levers can be used in a series; the only constraint is the friction and the sum of the gears' backlash.

linkages

Linkages are groups of rigid links connected by joints that allow them to perform certain restricted movements. They are mostly used to convert rotary or rocking motion into

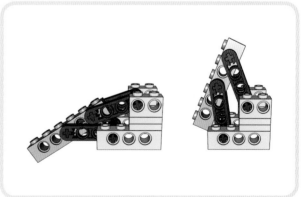

Figure 7-16: An outrigger mechanism from one of the LEGO mobile cranes uses levers that are not exactly parallel. The yellow part is the chassis, the levers are red, and the actual outrigger is grey.

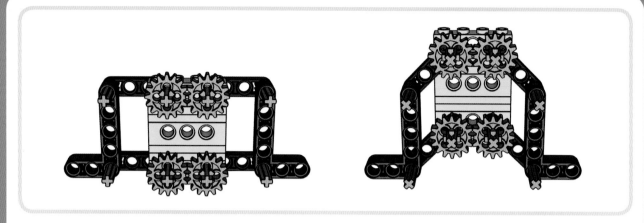

Figure 7-17: Two pairs of parallel levers connected by gears are installed on the element between them. The gears make the pairs rotate in opposite directions, moving the parts at both ends horizontally.

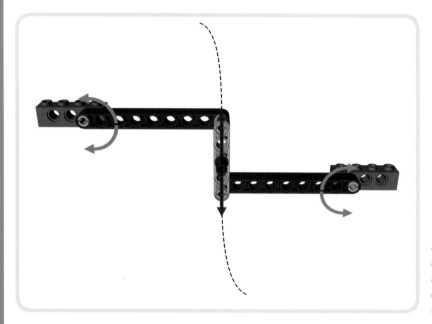

Figure 7-18: Watt's linkage consists of two long side links and one shorter central link. A rocking movement of any of the side links makes the central link move so that its center (marked by the red pin) follows a straight line.

linear motion, allowing elements of various machines to move along straight lines. They can also be used to achieve mechanical advantage using the law of the lever. The lever is, in fact, the simplest linkage possible.

NOTE In all the figures of linkages here, beams in the same color are of the same length. A dark grey color is used to mark the supporting structure, which remains stationary and to which the linkage is attached, and red pins mark the point of the linkage that performs the desired motion.

The key advantage of linkages is that their movement remains restricted without the need for external guiding elements, as shown in Figure 7-18. This makes them convenient for many uses. In the real world, linkages are used to control the movement of suspension components. Note also that usually only one particular point of a linkage follows the desired movement, and we can use pins located at this point to transfer this movement elsewhere—for example, to the base of the element we want to move using the linkage. A nearly infinite variation of motions can be achieved by varying the lengths and positions of just three or four beams!

Chebyshev linkage

The Chebyshev linkage, also known as Tchebycheff's linkage, consists of three links and is driven by the rocking motion of the lower links (light grey). This motion makes the central link (yellow) move so that its center (marked by the red pin) follows a straight line. The motion continues to the point at which the central link becomes vertical. The central link needs to be the shortest of the three to prevent it from colliding with the supporting structure (dark grey).

Hoeken's linkage

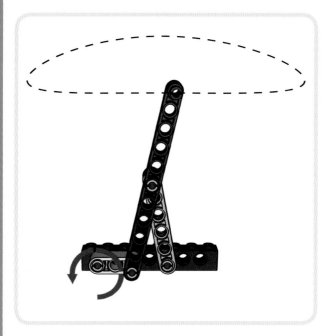

Hoeken's linkage consists of three links and is driven by the rotary motion of the shortest one (yellow). The proportions of the following three dimensions are crucial to make this linkage work: the length of the shortest link (yellow), the length of the medium link (light grey), and the distance between points of attachment to the supporting structure. The proportions should be 2 to 5 to 4. The longest link (blue) can be extended to any length beyond its upper joint. The tip of this link traces the shape of a flattened oval cut in half (the dotted line in the illustration), and the size of this oval is determined by the extended link's length. A little less than half of this link's movement is linear. Such an unusual motion pattern can be used, for example, to drive the legs of walking vehicles.

pantograph

A pantograph is a particular type of linkage with four links and two points, and its movement is quite interesting. In a pantograph, the point marked by the green pin mimics every movement of the point marked by the red pin, but on a larger scale. The difference in scale depends on the length of the longest link (light blue) and on where other links are attached to it (note that the longest link actually works like a lever).

The most interesting and popular use of this property is creating enlarged or reduced copies of drawings by attaching pens to both these points and "drawing" with one of them manually. This also works with handwriting; Thomas Jefferson used this method to duplicate his correspondence. Today, scaled copies can easily be created using a computer. However, pantographs still remain in use where certain tools require accurate manual control, as in engraving and sewing.

Peaucellier–Lipkin cell

The Sarrus linkage consists of four links in two identical groups that are perpendicular to each other. All links are of equal length, and the linkage is driven by the rocking motion of both lower or both upper links. The advantage of the Sarrus linkage is that it can be used to lift the structure connecting the upper links, providing an impressive range of movement as seen in Figure 7-19). Note that the perpendicular links work in different directions and thus exert stress on each other, which is why they need to be very rigid and preferably several studs wide for the linkage to work properly.

The disadvantage of the Sarrus linkage is that it requires one link from one group to be moved simultaneously with a second link from a second group. In other

The Peaucellier–Lipkin cell, also known simply as Peaucellier's cell, consists of seven links and is driven by the rocking motion of the central link (yellow). Note that the spacing between the cell's two points of attachment to the supporting structure needs to be equal to the length of the central link.

The Peaucellier–Lipkin cell works on the principle of inversion of a circle (with the central link tracing part of it), and it was one of the first linkages capable of producing perfectly linear motion. Its invention was crucial for the development of 19th-century industry and, most notably, for its use in steam engines.

Sarrus linkage

Figure 7-19: The Sarrus linkage's minimum and maximum range of lift

words, the motion of the links needs to be mechanically synchronized. Figure 7-20 shows one of the simplest synchronization methods. Note that the Sarrus linkage can consist of three or four groups as well, but two properly synchronized groups are enough to provide stable movement of the upper structure.

Figure 7-20: This Sarrus linkage uses mated bevel gears to synchronize links between the two groups.

Scott-Russell linkage

The Scott-Russell linkage consists of two links and is driven by the rocking motion of the shorter one (yellow). The longer link (blue) has one end attached to the supporting structure so that it can slide on it along a straight line. That makes the other end of that link move in a straight line as well. Both ends of that link move as if they were locked between guiding elements, but only one end actually is.

Note that the spacings between all joints of the linkage (marked by pins in the illustration) have to be equal. In this example, they are all equal to 3 studs.

scissor linkage

A scissor linkage, also known as a scissor mechanism, combines Scott-Russel and Sarrus linkages to create a compact mechanism capable of lifting with impressive range. It can consist of any even number of identical links—for example 2, 4, 6, and so on—and is driven by either the rocking motion of any link or by moving the end of the link that can slide within the supporting structure. Note that one of the top links also has an end that slides within the upper structure, but its movement can be restrained by simply making the upper structure's weight rest on it. In the illustration, the end has an axle pin with a bush attached to support the upper structure while sliding.

The two key advantages of the scissor linkage, its range (shown in Figure 7-21) and its stability, combined with its compactness make it a very popular mechanical solution. For example, it appears in car doors to make windows move up and down; in so-called scissor lifts; and even in high-end

Figure 7-21: A comparison of the same 10-link-long scissor linkage in a fully retracted and a fully extended position

computer keyboards, where it's used to stabilize keys. There is no limit to how many links can be used in a scissor linkage, except that every joint adds extra friction. There are also no special length or distance requirements, except that all links have to be equal.

Watt's linkage

Watt's linkage (shown earlier in Figure 7-18) consists of three links: a short central link (light blue) and two longer side links (blue). The linkage is driven by the rocking motion of either side link. As the side links rotate, the central links move so that the mechanism's center follows the dotted line, which remains straight most of the time. Note that while the ends of that line deflect to the left and right, you can limit motion of the linkage to the straight part only.

Watt's linkage is sometimes used in suspension systems to keep suspension components moving up and down rather than sideways. In most configurations, its side links are two or even three times longer than the central link.

8

custom mechanical solutions

While the LEGO Group produces an incredible range of specialized Technic pieces, they won't always meet our needs.
Sometimes we'll need to combine pieces to create mechanical solutions we find in the real world. This is the subject of
this chapter: mechanisms that extend the functionality of
your constructions beyond the limits of ready-made LEGO
pieces. Here you'll find mechanisms that transform one
type of motion into another, that take basic LEGO lights and
transform them into sophisticated signaling systems, and
much more.

These mechanisms are fun to build just on their own as
explorations of mechanical engineering concepts, but you'll
also find them quite useful when building larger models.

a stronger differential

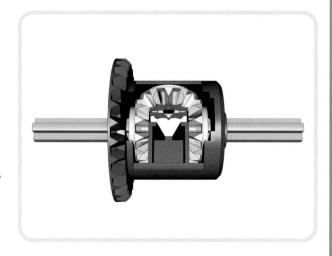

Figure 8-1: A ready-made LEGO differential, with the differential housing in
dark grey, three inner gears in tan, and two output axles in light grey

Differentials are an essential part of every driven axle in
a vehicle with wheels. They're also important in large and
heavy LEGO vehicles. The prebuilt LEGO differential consists
of a housing with a ring gear and with places for two axles
and three bevel gears inside, as shown in Figure 8-1. This is
the mechanism that we'll re-create, stronger and better.

NOTE There are three variants of ready-made LEGO
differentials. They are all discussed in Chapter 5.

In automobiles, a differential is located between the
wheels. The differential's housing is driven, and the differential transfers the drive to the wheels through its two output
axles. Note that the differential transfers the drive from the
housing through the central bevel gear, which is meshed
with bevel gears on the two axles. The central bevel gear

can balance the drive between the output axles, meaning
that it can drive one axle faster than the other. This ability
to balance the drive enables the vehicle to turn smoothly.
Figure 8-2 shows that the wheels of a turning vehicle travel
along different arcs. As a result, the inner and outer wheels
have to travel different distances. A differential is able to
balance this difference by driving the outer wheel faster than
the inner one.

As ready-made LEGO differentials are torque sensitive
and rarely appear outside of big, expensive sets, we can
build our own differential using a large Technic turntable,
as shown in Figure 8-3.

This kind of custom differential is much larger and much
sturdier than a ready-made one. Using a turntable allows the
mechanism to transfer drive to the differential without using
bevel gears and instead using the much stronger knob wheel.

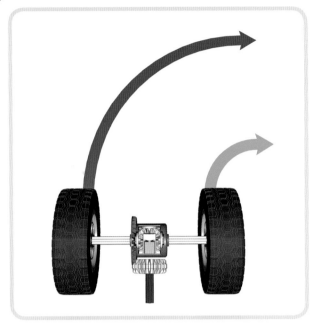

Figure 8-2: Differential in a turning vehicle. The red axle transfers drive to the differential housing, which then transfers it to the wheels.

Figure 8-3: A custom differential made of a large Technic turntable connected to a studless frame. The input axle is shown in red, the output axles are shown in green, and the dark grey beams are parts of the chassis's structure around the differential.

At the same time, the turntable provides a robust mounting point, holding the differential firmly to the chassis.

It's possible to build a vehicle without using differentials, but there are some disadvantages. Without a differential, at least one wheel will slip while cornering a turn, increasing friction and tire wear and impairing the vehicle's maneuverability.

If there is no differential in a driven, nonsteered axle, that axle will also be prone to slipping while making a turn. This can actually be desirable if your intention is to build a vehicle whose rear end slides dramatically when turning. In the real world, small, lightweight vehicles, such as go-karts, are usually built without differentials because the advantages of a differential are not worth the increase in the drivetrain's complexity.

If there is no differential in a driven and steered axle (like the front axle of a front-wheel-drive car), turning becomes much more difficult. The difference in the inner and outer wheels' speeds while cornering is much greater in steered axles than in nonsteered ones, creating so much friction that it exerts significant stress on the drivetrain and can even stall the motor. At the same time, the minimum turning radius becomes larger because the wheels, forced to rotate at equal speeds, lose their grip.

differential locks

With all the advantages of using a differential, there is also one disadvantage that is particularly important for off-road vehicles. As a differential transfers drive between its two outputs, it tends to transfer more of it to the less loaded one. This works fine when turning, but it can stop a vehicle entirely if one of the wheels slips or loses contact with the ground. A so-called *slip situation* occurs, in which the differential transfers all the drive to the wheel that has lost contact, completely stopping the one that's still touching the ground. When this happens, we can use a *differential lock* to force the differential to drive both wheels, overcoming the slip situation.

A differential lock joins a differential's two outputs together, effectively disabling the differential so that it transfers drive but doesn't balance it. It's important to understand that a differential lock does not *prevent* a slip situation: The lock is used when a slip occurs and *fixes* the slip. This is because a differential lock and a differential can't work at the same time. As a result, the differential lock

a custom differential

1

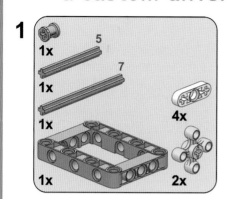

1x
1x
1x
1x
5
7
4x
2x

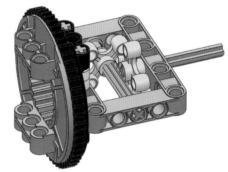

2

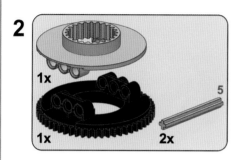

1x
1x
5
2x

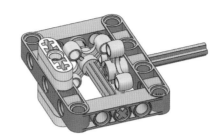

3

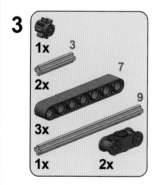

1x
2x
3x
1x
3
7
9
2x

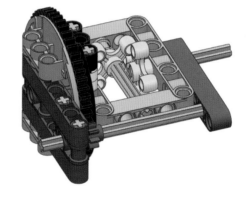

4

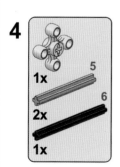

1x
2x
1x
5
6

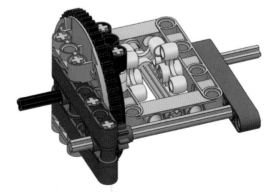

should remain disengaged to allow the differential to function normally and should engage only when a slip situation stops the vehicle. Real off-road vehicles come with manual or automatic locks that engage when a slip situation is detected and disengage when the vehicle drives out of it. LEGO differentials can be locked manually with relative ease; doing this automatically is also possible, but it's extremely complex and impractical. Figures 8-4 and 8-5 show simple manual differential locks for all three variants of ready-made LEGO differentials.

LEGO differential locks use transmission driving rings (#6539) that can be engaged and disengaged using a transmission changeover catch (#6641). The catch can be controlled remotely with a motor or with pneumatics. The latter solution is more convenient if there are many locks on your vehicle that move together with the suspension. Note that it's not necessary to put a lock on every differential on a vehicle—just one is usually enough to make the vehicle drive out of a slip situation.

Figure 8-6 shows a compact, robust nonsteered axle design based on the 5×7 studless frame. It allows the differential to be driven with a 3:1 gear reduction from the front or rear so that the drive can be transmitted through this axle to the next one. It also allows for easy locking and unlocking of the differential, using a lever that can be motorized or—as in this example—controlled by a small pneumatic cylinder.

As you can see, differential locks add to a chassis's width significantly. This is why they are unpopular in complex LEGO suspension systems (see Chapter 15), which are quite wide themselves. Still, given the fact that locks are not required on every axle, it's a good idea to install them on nonsteered driven axles, where they fit more easily than on steered ones.

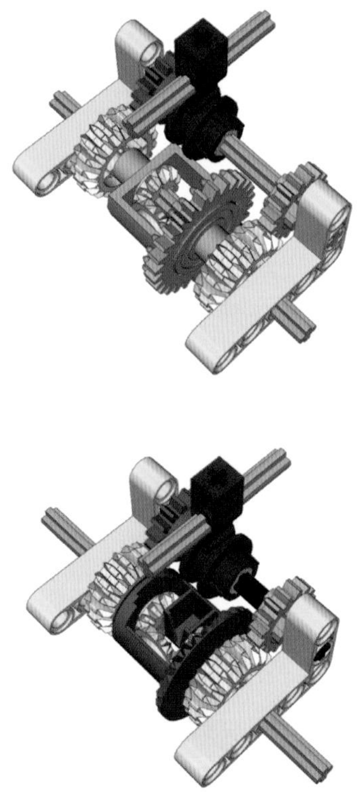

Figure 8-5: With the other LEGO differential variant, things are simpler: Each side of its housing can be engaged directly by a transmission driving ring, thus locking it to one of the outputs and efficiently disabling the differential.

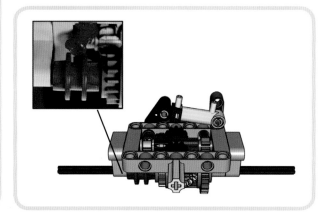

Figure 8-6: Compact nonsteered axle with a differential lock. Note that the transmission driving ring is moved by a common connector piece rather than by the changeover catch. The connector piece moves it without any backlash and is less likely to snap off under stress.

Figure 8-4: LEGO's oldest (left) and newest (right) differentials can have locks made of four extra gears and a transmission driving ring, which locks the two outputs together, disabling the differential. With the latest variant, the lock is 1 stud narrower than on the first.

an axle with a differential lock

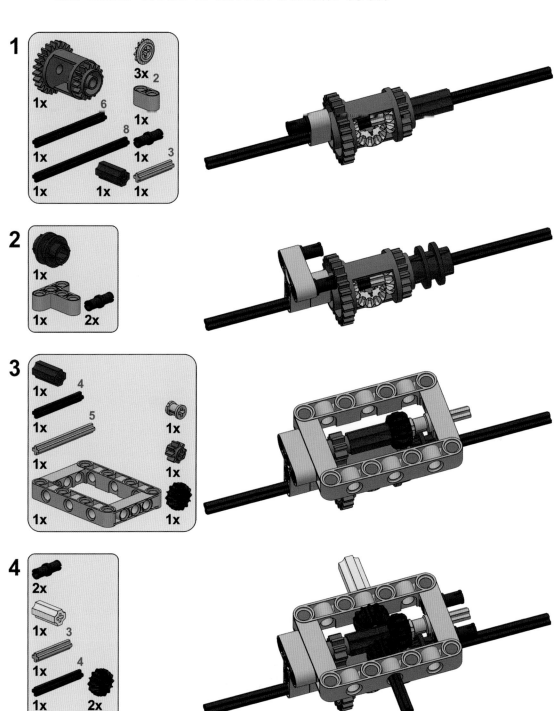

1
3x 2
1x
1x 6
8
1x
1x 1x 3
1x 1x 1x

2
1x
1x 2x

3
1x 4
1x 5
1x 1x
1x 1x
1x 1x

4
2x
1x 3
1x 4
1x 2x

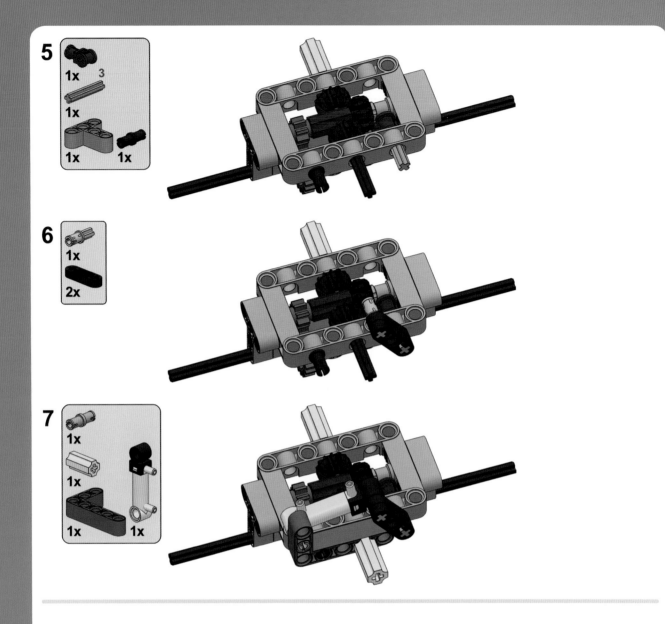

ratchets

There are certain mechanisms that we want to remain locked once they have stopped—for example, a winch on a crane or a rail-crossing barrier. If such mechanisms are motorized, a stopped motor will keep them stopped, but only until the load on the mechanism overcomes the motor's resistance and starts to drive it backward. This scenario is likely in the case of a heavy load, such as what a crane might carry.

One way to lock a mechanism completely is by using a worm gear (discussed in Chapter 5), but a worm gear reduces your speed dramatically and lacks the ability to unlock a mechanism. One better alternative is using a ratchet.

A LEGO ratchet has two elements: a freely spinning gear and a *pawl*, the small lever that stops the gear from spinning (see Figure 8-7). The pawl allows a gear to rotate in one direction but blocks it instantly when it starts to rotate in the opposite direction.

To work properly, a pawl needs to have a tip on its end that touches the gear's teeth at a specific angle. As Figure 8-8 shows, if we draw a line coming out of the mounting

Figure 8-7: A simple pawl (red) securing a 24-tooth ratchet (grey). The ratchet is free to rotate counterclockwise, as indicated by the green arrow, but the moment it starts rotating clockwise, the pawl will lock itself against the nearest tooth (although it's still possible to unlock it by hand).

Figure 8-8: The angle of the pawl should be such that the line coming out of its mounting point aims slightly below the gear's rim.

point of the pawl, this line should aim very slightly below the ratchet's rim. If the line aims too low, the ratchet will lock in both directions. If the line aims too high, the ratchet won't lock at all, bouncing off the teeth rather than stopping rotation.

The ratchet's shape also matters a good deal—luckily, a simple pin is perfectly suited for our needs. The pawl also needs to be *balanced* so that its tip tends to drop on the gear under its weight. Ratchets, therefore, are *gravity sensitive*.

NOTE It's possible to create a gravity-independent ratchet by attaching an elastic element, such as a rubber band, that keeps the ratchet pressed down on the wheel just as gravity normally would.

Figure 8-9 shows one possible use of a ratchet—as a means to store the potential energy of springs.

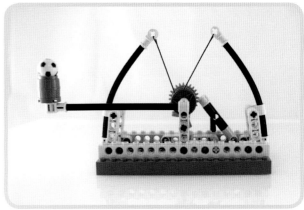

Figure 8-9: My working model of Leonardo da Vinci's leaf spring catapult used a ratchet as a trigger, keeping the catapult loaded and firing it when unlocked. The ratchet was strong enough to store the energy of two bent axles acting as a spring.

linear clutches

A linear clutch works just like the 24-tooth clutch gear described in Chapter 5—it slips under torque. By installing it between a motor and a mechanism, you can prevent the motor from stalling when the mechanism is blocked.

The difference between the linear clutch and the clutch gear is that the clutch gear needs to be meshed with a gear on another axle to work, whereas the linear clutch comes directly between two axles in single line. This saves a lot of space because the linear clutch can simply replace any axle that is at least 4 studs long. The linear clutch also fits between two universal joints that are at least 2 studs apart, and it doesn't need to be supported, so it can work at any angle.

The linear clutch makes use of axle pins with friction. As Figure 8-10 shows, two of these are inserted into a pin joiner, and then their axle ends can be inserted into axle joiners or universal joints, which can be connected to axles of any length. Note that using this clutch for a prolonged period of time will eventually wear down its parts.

Figure 8-10: Two axle pins (blue) inserted into a pin joiner (red) are the core of the linear clutch (top). They can then be inserted between two axle joiners (middle) or two universal joints (bottom).

eccentric mechanisms

An eccentric mechanism, also called a crank mechanism, is used to transform rotary motion into reciprocating motion and vice versa. It's a vital part of almost every car's engine, transforming the linear movement of pistons into the rotation of the driveshaft.

A typical eccentric mechanism consists of a disc and a short beam that connects the disc to a pushrod. As the disc rotates, the beam makes the pushrod move forward and backward along a straight line, as shown in Figure 8-11. Note that if the green pushrod is guided, it has only linear motion. In this case, it is guided by the yellow Technic brick.

The distance the pushrod travels depends on the disc's diameter. The bigger the diameter, the longer the pushrod's travel distance. We can also provide rotational motion using a shorter beam instead of a disc, as shown in Figure 8-12. Here, the distance the pushrod travels depends on the length of the shorter beam.

An eccentric mechanism can also be used to transform rotary motion into rocking motion (that is, partial rotary motion). This type of mechanism, shown in Figure 8-13, has no pushrod; instead, it has a second disc that performs a partial rotation back and forth. The range of its movement depends on the relationship between the two discs' circumferences, and we can adjust the degree of movement by using different-sized discs. For this type of mechanism to work, however, the diameter of the second disc has to be larger than the diameter of the first disc, and the beam's length has to be larger than the first disc's diameter.

Figure 8-11: An eccentric mechanism with a disc (light grey), a beam (red), and a pushrod (green). The pushrod's travel distance is equal to 2 studs—that is, the disc's diameter minus 1 stud.

Figure 8-12: An eccentric mechanism with a shorter beam instead of a disc

Figure 8-13: An eccentric mechanism with two discs connected by a beam. The smaller disc makes full rotations, and the larger disc makes only partial rotations back and forth.

As shown in Figure 8-14, we can also replace discs with beams in this type of eccentric mechanism. Because the second beam doesn't make a full rotation, the whole mechanism takes up less space. Note that this type of mechanism works only in one direction; you cannot drive the grey beam with the green beam.

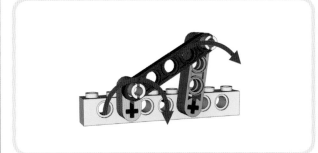

Figure 8-14: An eccentric mechanism with beams instead of discs. Because the second beam (green) makes only a partial rotation, the mechanism takes up less space.

Eccentric mechanisms can be put to a variety of uses, appearing in a car's windshield wipers, an oscillating fan, and so forth.

Scotch yokes

A Scotch yoke is a simpler alternative to an eccentric mechanism. It does the same job—converting rotary motion into reciprocating motion and vice versa—while using a smaller number of moving parts. The parts, however, are less common than those in an eccentric mechanism. A Scotch yoke takes more space than an eccentric mechanism but is less likely to fail under high torque.

A Scotch yoke consists of a rectangular frame hung between two sections of an axle. The frame has a slot inside it into which a single pin located on a disc adjacent to the frame enters, as shown in Figure 8-15. As the disc rotates, the pin can go up and down freely inside the slot, but its sideways movement is translated directly to the frame and thus to the axles.

Each rotation of the disc makes the frame move forward and backward by a range equal to the disc's diameter. The Scotch yoke's range of movement is equal to the disc's

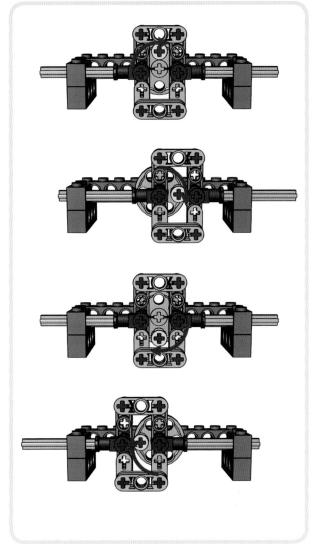

Figure 8-15: Working cycle of the Scotch yoke with a frame (green) and a disc with a single pin (yellow)

diameter, which means that it transforms the movement more efficiently than an eccentric mechanism would. We can increase the range by using a bigger disc and increasing the size of the slot inside the frame accordingly. The height of the slot has to be at least equal to the disc's diameter, which also means that the yoke's movement range is the minimum height of its slot.

a Scotch yoke

1

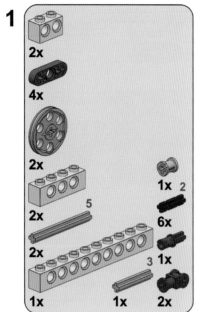

2x
4x
2x
2x
2x
1x

5
3

1x
1x 2
6x
1x
2x

2

4x

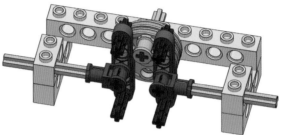

3

4x

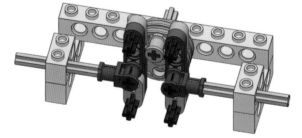

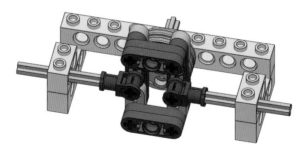

Oldham couplings

An Oldham coupling, also called an Oldham joint, is a coupling that transfers drive between an input and an output that are not aligned. While you can use universal joints or even gears to connect a misaligned output and input, these solutions may not always suit your needs. Using two universal joints tends to take a lot of horizontal space, and using gears may result in an unwanted change in torque and speed. An Oldham coupling maintains a 1:1 ratio and takes only a little space, though it is more complex, has a large diameter, and produces extra friction. To see an Oldham coupling in action, visit *http://www.youtube.com/watch?v=2M9cp_IJ4_I.*

Oldham couplings consist of two identical attachments—one for the input and another for the output—and a single sliding element between them. In the real world, the major advantage of an Oldham coupling is how short it is; in the world of LEGO, we can make an Oldham coupling 3 studs long, which is still only half the space required by two universal joints.

The coupling shown in Figure 8-16 can transfer drive between an input and an output that are misaligned by 1 stud horizontally and 1 stud vertically (the location of the input and output axles is shown in Figure 8-17). It is possible to build such a coupling using longer axles and thus increase the maximum displacement of its input and output. While the coupling will remain 3 studs long, however, its diameter will get significantly bigger.

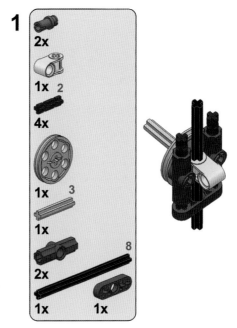

Figure 8-16: An Oldham coupling consists of two identical attachments (blue and red) and an element that slides between them. This Oldham coupling is only 3 studs long.

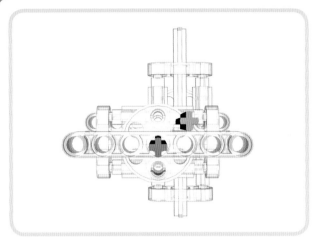

Figure 8-17: The maximum displacement between this Oldham coupling's input and output is 1 stud horizontally and 1 stud vertically. The coupling can be expanded to allow greater displacement at the cost of increasing its diameter.

Schmidt couplings

A Schmidt coupling, like an an Oldham coupling, transfers drive between an input and an output that are not aligned while maintaining a 1:1 ratio between them. It, too, is an alternative to using gears or universal joints to transfer drive.

A Schmidt coupling consists of three discs or triangles, each connected with three links to one another, making six links total. The first disc is attached to the input, the third disc is attached to the output, and the middle disc doesn't need any support—it can work while hanging in midair. Uniquely, this coupling's input and output can move relative to each other because the middle disc equalizes their movement. The coupling can therefore transfer drive between two elements while they are in lateral motion, which is not possible with traditional gearing or Oldham couplings.

We can build a Schmidt coupling with LEGO pieces by using piece #57585 as a base for the triangles, as shown in Figure 8-18 (note that only pins without friction should be used). The coupling is 5 studs long, but it's extremely robust and can handle greater torque than any alternative solution, including universal joints. It's also mesmerizing to watch. The coupling shown in Figure 8-19 can be moved by up to 5 studs, and we can increase this value by making

the triangles' arms longer. The links should be made longer accordingly—however, for the coupling to work, each link (shown in yellow) can be only a little longer than the radius of the triangle.

Figure 8-18: LEGO piece #57585 (light grey) can be used to create triangles of various sizes.

Figure 8-19: A Schmidt coupling with three triangles (in green, red, and blue) and six links (yellow). Note that the middle triangle (red) doesn't need any support—it can even move as the coupling works.

stepper motors

In the real world, stepper motors rotate by a constant angle every time they are turned on instead of rotating continuously. For example, we might have a stepper motor that performs one-quarter of a rotation every time its button is pressed. Such motors are very useful for complex automations of many sorts; real assembly lines are full of stepper motors.

While LEGO does not produce this kind of motor, we can build a custom one mechanically. By adding a simple mechanism to a motor, we can make it work like a stepper motor and use it for a variety of tasks; for example, we can control a sequential gearbox remotely.

To create a stepper motor, we need a knob wheel mounted on a motor's output axle and a beam fastened to that wheel with an elastic element, such as a shock absorber or a rubber band, as shown in Figure 8-20.

Figure 8-20: The knob on the motor's output axle (blue) has a beam (red) fastened to it at all times by a rubber band (green). This makes a regular motor behave similarly to a stepper motor.

By keeping the beam fastened to the knob at all times, we slow the motor down every quarter rotation (90 degrees). The motor takes a while to overcome the pressure and perform another quarter rotation; its constant rotary movement now becomes intermittent. By turning the motor on for just the right amount of time, we can control it precisely, making it turn by a desired number of rotations. To keep track of the number of rotations, we can watch the knob or simply listen to the sound of the motor, which is quite different from a motor running continuously. Note that this mechanism exerts some pressure on the motor, causing the motor's internal parts to wear down faster than usual.

Geneva mechanisms

A Geneva mechanism (see Figure 8-21), sometimes called a Geneva drive or Maltese cross mechanism, converts motion between its input and output so that every rotation of the input advances the output by a specific, constant angle. In plain English, that means it converts continuous rotary motion into intermittent rotary motion. A Geneva mechanism may appear odd, but it's quite common. For example, Geneva mechanisms appear in mechanical watches and movie projectors, where they stop every frame of the film for a fraction of a second.

Figure 8-21: A simple Geneva mechanism with an input (red) and an output (green). Each rotation of the input advances the output by a quarter rotation—that is, 90 degrees.

Building a Geneva mechanism with LEGO pieces is a tough job since real Geneva mechanisms use complex circular elements to achieve the desired motion. The following BI shows a relatively simple and small model.

Note that the output of this mechanism can rotate freely when not engaged by the input, while in a real Geneva mechanism, the output remains locked when not engaged by the input. Building a model with LEGO mechanisms in which the output remains locked like this is extremely difficult, and any attempts to do so will result in very large and complex mechanisms. The Geneva mechanism can be simulated in a simple way, though, by putting lots of friction on the green axle. This friction makes the mechanism stop unless engaged by the input.

a Geneva mechanism

1

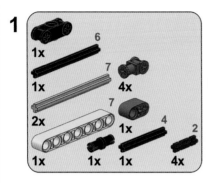

6 — 1x
7 — 1x
7 — 2x
— 4x
4 — 1x
— 1x — 1x — 1x
2 — 4x

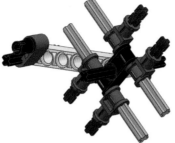

2

1x

2x
5 — 2x
1x — 2x

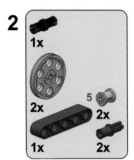 

reverse lights

Let's assume we have a vehicle on which we want reverse lights that turn on and off automatically when the vehicle backs up. We can create such lighting with a single switch connected to a driveshaft; we just have to block that switch to limit it to the on and off positions only. The Power Functions switch has an *on-off-on* switching pattern, and by blocking one of its extreme positions, we can limit it to *on-off*, as shown in Figure 8-22.

With the switch blocked, all we have to do is connect the axle that goes through it to the driveshaft, using a gear with a clutch so that the switch won't stop the driveshaft once switched, as shown in Figure 8-23. Note that the gear ratio matters here: Any gear reduction from the driveshaft will slow down the switching, and we don't want that. For the switch to react to changes in the driveshaft's direction quickly, we need a 1:1 gear ratio or higher.

Figure 8-22: In this simple way to limit a Power Functions switch to the on and off positions, the pin prevents the orange switch from moving to the far right on *position).*

Figure 8-23: A blocked Power Functions switch is connected to a vehicle's driveshaft (red) through a 24-tooth gear with clutch (white).

Any lights connected to the switch in this setup will turn on when the vehicle drives in one direction and off when it drives in another. There's a chance we will get the directions wrong and our reverse lights will turn on when the vehicle goes forward; to fix this, simply change the direction the axle inside the switch rotates by moving the switch to the opposite side of the driveshaft or by adding one more gear between it and the driveshaft. Of course, this mechanism adds the friction of the clutch to the driving system of the gear while the vehicle is moving. This friction causes a loss of power in the drivetrain, which gets bigger with higher driveshaft-to-switch gear ratios.

flashing lights

When we want LEGO lights to flash, we have two options: We can use old 9V bricks with lights (shown in Figure 8-24), which have the built-in ability to flash, or we can use LEGO LEDs from the Power Functions system, which require adding a custom mechanism.

Figure 8-25: A 1×4-stud 9V brick with lights connected to a 9V battery box. By rotating the brick on the plug 180 degrees, we can switch between its lighting modes.

Figure 8-24 Four types of 9V bricks with lights

Figure 8-26: A 1×4-stud 9V brick with lights (left) and a pair of Power Functions LED lights (right). Note the difference in the color and direction of the light.

Depending on the polarity of the power supply, 9V bricks with lights are programmed to provide steady light or to flash. To switch between the two modes, change the orientation of one of the plugs of the wire connecting the brick to the power supply—or, more simply, rotate the brick on the plug 180 degrees, as shown in Figure 8-25.

Bricks with lights, however, have a number of disadvantages when compared to LEGO LEDs. Most importantly, they are long out of production, so it's difficult and expensive to find a brick in good working condition today. Secondly, they use tiny incandescent light bulbs, which means that they consume a lot power, are prone to failure, and produce a strong yellowish light in all directions, as shown in Figure 8-26. LEGO LEDs are free from all these disadvantages, and they fit in much smaller spaces. Their only drawback is the lack of a built-in ability to flash, which we can add mechanically.

To make LEGO LEDs flash, we need a switch and a motor. Using an old 9V switch is the easy way, but we can use a Power Functions switch as well, which we can connect via an eccentric mechanism. Figures 8-27 and 8-28 show both versions.

With the old 9V switch, adding the ability to flash is simple: The switch can be connected directly to a motor whose rotary motion will keep turning it on and off, thus making the lights connected to the switch flash. The flashing frequency can be adjusted by adding a gear between the

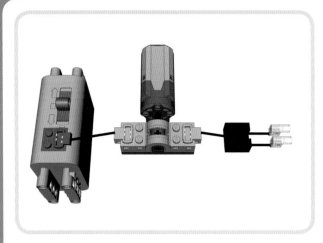

Figure 8-27: The old 9V switch

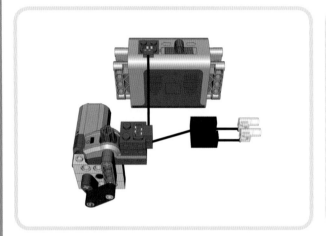

Figure 8-28: The Power Functions switch

To create turn signals, we need to extend our flashing-light mechanism by connecting two more switches to it. The resulting device will be controlled by a single motor and will have two groups of LEDs connected to it; one will flash or the other will, depending on the motor's direction.

Since we discussed how to make a flashing-light mechanism in the previous section, let's focus on the two extra switches. We need to hard-couple them so that turning one switch on turns the other off. The coupling can be done with two gears, preferably two 16-tooth gears (as shown on the left in Figure 8-29), because they are the smallest gears accurate enough, or two half bushes with teeth (as shown on the right in Figure 8-29). The important thing is to keep the two axles going through the two switches at slightly different angles so both switches can't be turned on or off at the same time.

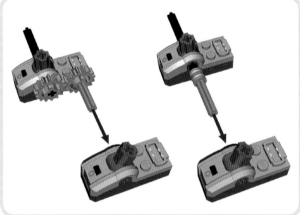

Figure 8-29: Hard-coupling two Power Functions switches with gears (left) and toothed half bushes (right). Note that the angle of axles coupled this way differs, preventing the two switches from being turned on or off simultaneously.

motor and the switch or by changing the motor's speed. Note that Power Functions extension/adapter wires are needed to use the old 9V switch with Power Functions LEDs and power supplies. The old 9V power supply requires no adapter.

The Power Functions switch needs to be motorized through an eccentric mechanism to make the lights connected to it flash. The eccentric mechanism keeps the switch going back and forth through its three positions (*on-off-on*).

turn signals

Now that we've covered how to make LEGO lights flash, we can take this knowledge one step further and create turn signals for our vehicle.

Next, with the two switches hard-coupled at different angles, we need to block one of them in the same way as with the reverse lights described earlier in this chapter (see Figure 8-30). We will limit the switching pattern from *on-off-on* to *on-off*. Since the switches are hard-coupled, both will be blocked.

Now we have to connect the axle of one of the switches to the input of the flashing-light mechanism. A gear with a clutch is needed to allow the input to keep running after the switches are switched, as shown in Figures 8-31 and 8-32.

The only thing left to do at this point is to connect all these elements electrically. A connection scheme for the variant with the 9V switch is shown in Figure 8-33. The

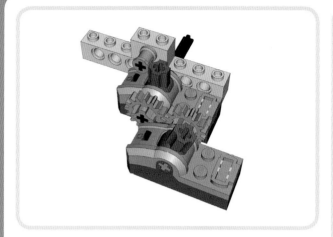

Figure 8-30: Two hard-coupled switches with one of them blocked. The hard-coupling makes the block work on both switches.

Figure 8-32: A more complex variant uses the Power Functions switch and an eccentric mechanism to make lights flash. The gear is identical to that of the previous figure.

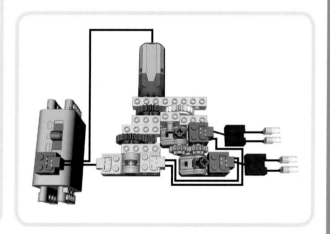

Figure 8-31: Two hard-coupled switches connected to a motorized flashing-light mechanism that uses an old 9V switch. Note the gear down between the motor and the 9V switch—it lowers the flashing rate of the lights to a realistic value.

Figure 8-33: Electric connection scheme for the simpler mechanism variant. For a remote-controlled model, you should connect the master switch to the same IR receiver as the motor.

variant with the Power Functions switch follows the same pattern: The *master switch* (the one used in the flashing-light mechanism) is connected to the same power source/control module as the motor. The two *child switches* (the hard-coupled ones) are connected to the master switch and have lights connected to them. Thus, as the master switch creates a flashing effect, the child switches control which

group of lights is flashing at the moment. You can switch between the two groups by changing the motor's direction.

Note that there is no limit to the number of flashing lights we can control with this method. And the same motor that controls this mechanism can be used to steer the vehicle that houses it, making the turn signals work automatically as you steer your model!

complex turn signals

1

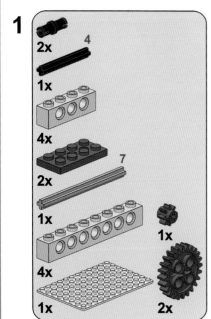

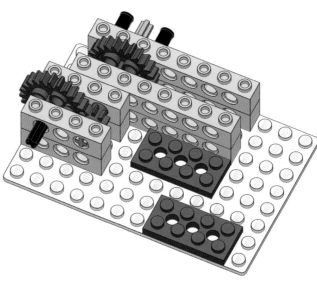

2

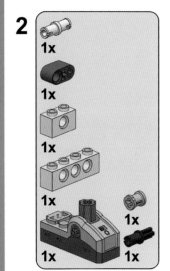

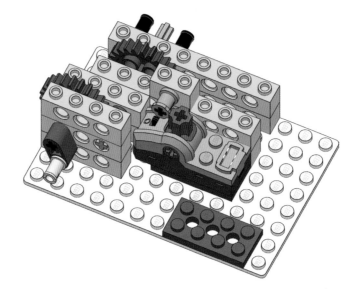

3

1x
2x   6
1x   1x   3
1x   1x
1x   1x

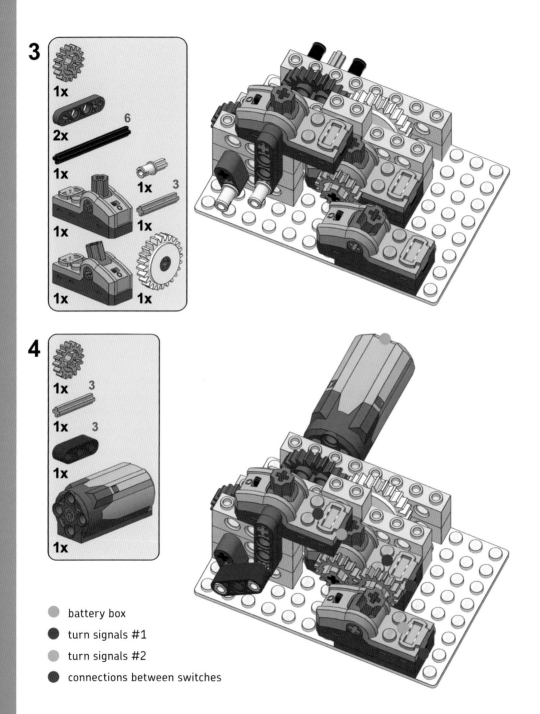

4

1x
1x   3
1x   3
1x
1x

- ● battery box
- ● turn signals #1
- ● turn signals #2
- ● connections between switches

double-axle turntable transmission

Transmitting drive through a Technic turntable is quite easy with just one axle—we just have to put the axle through the turntable's center. However, one axle is not enough for some vehicles. Tracked excavators, for instance, need two separate axles to drive the right and left tracks, and their propulsion motors are often located in the superstructure, which is separated from the chassis by a turntable. In such a case, we can use a transmission driving ring (as shown in Figure 8-34) or an empty differential housing (as shown in Figure 8-35).

The disadvantage of such a transmission system, other than its complexity level, is that when the superstructure rotates relative to the chassis, one of the axles is affected by its movement: the blue one in Figures 8-34 and 8-35. The axle is actually driven by the superstructure's movement, causing the whole chassis to turn. However, as the superstructure's rotation is usually slow, the effect is negligible, and it can be further minimized by gearing down both axles below the turntable. The advantage is that this transmission system allows you to build a tracked vehicle with all the electric elements in the superstructure. This means that no wires go through the turntable, which enables the superstructure to rotate any number of times without the risk of damaging any elements going through it.

Both variants can be built in a similar way. However, as the transmission driving ring variant is more practical, we will focus on it. The building instructions for this variant are shown next. Notice that the chassis and the superstructure can be easily built around this variant.

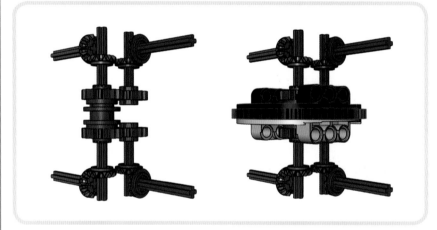

Figure 8-34: Scheme for transmitting drive through a turntable for two axles independently. Elements transmitting the drive are marked red and blue to show their independence. This variant uses a transmission driving ring to transmit drive over the blue axle that goes through the turntable's center. Note that there is no axle joiner inside the driving ring, so it rotates freely on the axle.

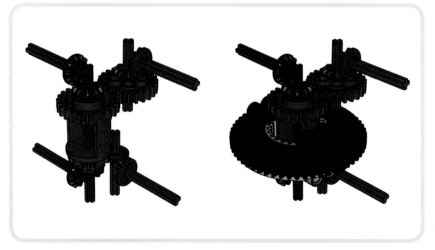

Figure 8-35: The same transmission system with an empty differential housing instead of a transmission driving ring. This variant is simpler but less practical because of the large 24-tooth gear on the housing.

a double-axle turntable transmission

1

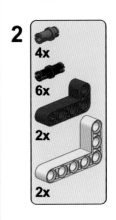

10x

2x

1x

1x

2

4x

6x

2x

2x

3

11

2x

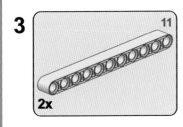

4

2x

2x

5

2x

1x

1x 3

1x

1x 7

1x 3x

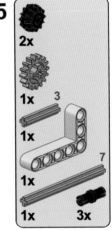

6

1x

1x 11

1x 2x

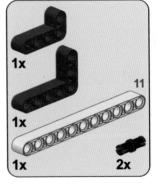

7

7
1x

8
1x 2x

8

2x

2x

1x

9

2x

1x 3

1x

2x 2x

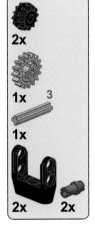

10

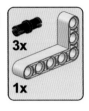

3x

1x

11

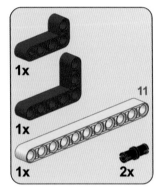

1x

1x

11

1x 2x

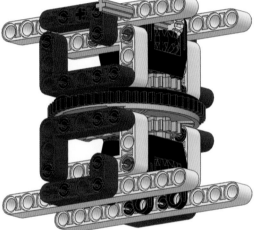

12

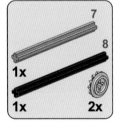

7

8

1x

1x 2x

a sturdy universal joint

While ready-made LEGO universal joints have a number of advantages, they are prone to failure when subjected to high torque. We can build a custom universal joint out of basic pieces that will act the same while being more robust, at the cost of bigger size (shown in Figure 8-36).

Figure 8-36: A custom universal joint is more robust but also larger than ready-made ones.

a universal joint

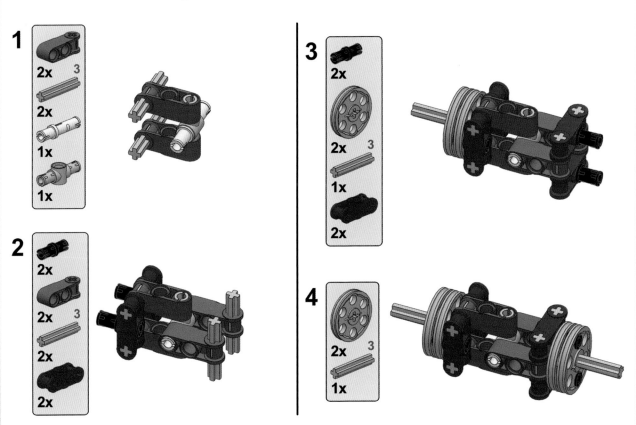

the LEGO pneumatic system

the Old system

The LEGO pneumatic system is a miniature model of real-life pneumatic and hydraulic systems. It consists of three basic modules: a *pressure generator*, such as a manual pump or a motorized compressor; a *control module*, one or more valves that direct the flow of air; and *cylinders*, which convert pressure to linear movement. The modules are connected by elastic pneumatic hoses.

The basic working principle of a pneumatic system is based on the tendency of air to move from areas of high pressure to areas of low pressure. The pressure generator fills the pneumatic system with pressurized air, and then the air is directed to the cylinders using the control module, which makes the cylinders extend or retract. When the pressure of the system is equalized, all movement stops.

Every pneumatic system has limited capacity for air pressure. In the case of LEGO models, that limit is normally three bars, which is roughly equivalent to three times atmospheric pressure. If a LEGO pressure generator exceeds this capacity, the pneumatic hoses may pop off the ports of pneumatic pieces.

Because the LEGO pneumatic system relies on hoses and connectors, it is not perfectly closed and is subject to microleaks. *Microleaks*, small amounts of air leaking out of the pneumatic system, usually occur at the ends of pneumatic hoses (or in the middle if they are damaged). These microleaks result in reduced efficiency. And of course, as with any mechanical system, complexity is the enemy of efficiency in pneumatics.

NOTE Although LEGO connectors in the pneumatic system are technically called *inlets* and *outlets*, I'll call them *ports* for the sake of simplicity.

There are actually two different LEGO pneumatic systems: Old and New. Each works a bit differently, as described in the next sections.

Introduced in 1984, the Old LEGO pneumatic system (shown in Figure 9-1) is relatively complex. Its control module includes two interconnected pieces and one pneumatic hose that connects the pressure generator to the cylinders. Although the last LEGO set that included the Old system was released in 1987, this durable system continues to be widely available.

The *pump* shown in red at ❶ usually has a spring. When pushed, it pumps the surrounding air through its port, and the spring returns the pump to its initial rest position when released.

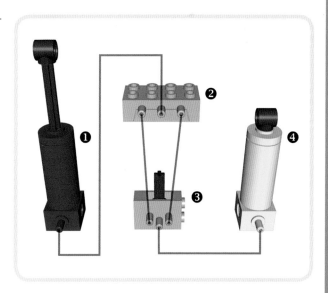

Figure 9-1: The Old-style pneumatic system uses two blocks to control airflow. The grey lines in this diagram represent hoses.

The light-grey element at ❷ is a *distribution block*, which includes a special *one-way valve*. Air is delivered from the pump into the distribution block's middle port, and the one-way valve forces the two side ports to pump air in only one direction: The port on the left takes air in, and port on the right expels the air. Thanks to the distribution block, we can not only increase the pressure in the LEGO pneumatic system but also decrease it by expelling air from the system.

The light-grey element at ❸ is a *valve*, which is connected to the distribution block by two hoses. A single distribution block can be connected to many valves using forked hoses. The total number of valves depends on how many pneumatic cylinders are meant to be controlled independently.

The valve has a lever that can be switched to one of three positions. One position extends all connected cylinders, another retracts the cylinders, and the third (middle) position cuts the connection that goes through the valve, effectively locking all cylinders. This third position is called *neutral*, and it is needed when you have many valves in a system because it prevents the valves from interfering with each other. Additionally, with the valve in neutral, the pressurized air remains sealed and thus can be used more efficiently in other parts of the system.

The yellow element at ❹ is a cylinder, which extends when air is delivered to it and retracts when air is sucked from it.

NOTE When a cylinder is subjected to suction, the air pressure inside it drops until it becomes lower than the atmospheric pressure surrounding it (one bar), at which point the cylinder starts to retract. For this reason, the LEGO pneumatic system can exert up to three bars of pressure for extension, but only up to one bar of pressure for retraction.

Compared with the New pneumatic system (discussed below) the Old pneumatic system does offer one advantage: It requires only one hose to connect a cylinder to a valve. But it also has several disadvantages. One is that it applies much less force to retract a cylinder than it does to extend it because air is expelled from the cylinder during extension and drawn in during retraction. Since the force exerted by the cylinders in a pneumatic system depends on whether they extend or retract, this is often considered a significant disadvantage, and this disadvantage is one of the main reasons why the New system was created.

Also, the control module in the Old system is complex, requiring two hoses for every valve connected to the distribution block. Finally, the Old system has many unique pieces (the pump, distribution block, and cylinders) that haven't been produced since 1987, making it virtually obsolete.

the New system

LEGO introduced the New pneumatic system (shown in Figure 9-2) in 1989 with the goal of simplicity and efficiency. The New system eliminated the distribution block and redesigned the pumps and cylinders, though it does use the Old valves. This new system is much more like real pneumatic and hydraulic systems.

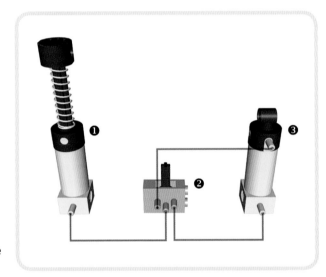

Figure 9-2: The New pneumatic system uses a simple design.

The yellow element at ❶ in Figure 9-2 is a pump that works only with the New system. The light-grey valve at ❷ is the same as that in the Old system except that it is connected a bit differently: Air is delivered into it through the middle port, and its side ports are connected to the cylinder. Either valve's port can be connected to either cylinder's port; this connection determines which of the valve's two extreme positions makes the cylinder extend or retract.

The yellow element at ❸ is a cylinder. It extends or retracts depending on which port the air is delivered to.

Unlike the Old system, the New one expels air through the valves, resulting in distinctive hissing sounds when valves are switched under high pressure. Also, because the New system doesn't use suction, retraction is only slightly weaker than extension.

NOTE You can swap the cylinders between the Old and New systems, but the cylinders from the Old system will perform poorly due to their different internal construction.

Compared with the Old system, the New system offers the advantage of using a simple control module, and the same force is exerted by the cylinders regardless of whether they extend or retract. Its main drawback is that two hoses are required for every cylinder connected to the valve, which can make multicylinder pneumatic systems very complex.

The New pneumatic system is used by most LEGO builders today, though some choose the Old system in order to reduce the number of hoses needed to connect cylinders or simply because they prefer the red cylinders.

Although the principles of the New system haven't changed since 1989, some new pieces have been added and existing pieces have been updated.

an inventory of pneumatic parts

This section describes all existing pneumatic pieces, in order of function, from pressure generators, control modules, and cylinders to miscellaneous pieces. Since most of the pieces in the New and Old systems are interchangeable, I've listed them together.

pneumatic pump (Old)

This is a large manual pump with a single port and a spring-loaded rod. It comes in two lengths and in both red and yellow. It draws air in from the outside when the rod is pushed; when the rod is released, the spring returns the pump to its initial, neutral position.

The pump's bottom can be mounted on studs, and both its ends have regular Technic holes. The lower end (the one with the port) is 2 studs wide, and the upper end is 1 stud wide. The pump's upper end makes manual pumping uncomfortable: When pumping fast for a prolonged time, it quickly becomes hot due to the compression of the air inside it.

pneumatic pump (New)

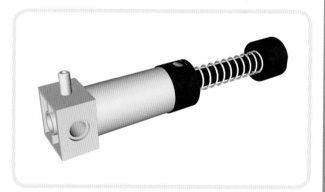

This is the large manual pump from the New system. This part is always yellow in LEGO Technic sets and transparent light blue in LEGO Education sets.

Like the Old system's pump, it contains one port and a spring-loaded rod. It works just as the old pump does, and its dimensions are almost identical, except for the addition of a contact pad on its upper end. This contact pad is designed to make manual pumping much more comfortable, and it does, but the pump is still prone to heating up just like the Old one.

small pneumatic pump (New)

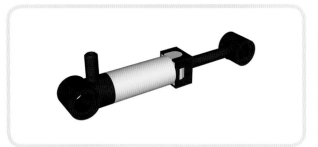

This small pump with one port has a rod that extends by 2 studs and no spring. It is best used with motorized compressors rather than manual pumps. Because it's so much smaller than the other pumps, it takes longer to provide comparable pressure, which is why compressors often include more than one such pump. It is also much less prone to heating.

This pump comes in yellow, blue, and a transparent light blue. In 2011, a new version was released with the 8110 set; it's light grey and is half a stud longer, resulting in slightly increased capacity.

distribution block (Old)

The distribution block is a light grey piece that's the same size as a 2×4×1 LEGO brick. It is used exclusively in the Old pneumatic system for sucking air out of the cylinders and

hasn't been produced since 1987. It has three ports on one side, and air is delivered to the middle one. A one-way valve inside affects how the ports work: The middle port allows air to flow both ways, the left allows air to flow in only, and the right allows air to flow out. If you use the ports incorrectly, the valve will close, stopping all air circulation inside the block. The valve will reopen once you connect the ports properly.

valve with studs

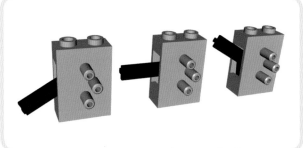

The valve is the size of two 1×2 bricks and a 1×2 plate stacked, and it is always light grey. It has three ports on one side, with air delivered to the middle one.

A lever (roughly 1.5 studs long) on one of the valve's narrow sides can be switched to one of three positions. The middle position, called neutral, cuts the connection inside the valve, effectively disconnecting the side ports from the rest of the pneumatic system. The top and bottom positions control the flow of air through the valve's side ports, as shown in Figure 9-3, making cylinders connected to these ports extend or retract. (The valve does not actively take in air; it only receives air through its ports and expels it through the hole that houses the switch.)

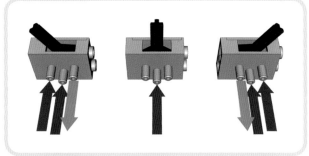

Figure 9-3: The direction of airflow through the valve's ports: Blue arrows show air coming from the pump, green indicates air coming out from the valve to the cylinder, and red indicates air returning from the cylinder to the valve.

A valve can be attached on the top or bottom of any studded LEGO piece. It can also be mounted between two 1×2 Technic bricks, which can then be connected with pins to any piece that has at least five pin holes (see Figure 9-4).

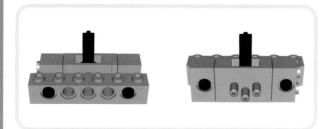

Figure 9-4: By placing a 1×2 Technic brick on each end of the valve (front and back shown), you can connect the valve to a brick or beam that is at least five pin holes long.

valve with no studs (New)

Introduced in 2003, this New valve works the same as the valve with studs. Unlike the Old valve, it comes in dark grey, but it has similar dimensions. Aside from the color, the only difference is its lack of studs and the addition of two pin holes, 1 stud apart, at one side of the valve. These changes make it better suited for studless constructions. Also, because the valve's points of attachment are on one side and the valve's lever is on the other, the lever remains conveniently exposed when the valve is attached to something.

large cylinder (Old)

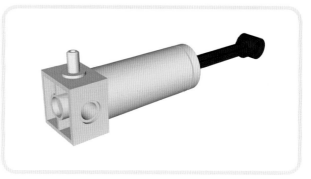

This cylinder from the Old system, which hasn't been produced since 1987. It includes a single port and a plastic rod that extends by nearly 4 studs. Available in yellow and red, its dimensions are the same as those of the Old large pump. Unlike the Old pump, however, it has no spring. The cylinder's upper part expels air when extending and draws it in from the outside when retracting, and the cylinder exerts more force when extending than it does when retracting. It's only partially useful with the New pneumatic system because it can be extended but not retracted.

6L cylinder (Old)

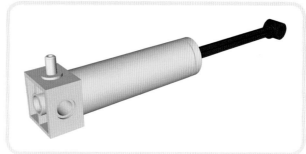

This yellow cylinder is basically just a longer version of the Old system's large cylinder. It has a single port and a plastic rod that extends 6 studs, and it has no counterpart in the New pneumatic system; in fact, it is the only pneumatic cylinder this long. Its plastic rod and long reach make it more likely to break under stress than any other cylinder.

As with all Old-style cylinders, its upper part expels air when extending and draws it from the outside when retracting, and it exerts more force when extending than when retracting. And, just as with the regular large cylinder, its usefulness in the New system is limited because the New system doesn't allow it to retract.

small cylinder (New)

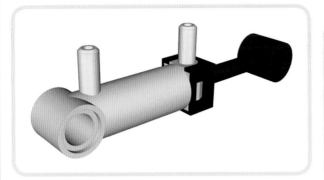

The New system's small cylinder has two ports and a plastic rod extending 2 studs. In the Technic sets, it's always yellow, though it comes in a transparent light blue in the Education sets.

This rare and expensive pneumatic piece is easily confused with the small pneumatic pump. This piece is unable to exert large force due to its small capacity, but it's valued for its small size. As with all cylinders in the New system, it is completely airtight.

large cylinder with square base (New)

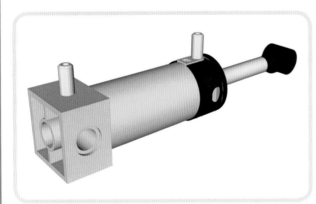

The New system's large cylinder is one of the most common pneumatic pieces. It has two ports and a metal rod extending by nearly 4 studs that makes it very robust. It is similar in size to the large pneumatic pump.

large cylinder with round base (New)

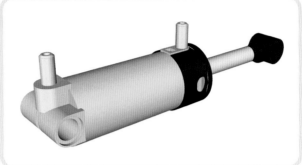

This updated version of the large cylinder, introduced in 2002, has two ports and a metal rod extending by nearly 4 studs. The only difference between this cylinder and the Old one is that it has a round rather than a square base; the round base takes up less space and cannot be mounted on studs. However, the rounded design allows the New cylinder to tilt in tight spaces, which has made it very popular.

The square, Old version of this pump requires a large margin of free space around its lower end in order for the cylinder to tilt, which makes it less realistic. Real hydraulic cylinders are almost always mounted on a pin joint so that they can pivot during their stroke, which prevents loads from bending the actuator. The round base on the New cylinder allows for this type of action, making it more realistic than the square version.

pneumatic tubes and hoses

The 4 mm thick elastic rubber hose is a vital part of the Technic pneumatic system. It comes in various lengths and colors—black, grey, and blue—and is easy to insert through Technic holes and connect to ports of the pneumatic system.

When working with hose, remember that LEGO pneumatic systems cannot maintain high air pressure for prolonged periods and each hose leaks somewhat, so the system becomes increasingly inefficient with each hose you add. Additionally, hoses tend to pop off ports when the pressure exceeds three bars, and if a hose is stretched or damaged, it can pop off even below three bars. The oldest hoses, rarely found today, were made of a material that slowly broke down when exposed to UV light, causing them to develop cracks and leaks. The newer hoses are made of silicone and are mostly immune to these problems.

The 4 mm hoses make it easy to circulate air through any pneumatic system, no matter how complex, and they take up very little space in LEGO constructions. Their flexibility and resilience allows them to span components that need to have relative motion, but their inner ducts are narrow and can easily become blocked. To avoid blocking the tubes, be sure that the surrounding structures do not press on a hose and that no hose is stretched or bent sharply.

Figure 9-5 shows a pneumatic hose connected to the upper port of a (New) large cylinder. Note that when a hose is attached to a port, it becomes thicker than 1 stud. As a result, the part of the hose with the port inside it can't fit through a Technic hole.

Figure 9-5: A hose connected to a cylinder port

In addition to ports, pneumatic hoses can also be connected to 3 mm thick rigid tubes in order to join several pneumatic hoses to create longer ones.

In real hydraulic and pneumatic systems, *hose* is always used to describe a flexible part, and *tube* is used to describe a rigid part. In keeping with this terminology, I'll refer to the flexible silicone parts as hoses and the 3 mm rigid parts as tubes. Figure 9-6 shows how a 3 mm tube can connect two pneumatic hoses. But these tubes can also be connected to any studded structure, such as a brick, in a way that would not be possible with the regular pneumatic hose.

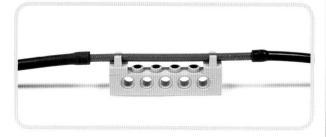

Figure 9-6: A tube connecting two hoses, connected to a Technic brick by two 1×1 tiles with clips

NOTE Real machines equipped with pneumatic or hydraulic systems often use rigid tubes to traverse structures that do not bend, such as the boom of a crane. The 3 mm tube makes this type of construction easy to model with LEGO pieces.

T-piece (Old)

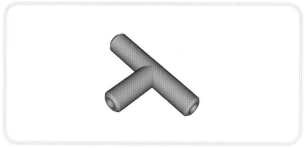

The Old version of the T-piece, which hasn't been produced since 1996, is simply a small, T-shaped piece with three ports. When air is forced into one port, it flows into the two other ports, making the T-piece work as a pneumatic parallel connector.

T-pieces are used to divide pneumatic hoses in two by connecting a hose to each port (see Figure 9-7). Two of the hoses act as a single section with the T-piece in the middle, and the third one acts as its branch. Because every T-piece adds one new branch to a pneumatic hose, in order to split a hose into four, you need three T-pieces: one to split the hose in two, and two more to split each of the two resulting hoses into two again. The rule is a universal one: splitting a single hose into n hoses requires $(n - 1)$ T-pieces.

Figure 9-7: Two T-pieces allow a single hose (blue) to branch into three individual hoses (red).

NOTE Splitting hoses lowers the effectiveness of the whole pneumatic system because changing the direction of airflow by 90 degrees produces drag.

T-piece (New)

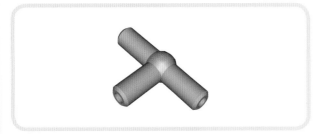

The updated version of the T-piece has a ball-shaped center, which makes it easier to disconnect from hoses. It works the same as the Old T-piece, but it is stronger and slightly more effective in reducing drag. T-pieces are always light grey.

hose connector with an axle joint (New)

This piece was introduced with the 8110 set in 2011. It looks a bit like the T-piece, but instead of splitting hoses, it's used to extend them.

Designed to connect two sections of pneumatic hose in a way that makes the hoses easy to remove, this piece allows you to easily connect or disconnect two pneumatic systems. Due to its design, this piece is especially handy for creating pneumatic *power take-off (PTO)*, a connection that powers external attachments like a pneumatic snowplow or a knuckleboom crane, as in the original 8110 set. Many agricultural machines also come with PTOs; for example, a tractor might swap between different attachments.

cylinder bracket

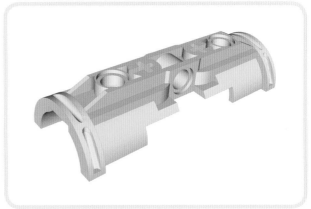

The new pneumatic system doesn't include 6L cylinders, and the regular large cylinders, which have nearly 4 studs of extension range, are too short for certain purposes. The solution is to join two cylinders with the bracket shown in Figure 9-8 so that they work like one cylinder with rods extending from both ends, effectively doubling both the length and extension range.

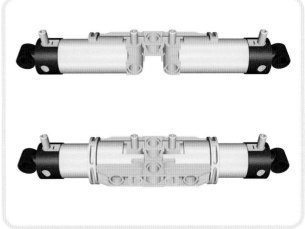

Figure 9-8: It takes two brackets to secure two cylinders.

The brackets are symmetrical, so you can have one cylinder with ports facing up and the other with ports facing down, but having all ports on one side will make it easier to connect hoses.

NOTE For the cylinders to work as one, you have to couple their lower and upper ports separately with hoses forked using T-pieces.

Figure 9-9 shows two brackets secured around two cylinders by two axles and two 3L beams with pins. The brackets are not physically attached to the cylinders or to each other. To attach them, either insert axles through their axle holes or add pins to their central holes and connect them with 3L beams. The pins-and-beams method is more reliable because it prevents the brackets from coming apart; however, it uses the brackets' central holes, which are often better used for routing hoses.

Figure 9-9: Two brackets secured around two cylinders

airtank

The airtank stores compressed air. This part is blue in Technic and white in the Education system. It comes in handy particularly when you want to create a pneumatic system that doesn't require constant pumping. While with a little tinkering you can connect pneumatic hoses to plastic bottles or bags to store air, the airtank is the only original LEGO piece designed for this purpose.

NOTE Each pneumatic system has a capacity equal to the volume that can be filled with pressurized air. This volume is typically related to hoses: Adding several long hoses adds to the capacity significantly. The airtank's capacity, however, is far greater than that of any number of hoses.

To have the air stored in the airtank available for the whole pneumatic system, place the airtank between the pressure supply and the control module.

According to LEGO, it takes 30 to 35 repetitions with a large pneumatic pump to fill the airtank completely. At roughly 40 repetitions, the pressure will reach the critical three bars, causing either the pump to stop working or the hoses to pop off its ports. (If a breach occurs, the pressurized air will escape the airtank in a split second.)

Despite its apparent simplicity, the airtank's shape is actually quite complex. Its bottom has a 2×4 connecting area that can be used with any bricks or plates. To attach it to anything larger than a 2×4 piece, try adding a 2×4 plate as a buffer (see Figure 9-10).

The airtank's connecting area also includes three 1-stud-deep axle holes, which you can use to mount the airtank on axles or axle pins. You can do the same with the single axle hole above each of the airtank's ports.

Figure 9-10: Because of the shape of the airtank's bottom, a spacing of at least a single plate is required to connect it to anything larger than a 2×4-stud area. A 2×4 plate is used here. Note that despite the presence of the large red plate, it's still possible to connect hoses to this airtank, thanks to its angled ports.

manometer

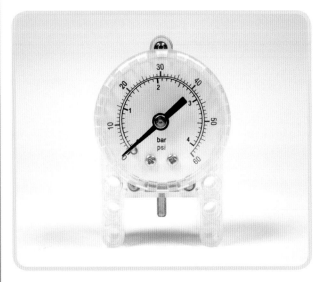

The manometer was released in 2008. It is designed to measure the air pressure in a pneumatic system in both pounds per square inch (psi) and bar units. It is enclosed in a semitransparent 5×8×3 case, with a single metal port at the bottom.

To use the manometer to measure air pressure in the pneumatic system, place it between the pressure supply and the control module. It can be connected with a single section of pneumatic hose to practically anything, whether that's the airtank or any two sections of a hose using the T-piece. Figure 9-11 shows two examples of manometer placement.

The manometer's usefulness is limited. If you choose to use it, remember that it is best used with the airtank. If you choose to use the manometer on a pneumatic system without an airtank, its readings will change drastically with each movement of a pump or valve.

modding the pneumatic system

The pneumatic system is ripe for experimentation. Here are some common ways to tinker with it.

non-LEGO hoses

It's easy to replace the original LEGO pneumatic hoses with custom ones, as long as the custom hose is elastic and 4 mm thick (if you want to be able to insert it through Technic holes) and as long as it has reasonably large inner ducts. Some industrial hoses may come in handy for this purpose—for example, the fuel hoses used for radio-controlled models. Medical drip hoses—that is, IV lines—can be used too, but they tend to be sticky and to collect massive amounts of dust.

non-LEGO airtanks

Although the LEGO airtank is quite useful, you can replace it with practically any airtight container. Plastic bottles or bags and even balloons can work very well as long as you connect them to the pneumatic system in a way that keeps them airtight.

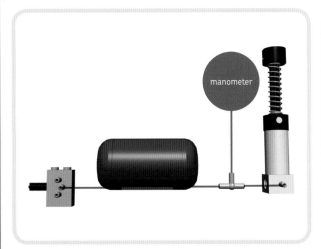

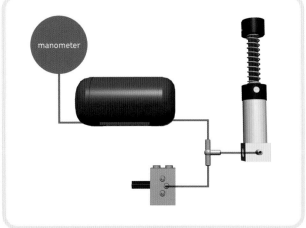

Figure 9-11: Two diagrams showing a pneumatic system with an airtank and a manometer. Notice that both the airtank and the manometer work exactly the same way in both cases.

removing springs to create motorized compressors

Since the large pneumatic pumps are so much more power-ful than the small ones, they can be used to advantage in motorized compressors. The one problem you'll encounter is that the spring in the large pump resists the force of the compressor's motor and slows the entire mechanism down. To solve this problem, remove the spring by pulling it off the Old large pump or, with the New pump, cutting it (because the contact pad gets in the way).

pneumatic suspensions

In heavy models, you can use the large pneumatic cylinders instead of shock absorbers to create a kind of pneumatic suspension. Depending on the pressure of the air inside them, the cylinders will tend to retract under the load and extend back to their neutral position once the load is reduced or gone.

The advantage of pneumatic suspensions is that they're tough and they allow you to adjust ground clearance simply by changing the air pressure. But they also have a few disad-vantages: Their performance is worse than that of traditional shock absorbers, they're best used with heavy models, and their pneumatic system needs to be refilled from time to time due to microleaks.

turning your pneumatic system into a hydraulic one

In real life, pneumatic systems are less popular than hydraulic ones. Liquid-filled hydraulic systems are widely used by machines that handle heavy loads, especially construction equipment like excavators, cranes, front-end loaders, backhoes, skid-steer loaders, forklifts, dump trucks, and so on.

If your constructions need to handle heavier loads, you can turn the pneumatic system into a hydraulic one by replacing the air with liquid, although this has to be done carefully. Liquids are much denser than air and much less prone to compression.

Of course, there are certain risks in filling the LEGO pneumatic system with fluid, the most important of which is that you may damage large cylinders: They have metal rods, which can corrode depending on the fluid you use. Also, the rods are covered with grease for lubrication, which may react with the fluid you choose or be removed by it. And even if you use a "safe" fluid, there is still the matter of drying the cylinder after use—a difficult task given that the cylinder is almost fully closed.

The following is a list of tips for using fluids in LEGO pneumatic systems. I'm not recommending that you fill the system with fluid, and if you do so, you may damage your pieces in the process. Remember that if you decide to experiment with fluids, you do so at your own risk. Be advised that when things go wrong, it can get pretty messy!

* The best choice of liquid is a mineral oil—a noncorrosive, nonreactive, odorless fluid that is safe for human contact. Mineral oil is 20 percent thinner than water, inexpensive, and available at most drug stores.
* You should only convert the New LEGO pneumatic system to hydraulics because the valve is the only exhaust in the system; the fluid will exit only from there instead of exiting from cylinders, as in the Old system.
* You'll need a constant supply of fluid, and the LEGO pumps must be fully submerged in the fluid in order to pump it.
* The fluid's viscosity will improve the way the cylinders handle heavy loads, but this also means that you will need to apply much greater force while pumping.
* The integrity of the seals in the pneumatic system is very important when fluid is used. Any leaks can introduce air into the system, which could block its function completely.
* Any leak in a fluid-filled pneumatic system can affect its surroundings. Make sure that there are no electric or metal pieces near the pneumatic system in your construction. Also, try to build the system so that if a hose pops off, you can access the hose quickly and block it or lift its end to stop the fluid from leaking out.
* Never use the manometer with fluids; you're likely to damage it permanently.
* It's very difficult to dry the insides of pneumatic pieces unless you disassemble them. Pumping warm air through them continuously for a prolonged period of time will help; you can also try leaving them for a while in a bag of uncooked rice, as rice absorbs moisture.

10

pneumatic devices

This chapter presents devices that make creative use of pneumatic systems: motorized compressors, remote-controlled valves, and pneumatic engines. All these devices take advantage of the fact that the pneumatic system has been designed to be customizable, and there's almost no limit to potential modifications.

In this chapter, we'll start by discussing the most basic and versatile devices and then move on to more sophisticated and specialized ones.

motorized compressors

A *compressor* is a stand-alone mechanism that provides a continuous supply of pressurized air—for example, the massive air compressor you can find at the gas station (for reinflating tires) or the portable model you might use to inflate an air mattress. The most practical and popular method of building a Technic compressor is by driving small LEGO pumps with a motor. This method allows us to control a compressor remotely, and it ensures that the compressor works at a constant rate, making the cylinders in a pneumatic system move smoothly.

It's convenient to keep the motor attached directly to a compressor. This allows us to place the whole mechanism practically anywhere in our construction, as we are not bound by driveshafts, gears, or any other rigid elements. Our only limitation is finding a home for the electric wire and pneumatic hose.

There is one issue worth keeping in mind when building a motorized compressor: its *ripple*. LEGO pumps work in a cycle: They are retracted, pumping air into their outlets, and then extended, taking air from outside. In other words, they don't provide air constantly but only during exactly half of the cycle. This cycle has two consequences that become more significant as the number of pumps working simultaneously increases: fluctuating air flow and vibrations, which result from the pumps' rods being repeatedly pushed back and forth.

Some builders are fond of building monstrous compressors with eight or more pumps driven by the RC motor (shown in Figure 10-1). This is not always the best solution, as RC motors are large, loud, and power consuming. Another solution is to divide pumps into groups that work alternately. For example, instead of four pumps working as one, we can use two pumps that are retracted while the

Figure 10-1: An eight-pump compressor driven by the RC motor. This design is a real monstrosity in the world of LEGO compressors.

other two are extended. Ideally, we should have multiple pumps that are fully out of phase because this limits both the load on the compressor's motor and the vibrations the compressor creates. Supporting the pumps' ends as rigidly as possible also reduces vibrations.

You might ask why we would want to use so many pumps in the first place. It's because a single pump has a very small capacity and is, therefore, not very powerful, taking quite a while to fill just a single large pneumatic cylinder. How fast your pneumatic system operates depends on the volume of pressurized air delivered to it, so using many pumps is a natural solution. The rule of thumb is that for a pneumatic system in which one or two large cylinders are working at the same time, it takes at least two pumps for a PF Medium motor to provide air pressure at reasonable rate.

NOTE All of the compressor designs in this chapter are intended for pumps that are 5.5 studs long when extended, not for the newer 6-stud-long version. This longer version is found only in a single set and is therefore quite rare.

Figures 10-2 through 10-6 show various compressor designs that drive more than one pump.

The rocking compressor, shown in Figure 10-6, can hold from 2 to 18 pumps, depending on the length of its axles. It moves the pumps in a reciprocating motion, rather than the rotary motion used in other compressors, which results in a more compact build. Moreover, it has a gearing with four possible gear combinations (see Figure 10-7).

Figure 10-3: A compressor that can hold two or four pumps while making use of two 36-tooth gears. The orientation of the gears relative to each other is maintained by two 12-tooth gears on a separate axle, which also transfers drive between them. It's possible to connect two or more such compressors side by side to increase the number of pumps.

Figure 10-4: It's perfectly possible to split pumps in a compressor into three groups.

Figure 10-2: A compressor with two pumps that work alternately, both attached to two wedge belt wheels. The design is small, but it's difficult to add more pumps to it. In this compressor, the pumps are 90 degrees out of phase rather than 180 degrees, so the pressure is still "uneven." In other words, one pump is not fully extended while the other is fully compressed.

Figure 10-5: You can even split pumps in a compressor into four groups at various points of the working cycle. But such compressors are significantly more complex while working only a little more smoothly.

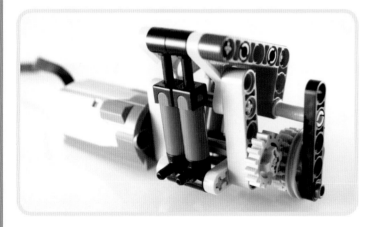

Figure 10-6: Finally, here's a design called a rocking compressor. While it doesn't extend pumps to their maximum, it can hold up to 18 pumps in two alternating groups.

2:1

1.25:1

1:1.25

1:2

Figure 10-7: The four gear combinations suitable for the rocking compressor, with their ratios labeled

a rocking compressor

Here's a look at the complete building instructions for a simple design. The blue axles limit the number of pumps, but making the axles 1 stud longer adds space for two more pumps. For clarity, the instructions show the compressor without pumps, but the pumps should be mounted on the blue axles.

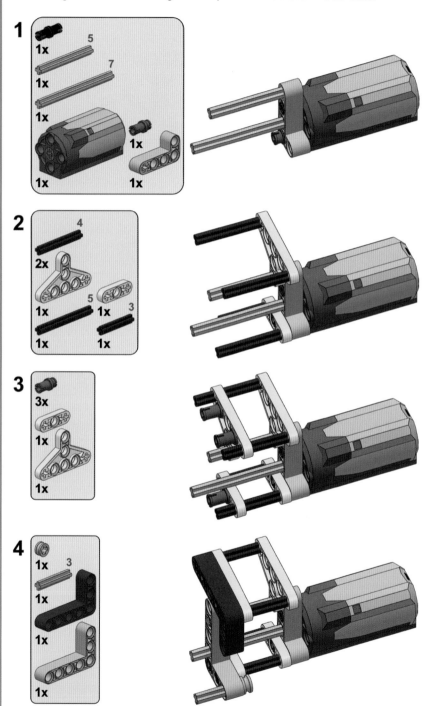

5

1x

1x

1x

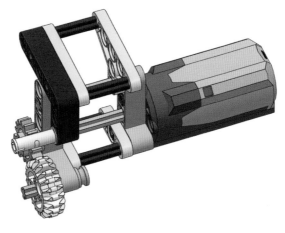

6

1x

1x

1x

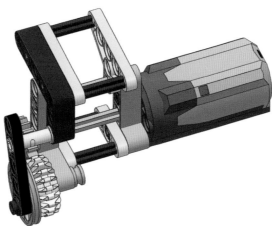

motorized valves

The purpose of motorizing a pneumatic valve is simple: remote control. A valve can be connected to a motor in a simple way, preferably with the use of a 24-tooth gear with a clutch, which prevents the motor from stalling (see Figure 10-8). Once the 24-tooth gear can no longer drive the valve, the grey circle inside the gear begins to rotate instead, which prevents damage to the motor or to the gearing.

Polish builder Maciej "dmac" Szymański discovered that if we use this exact combination of motor and gears with a regular 24-tooth gear (without a clutch), we'll get a return-to-center motorized valve—that is, a valve that returns to

Figure 10-8: A simple way to motorize a pneumatic valve is to use a gear with a clutch for the motor's safety.

central position the moment the motor stops, thereby shutting down the valve (see Figure 10-9).

But precision is often crucial when switching pneumatic valves. The designs above lack precision, while the design shown in Figure 10-10 offers plenty of fine-grained control. This is useful for retracting heavily loaded cylinders, when the valve has to be opened little by little to prevent cylinders from yielding to the load.

Figure 10-9: With a regular 24-tooth gear instead of the clutch gear, we get a return-to-center valve.

Figure 10-10: This high-precision valve-switching mechanism makes use of a worm gear and a 40-tooth gear to ensure accuracy. The red bush on the valve's lever improves it further by reducing backlash. Note that there is no safety clutch in this assembly; because the mechanism multiplies the motor's torque by a factor of 40, there is a chance that some pieces may be damaged if the motor doesn't stop at the right moment. To lessen this risk, a clutch can be added between the valve and the motor.

autovalve

An autovalve combines the functions of a motorized valve with those of a compressor. It makes use of the compressor's ability to function regardless of the input's direction of rotation—we'll use the motor's direction of rotation to control the valve itself. After switching, the motor can continue to drive the compressor as long as is needed.

The autovalve's working principle is based on a so-called *sliding worm gear*, as shown in Figure 10-11. The motor drives the compressor through an axle on which a worm gear is located. The worm gear drives one of two identical short axles with a 12-tooth gear and a short beam (shown in green). The beams act as pushing elements: Each of them can push the valve's lever in one direction and then continue rotating freely. But when driven in the opposite direction, the beam locks against the lever, stopping the respective axle and making the worm gear slide away from it. The worm gear slides until it meshes with the other axle's gear, at which point it starts to drive it and the other pusher located on it, effectively switching the valve.

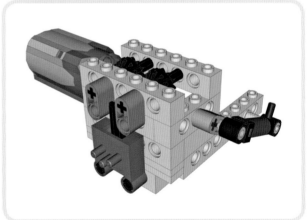

Figure 10-11: An autovalve uses a sliding worm gear to control a compressor and a pneumatic valve with just one motor.

The disadvantages of the autovalve include a long switching time, which can be remedied by driving the input faster, and the limit of one valve and one compressor per motor. Still, the compressor can be connected to any pneumatic system, with more valves controlled separately (see Figure 10-12).

To see an autovalve in action, visit *http://www.youtube.com/watch?v=0sDJ4iTs-P8*.

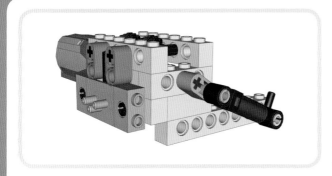

Figure 10-12: An autovalve can be created with both types of pneumatic valves (the older one is shown here) and with any compressor whatsoever—the single-pump compressor here is just an example.

a motorized valve

1
4x
2x 2
2x
1x
2x 5
3x

2
3
1x
2x

3
2x
1x

4
2
2x
2x
2x 2x

5
1x
1x

an autovalve

1

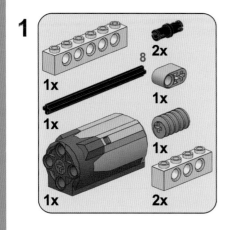

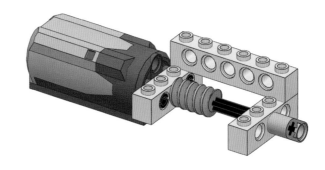

2

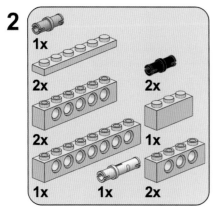

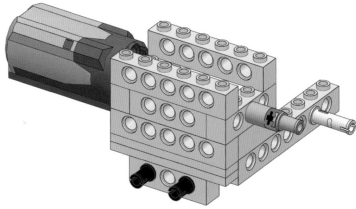

3

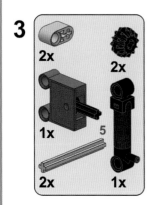

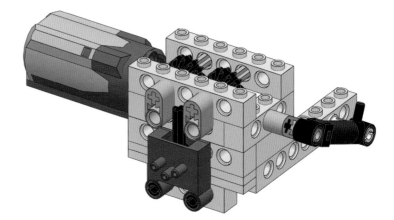

automated pressure switch

Having a motorized compressor in your pneumatic system doesn't necessarily solve your pressure problems. Complex pneumatic systems with many cylinders working in turns can require large amounts of pressurized air in the system at one moment and no air moments later. While the amount of air pressure that goes into a system can be managed by building a compressor fast and/or large enough, constantly turning it on and off can be an onerous task.

The solution to this problem is a pressure switch, also known as a pressure limiter. We can build one using a PF switch, a small pneumatic cylinder, and a rubber band.

How does a pressure switch work? Take a look at Figure 10-13, which shows how the switch connects the compressor motor to the power supply. The cylinder's lower port is connected to the pneumatic system, while the upper one is left open. A rubber band is put over the cylinder, keeping it retracted. If the pressure in the pneumatic system is high enough, the cylinder will overcome the rubber band and

extend. If the pressure drops, it will yield to the band and retract. This means that if we connect the cylinder to the PF switch, the switch can effectively control the compressor's motor, turning it on automatically when pressure is low and then turning it off when it's high enough. Such a mechanism is best used with an airtank, filling it automatically when necessary.

The pressure switch works best when close to the airtank, which, in turn, should be close to the compressor, as shown in Figure 10-14. Some builders create complete modules with the motorized compressor, airtank, and pressure switch all put together. I prefer to take advantage of the elastic elements—that is, the wires and hoses—to be able to adjust the location of these elements more freely. A singular module has fixed dimensions, while separate elements connected only by wires and hoses can be fitted into limited space in different ways, allowing for less massive and more creative housings.

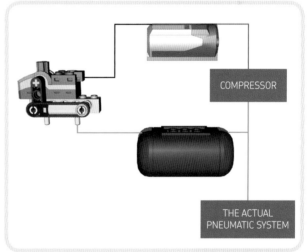

Figure 10-14: The general scheme of the pressure switch and its connections to other components of the pneumatic system. Black lines mark electric wires, blue lines mark mechanical connections, and green lines mark pneumatic hoses.

Figure 10-13: A close-up view of a pressure switch. The switch usually needs adjusting to activate at the desired pressure threshold. It can be fine-tuned by adjusting the rubber band's strength, the angle of the cylinder relative to the lever, and the length of the lever. It is also possible to use old 9V switches, which offer less resistance, or to use multiple cylinders. Large cylinders can be used as well, although their large capacity makes them less sensitive and therefore less useful in system that must react to small changes in air pressure.

A properly built and adjusted pressure switch leaves you with only pneumatic valves to take care of; the compressor works automatically, and the pressure in the airtank is maintained at all times. Note that there is no particular place where the *switch-airtank-compressor* combination should be connected to the rest of the pneumatic system. Such a connection can be placed between the compressor and airtank, between the airtank and pressure switch, after the airtank (as shown in Figure 10-13), or after the pressure switch—it will work just the same regardless of placement. You can also connect a LEGO manometer to observe the relationship between air pressure and the functioning of the switch.

pneumatic engines

The functioning of pneumatic cylinders is somewhat similar to that of the pistons in an internal combustion engine, allowing us to build a compressed air engine with cylinders driving the crankshaft. Such an engine, sometimes called a LEGO pneumatic engine (LPE), is powered by pressurized air delivered to the cylinders. Pneumatic engines are advantageous in terms of their performance, resemblance to combustion engines, and sound, which is quite loud and car-like compared to that of electric motors. What makes these engines appealing to many builders is their complexity, which creates almost endless possibilities for improvements. While the complexity of these engines may be appealing, they're also quite a challenge to build. Disadvantages of pneumatic engines include their size and their need to be constantly connected to a compressor. Moreover, pneumatic engines work only in one direction, and they get warm from the friction of many moving parts and from air being compressed inside the cylinders.

The working principle of a pneumatic engine is simple: A cylinder is connected to a shaft with a cam so that extending it rotates the shaft by a half rotation and retracting it rotates the shaft by another half rotation (see Figures 10-15 and 10-16). The same shaft uses another cam connected to a valve to switch the cylinder between extending and retracting continuously, thus creating a complete working cycle. The cycle, therefore, involves both cylinder and valve and goes as follows: Cylinder extends to maximum, valve is switched, cylinder retracts to maximum, valve is switched.

The problem with the cycle is that both cylinder and valve have *dead spots*, or points of the cycle at which they can stop, as shown in Figure 10-17. For a cylinder, it's the point when it's extended or retracted to maximum, and for a valve, it's the point when it goes through neutral position and no air comes through it. If we make an engine with just one cylinder and one valve, these dead spots will overlap and effectively stop the engine after it makes just half a rotation. This can be prevented by using a heavy flywheel and a modified valve.

Figure 10-15: A simple way to connect the cylinder to a shaft is to use a cam made of a short beam. However, a cylinder can extend by 4 studs, but here it's allowed to extend by only 3.

Figure 10-16: To make the cylinder extend fully, we need its tip to be mounted 1.5 studs away from the shaft. A piece called a Technic cam allows this.

Figure 10-17: A simple cylinder and valve combination with two cranks: one made of Technic cams, converting the cylinder's motion into the crankshaft's rotation, and another made of a wedge-belt wheel, using the crankshaft's rotation to switch the valve back and forth. Note that both cylinder and valve are in dead spots here.

Modifying LEGO pieces is actually quite common among advanced LPE builders. The best pneumatic engines from these builders can far outperform any LEGO electric motor in terms of both speed and torque, but that performance comes at a cost. In such engines, cylinders' ports are often drilled to increase throughput; the valves' internal structure is cut to reduce their switching resistance; and many moving parts, such as cylinders and camshafts, are lubricated. Industrial tubing with clamps replaces LEGO hoses and is sometimes glued to the ports. Finally, these engines are powered with non-LEGO compressors, such as electric compressors for car tires. LEGO pneumatic pieces were simply not designed to move quickly, and there is a lot of friction involved in the many moving pieces of a pneumatic engine, which justifies modifications for some builders.

Getting back to our single-cylinder engine, a modified valve and a flywheel can make it work: The flywheel will provide the momentum necessary to get the engine through dead spots, while the valve will offer minimum resistance and thus minimum risk of getting stuck in a dead spot (see Figure 10-18). Such an engine needs to be started by spinning the flywheel manually, but it will keep running for as long as it receives sufficiently high air pressure.

Figure 10-18: This is the engine from Figure 10-17 with a flywheel added to keep it running through overlapping dead spots. Starting such an engine is a little finicky, but it works fine once it gets going.

a single-cylinder engine

Here are the building instructions for the engine shown in Figure 10-18. Like every set of engine instructions in this chapter, these instructions have both the cylinder and hoses removed for clarity. In this BI, a photo shows the cylinder's position and a connection scheme for the hoses. Remember that engines like this work best with a large volume of continuous air pressure, and they are difficult to drive with a LEGO compressor.

1

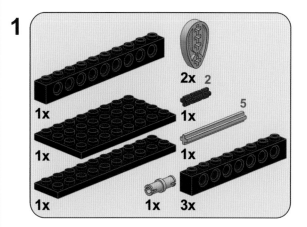

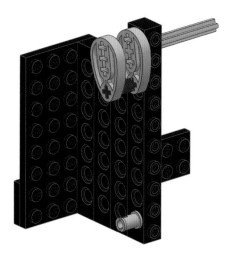

2

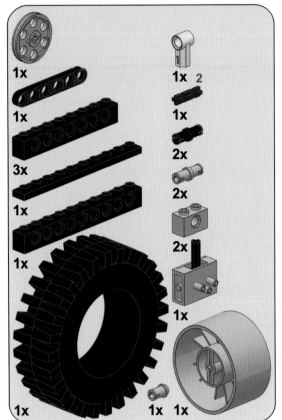

1x
1x
3x
1x
1x

1x

1x 2
1x
2x
2x
2x

1x

1x 1x

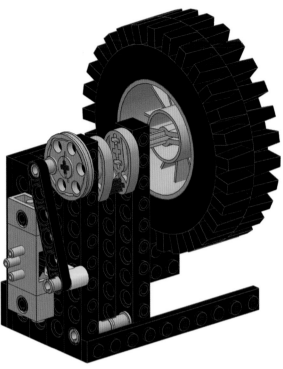

3

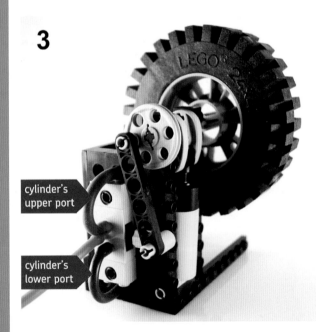

cylinder's
upper port

cylinder's
lower port

Engines with two, four, six, or more cylinders can be built as follows: The cylinders are split in two groups, each group connected to one valve so that there are two valves in the engine for any number of cylinders. At any given time, one group of cylinders is retracting while the other is extending. These groups should be mixed so that no two cylinders of the same group are next to each other. All the cylinders are connected to a common camshaft, but with cams rotated 90 degrees relative to the adjacent ones (see Figure 10-19). This reduces the overlap of the cylinders' dead spots. Finally, each valve is connected to the end of the camshaft closest to the group of cylinders connected to the other valve, as shown in Figure 10-20. This arrangement ensures that we don't overlap dead spots between a valve and the cylinders connected to it.

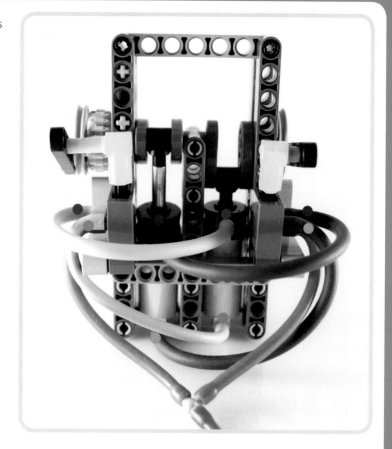

Figure 10-19: A two-cylinder engine built in accordance with the rules above. The colored dots show which ports are connected. Note the position of the cams. The engine can start all by itself and runs relatively smoothly. The tan gear can transfer drive from the engine. More cylinders can be added to the engine, and it reaches optimum smoothness with four cylinders, each with a cam rotated 90 degrees relative to the next one.

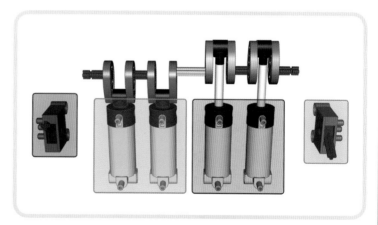

Figure 10-20: A simplified layout of a four-cylinder pneumatic engine: All cylinders, running the same camshaft, are split into two groups (marked green and blue), each connected to a single valve. The valves are connected to the sides of the camshaft nearest to the opposite group.

a two-cylinder pneumatic engine

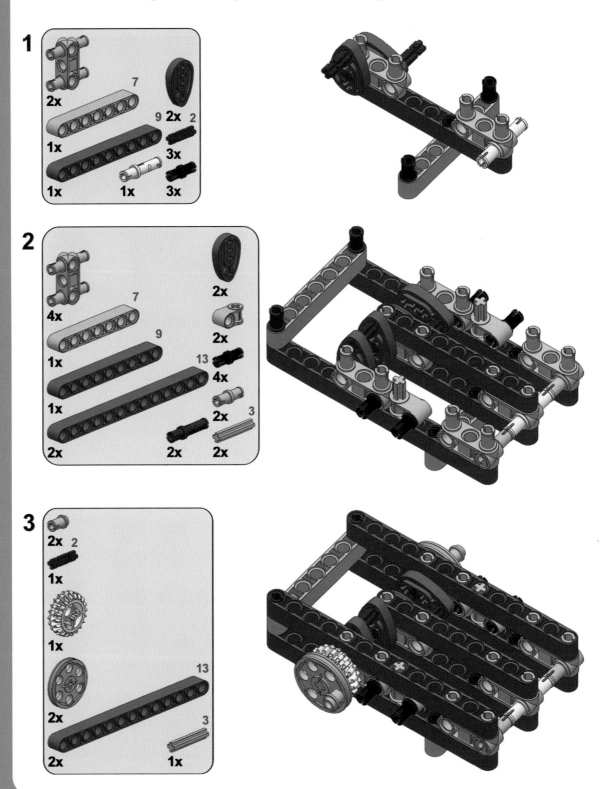

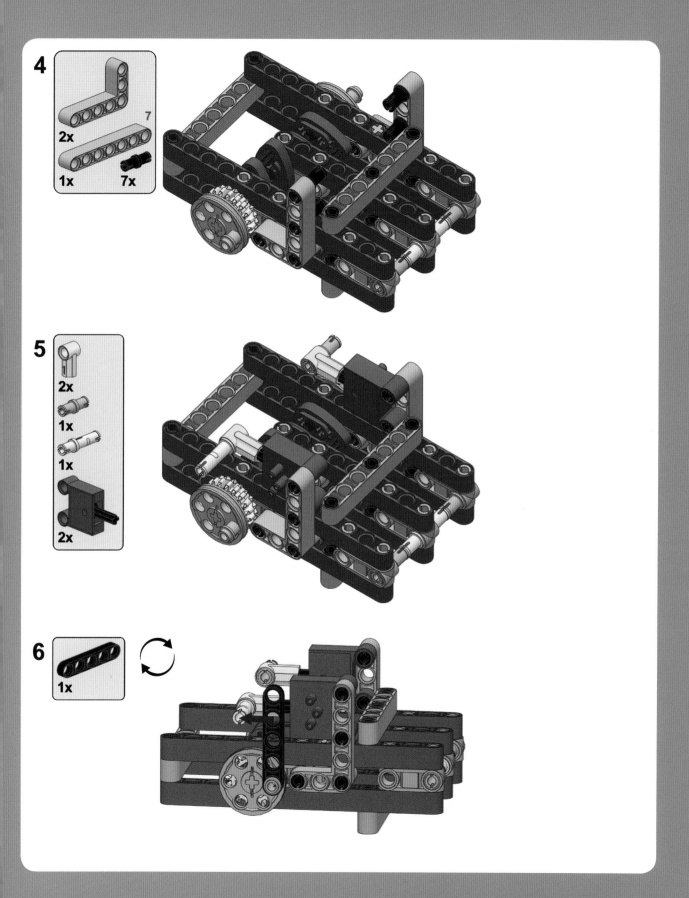

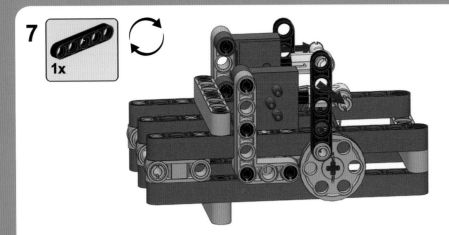

7 **1x**

In general, the more cylinders we add, the smoother the engine will run. The engine reaches optimum performance when we use at least four cylinders, each with its cam rotated 90 degrees relative to the adjacent ones (see Figure 10-21). On the other hand, adding more cylinders will result in a greater combined engine capacity, which will in turn increase fuel consumption. Note that the efficiency of LEGO compressors is poor compared to the capacity of such an engine. Note also that the engine's efficiency can't be improved by using airtanks because the engine needs a constant supply of equally pressurized air and airtanks provide only a single, short blast of very highly pressurized air. You can, of course, build an engine with a separate valve for each cylinder. Some builders do that for smoother operation, but it drastically increases the overall complexity of the engine.

One last issue is that cams are quite fragile when subjected directly to the cylinder's power. This problem can be remedied by using sliders—that is, elements that move together with the tip of the cylinder and thereby transfer movement to the cams (see Figure 10-22). Sliders keep a cylinder's tip moving in a straight line, and this creates a more favorable distribution of force, leaving the cams less stressed. The use of sliders is also more efficient because the cylinder's power is not wasted by tilting it sideways; instead, all of the power is transferred to the cam. Additionally, with cylinders maintaining the same position, it's possible to pack them more tightly. Sliders are very popular in complex engines—especially in those in the V system—as they allow a sturdier overall construction.

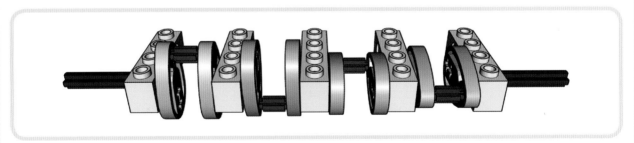

Figure 10-21: The "optimum crankshaft," with four cams, each rotated 90 degrees relative to the next one, provides the smoothest operation possible for a pneumatic engine.

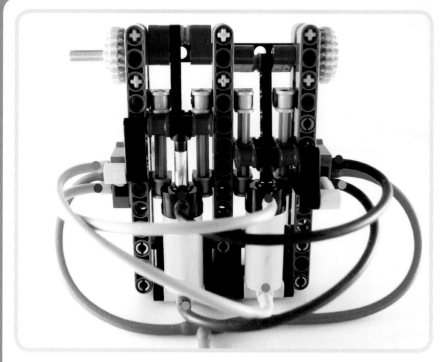

Figure 10-22: A two-cylinder engine with sliders. The colored dots show which ports are connected. The sliders are built around the red pieces, each moving along two light grey axles. They keep the cylinders' motion in a straight line and then transfer the motion to the cams (blue). Note that the extension of the cylinders is limited to 3 studs rather than 4, but thanks to this limitation, the sliders can also be used to control the valves.

a two-cylinder pneumatic engine with sliders

1

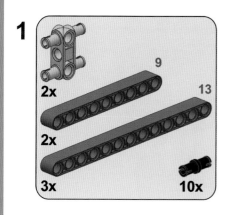

2

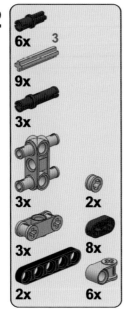

6x

9x 3

3x

3x   2x

3x   8x

2x   6x

3

4x

2x

4x 3

4x   9

2x   2x

4

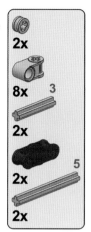

2x
8x 3
2x
2x 5
2x

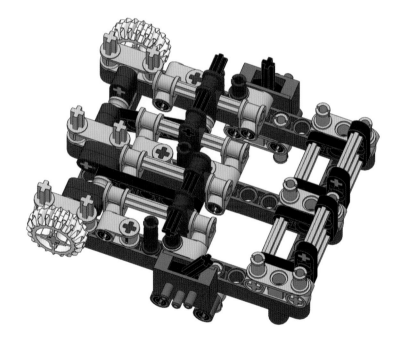

5

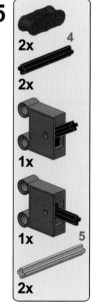

2x 4
2x
1x
1x 5
2x

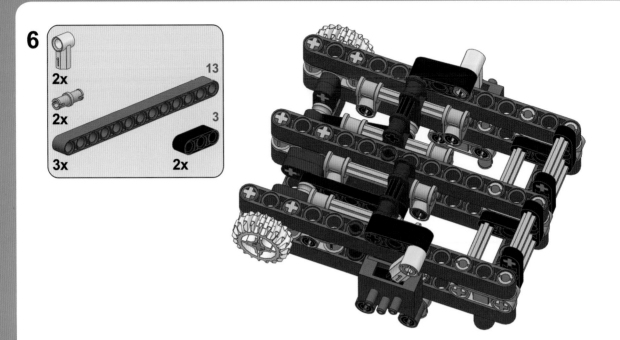

6

2x

2x

13

3

3x

2x

Engines in the V configuration are engines with cylinders aligned in two planes that form the shape of a letter *V* when viewed along the axis of their common camshaft. These engines can be built in two ways, both of which require building two identical modules with cylinders lined up and connecting them at a right angle. The first way is to build them with two separate crankshafts, each for one module, and to then use gears with a single central shaft to connect the modules. The second way is to use a single common crankshaft for both modules and to then connect two cylinders to each single crank pin. Since we want to keep the modules aligned (as they are in real engines), it's easier to use half-stud-thick beams to connect sliders to the cams rather than use 1-stud-thick cylinder tips (see Figure 10-23).

The possibilities with pneumatic engines are vast and include engines in W, boxer, and even radial systems. You can find many ingenious variants shown in detail by visiting Dr. Dude's YouTube channel: *http://www.youtube.com/user/DrDudeNL/*. Dr. Dude, a Dutch builder, has been a fan of the LEGO Technic set—and of big Technic cars in particular—for over 30 years.

Figure 10-23: Two cylinders connected to a single cam directly (left) and through sliders (right). You can see that the sliders allow the cylinders to stay aligned, while direct connection forces one of them to be moved by 1 stud.

builder showcase

Many LEGO builders produce impressive pneumatic engines, but one of them is the unquestionable master in this field: Alex "Nicjasno" Zorko. Alex builds big and heavy models of sports cars and found LEGO motors too weak to drive them. He has developed incredibly advanced motors, including "simple" inline engines, a V6 that operates at speeds well above 2000 RPM, and a V8 strong enough to make even a very heavy model drift (shown in Figure 10-24). Alex shows his models at *http://nicjasno.com/* and sells his engines at *http://lpepower.com/.*

Figure 10-24: Alex "Nicjasno" Zorko's V8 motor

a working water pressure pump

While LEGO Technic creations don't mix well with fluids, it is possible to build a pneumatic pump that will work with water while ensuring that no sensitive pieces come into physical contact with liquid. This pump uses pressurized air to push water, making it fairly safe and simple to use in, for example, a LEGO fire engine model.

To create a water pressure pump, we need an airtight container that will initially be filled with water and will then have pressurized air delivered to it. Using LEGO pieces for such a container may not be the best idea; a small bottle with a metal or plastic cap is a better alternative.

The working idea of this pressure pump is that by delivering air into a closed, water-filled container, we can force the water out. The container therefore needs an entry for the air and an exit for the water. The entry can be anywhere in the container; the exit should be at the bottom to stay in contact with water as long as possible.

We can adapt our bottle by making two holes in the cap and putting two hoses through them, as shown in Figure 10-25. One hose (dark grey) will deliver air and can end just below the cap or go deeper into the bottle—it doesn't matter. The other hose (blue) will be the water's way out, and it should reach all the way to the bottom. It's a good idea to make the other hose stiff so that it doesn't float in the water; a rigid LEGO hose or a regular drinking straw can be used. The hardest part is making the cap airtight with hoses going through it. You can achieve this by using modeling clay, masking sol, or molten wax from a candle.

Now you can connect the first hose to any compressor, and the water will spurt from the other one. Note that water is much less compressive than air, so it will take very high air pressure to make water really spurt. You can make your pump more effective by delivering air to it faster and by making the exit hose narrow. You can also use an airtank full of pressurized air and connect it to the first hose through a pneumatic valve; opening the valve will empty it into the bottle in an instant.

Just make sure the water doesn't come out anywhere near the electric components of your construction!

Figure 10-25: A small plastic bottle with a metal cap makes for a very good container. The dark grey elastic hose delivers air, while the blue rigid one lets the water out (note that it can be extended by putting another elastic hose on its end). The cap was punctured in two places to let the hoses through and then sealed with modeling clay (pink).

building strong

There was a time when Technic bricks alone could support and hold together almost any motorized mechanism. But eventually LEGO introduced stronger motors with enough torque to push even Technic brick connections apart. Having more torque at our disposal is an advantage in all aspects except one—it requires *structural reinforcing*, adding extra pieces whose primary purpose is to hold other pieces together (see Figure 11-1). A properly reinforced mechanism stays together regardless of its motor's strength and how much load is applied to its output, even if the load stalls the motor.

This chapter explores how to find places in a structure where reinforcing is crucial; how to identify strong and weak LEGO pieces; and how to create casings, chassis, frames, and trusses to support your models.

why things fall apart

In order to find where and how to reinforce our structures, we first have to understand why pieces come apart. When we house a mechanism inside a structure, it has an input, an output, and points of attachment to that structure; most often this means we have axles with gears that are housed in a structure's pin holes, as shown in Figure 11-2. Whenever a mechanism works, it handles a load that exerts stress on its output and has to be overcome by the force applied to its input. For example, if our mechanism is a drive-train, the motor driving its input has to overcome the stress exerted by its wheels—the rolling resistance and friction. This means that there are basically two forces in our mechanism, one applied to its input and one applied to its output, and that they work against each other. In other words, the output *resists* the input, creating stress that is carried through every component between them.

Figure 11-1: The two red beams hold the yellow Technic bricks together. Without these beams, the powerful PF XL motor would push the lower brick away the moment it started running.

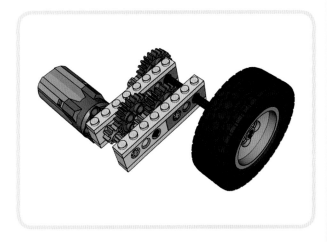

Figure 11-2: An example of a mechanism with a motor driving a wheel. The mechanism consists of six gears in three pairs on four axles, and it's housed inside Technic bricks held together by plates.

Let's think of this mechanism as a *chain*, with input and output being the first and last links. The initial force applied to the input (the first link) will be transferred through the chain and will stop on *the link of least resistance*. If the structure around our mechanism is solid, all links will have more resistance than the mechanism's output (the last link of the chain), and the mechanism will work as intended: Only the output will yield to the input. But if any link of our chain before the output has *less* resistance than the output, it will be dislocated and separated from the next link, thus breaking the chain and preventing the mechanism from working.

finding weak links

So let's find the weak link in our chain. In our example from Figure 11-2, we have a motor connected to the axle, an axle connected to the 8-tooth gear, an 8-tooth gear connected to the 24-tooth gear, and so on, all the way to the output and the wheel.

Most of the axle pairs (or other connections) in this chain are within a single LEGO brick. But the connection marked by red arrows in Figure 11-3 involves two 2×4 Technic bricks, meaning that when stress is applied, it can break apart (as shown in Figure 11-4). When deciding where to reinforce your model, look for the *seams* that could separate under stress.

Also note that a pair of gears that increases the gear ratio (the driver gear is bigger than the follower) is more likely to come apart than a pair that decreases the gear ratio (the driver gear is smaller than the follower). There is simply more force exerted on the follower gear when gearing up, and such a pair of gears is a good candidate for reinforcing.

Figure 11-5 shows one obvious way to reinforce our mechanism: We simply replace the two pairs of 1×4 bricks with two 1×8 bricks. On the upside, the weak seam is now gone, every link in our chain is solid, and we no longer need to use plates. Additionally, this solution adds no weight and takes up no extra space. The downside is that using long, solid bricks can be an invasive way of reinforcing, and building in this way is time-consuming and extremely inconvenient with complex gearing, as you'll have to place all elements at the same time.

Figures 11-6 and 11-7 show another way we can reinforce our mechanism: by adding support beams. This increases the weight of the mechanism and takes more space, but it involves only minimal changes to the original structure. Note that structures like the one shown in Figure 11-7 have the downside of added friction because the yellow bricks are partially supported by the axles—building compact mechanisms can come with a cost.

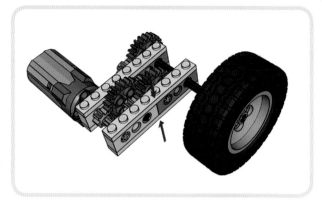

Figure 11-3: The critical connection in the mechanism from Figure 13-2 is marked by a red arrow here. This connection lies between two separate bricks and is held together merely by the clutching force of two 1×8 plates (yellow); therefore, it can be broken easily.

Figure 11-4: Without reinforcement, the weak link breaks apart the surrounding structure. The red gears are no longer meshed, and the mechanism fails.

understanding where to reinforce

The direction of a stressed gear's displacement depends on its location and its direction of rotation. When one gear drives another that resists it, the driver gear pushes against the follower gear just as the follower gear pushes back. This principle, which you might remember from high school physics, is a case of Newton's law of action and reaction, which states that forces are generated in equal and opposite pairs. Figure 11-8 shows a driver gear on top, rotating clockwise (as marked by the black arrow), and a follower gear on the bottom, being pushed down and to the side at the same time (as marked by the blue arrows).

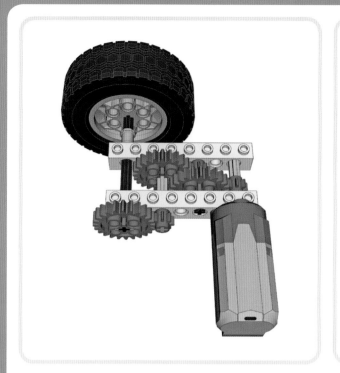

Figure 11-5: The two pairs of 1×4 bricks from our original structure have been replaced with two single, solid 1×8 bricks.

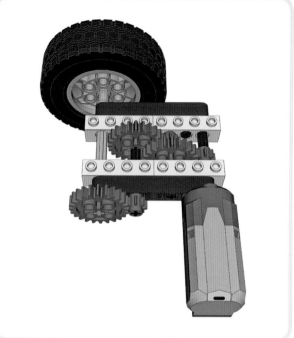

Figure 11-7: If vertical space is limited, horizontal beams (red) can some-times be used. In this case, doing so requires using a few longer axles and moving the motor 1 stud away from the bricks. Note that in order to create a rigid connection, each of the bricks is attached to the beams at two points.

Figure 11-6: Vertical beams (red) are a popular means of reinforcement.

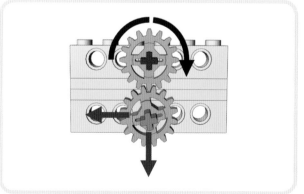

Figure 11-8: Directions of forces (blue) exerted by a driver gear (top) on the follower gear (bottom)

Now, if there were nothing holding the bricks in Figure 11-8 together, the follower gear would be pushed downward and to the left. The key to reinforcing properly is to limit displacement in *both* directions: Pieces that can't be separated can still be rotated, displacing and misaligning important elements of our drivetrain.

This same principle applies when two gears are mated at a different angle, as shown in Figure 11-9. Note that the gears in this figure can't come apart because their axles are both housed in a single L-shaped beam.

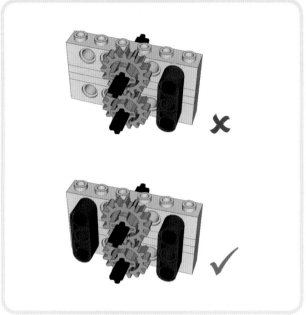

Figure 11-9: The directions of force exerted on the follower gear, which is located below and to the side of the driver gear

the right way to reinforce

Now that we know how to find weak links in our mechanisms, let's look at some examples of reinforcing. Figures 11-10 to 11-14 show reinforcing done poorly and done properly.

As you can see, reinforcing gears can be boiled down to making sure the axles are securely supported. But since axles can be long and prone to bending, there are two rules to follow here:

* The axle should be supported at least at two points.
* The axle should be supported as close to the gears on it as possible, preferably from both sides of the gears.

Figure 11-15 illustrates the first rule, and Figure 11-16 illustrates the second rule. Axles are in fact much less rigid than beams or bricks, and they can bend, twist, or even slide through the gears when subjected to sufficient stress.

Figure 11-10: Holding one end of the bricks together doesn't create a rigid connection, but holding both does.

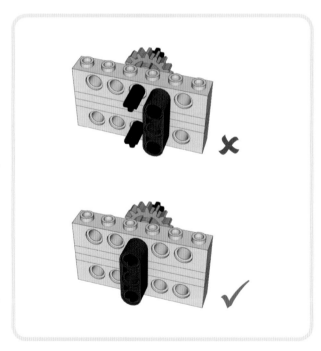

Figure 11-11: It's possible to reduce the number of reinforcing pieces by aligning them to the meshed gears rather than pairing them.

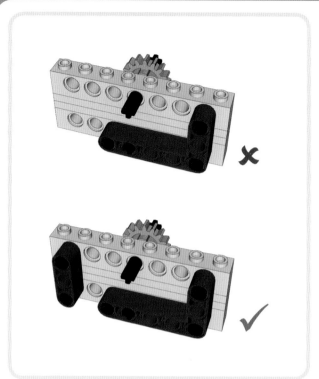

Figure 11-12: The L-shaped beam alone is not enough to create a rigid connection because it has only one point of attachment to the upper brick.

Figure 11-13: Beams that have only one point of attachment to adjacent bricks don't create a rigid connection. At least two points of connection to each brick are needed.

Figure 11-14: Plates help to create rigid connections. Use them as spacers between the points of connections of two bricks to prevent the bricks from oscillating.

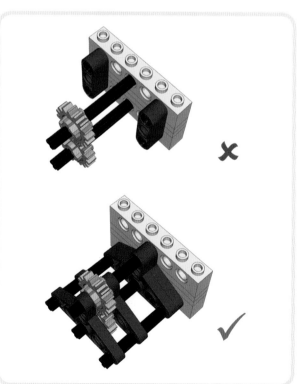

Figure 11-15: Both ends of the axles need to be reinforced to prevent the gears on them from coming apart.

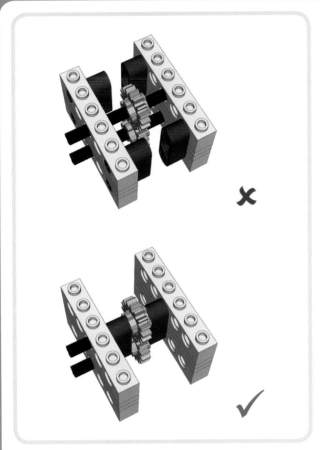

Figure 11-16: Empty space on the axles adjacent to the gears allows them to slide or enables the whole axle to bend. This empty space should be used for reinforcement.

Figure 11-17: Axles are much more elastic than they might seem. This one has been twisted permanently by a PF XL motor.

Figure 11-17 shows a permanently twisted axle. Note that the longer the axle, the more easily it gets twisted—that's why it's always a good idea to swap a single long axle for a few shorter ones connected with axle joiners. Another good idea is to add substantial gear reduction near the output so that only a small portion of the drivetrain is subjected to high torque.

Reinforcing perpendicular bevel gears is a more difficult task, as even a minimal displacement in structure disengages the gears. This is because their teeth come into contact over a small area. We need to make sure the gears are firmly kept in place. A number of LEGO studfull and studless pieces are designed specifically to reinforce perpendicular gears, as shown in Figures 11-18 to 11-20.

When you have no dedicated LEGO pieces to reinforce perpendicular gears, you can still use basic pieces to do so. Figures 11-21 and 11-22 show examples of this approach using studfull and studless pieces.

things to remember when reinforcing

There are a few more rules of reinforcing worth keeping in mind:

* Minimal reinforcement is the best reinforcement. Extra pieces add weight and take up space.
* If a seam or joint can separate, it eventually will—and usually when you least expect it. (And Murphy's law says that it will be deep inside your MOC where you can't fix it!)
* Real reinforcement doesn't yield until pieces physically break.
* When building, think about disassembly, too. A reinforcement that has to be cut to be taken apart will cost you pieces.

The last rule is no less important than the ones preceding it. It's fairly easy to connect LEGO pieces in such a way that the resulting structure is impossible to disassemble without cutting some of the pieces. Figure 11-23 shows some examples. As you'll see, you should take precautions when inserting axles—always make sure it's possible to pull or push them out.

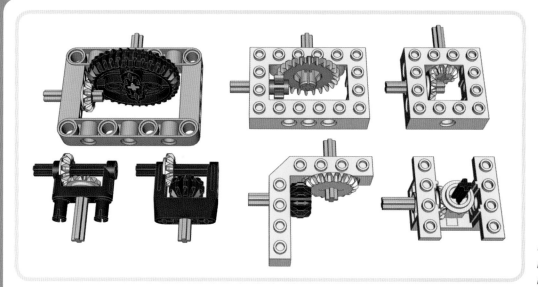

Figure 11-18: LEGO pieces for reinforcing perpendicular gears

Figure 11-19: Piece #6585 is a particularly interesting brace that can reinforce both horizontal and vertical gears. Technic bricks and plates can be connected to it to support their axles.

Figure 11-20: There are also so-called Technic gearboxes, which have special sturdy bevel gears enclosed. They are robust and can have axles inserted into them, but they are rare.

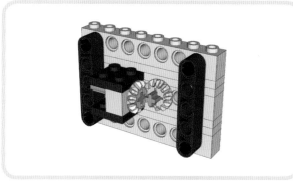

Figure 11-21: Perpendicular gears reinforced with bricks held together by beams. Note the use of 2×3 plates (blue) to hold the perpendicular brick.

Figure 11-22: Perpendicular gears reinforced with L-shaped beams. Note that one end of the beams is held together by a vertical beam. This is because there are only axles on this end of the beams and the axles don't hold the beams together. The other end of the beams has a connector with pins that hold the beams together with a force very unlikely to be overcome by gears.

Figure 11-23: Dangerous structures: Once the axles marked by arrows are pushed in, these structures are impossible to take apart without cutting pieces.

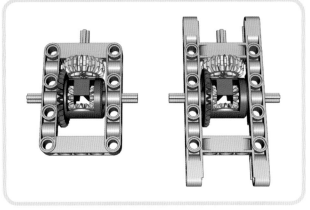

Figure 11-24: The studless frame comes in a regular (left) and an extended (right) variant. Both create a perfectly rigid reinforcement for the newest type of LEGO differential.

reinforced differential casings

Differentials are often subjected to high torque because there is usually no gear reduction between them and the wheels. To make things worse, they are usually meshed using perpendicular gears. It was only in 2009 that LEGO released pieces designed specifically to remedy this problem: studless frames. But studless frames aren't very common and work only with the newest type of differential gear, as shown in Figures 11-24 and 11-25.

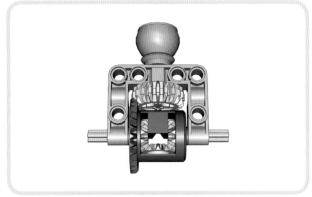

Figure 11-25: The larger part of the ball joint comes with an attached C-shaped frame, large enough to house the newest type of LEGO differential.

four reinforced differential casings

The following are examples of sturdy casings for all types of differentials, made of common pieces. They are inevitably inferior to studless frames because of their greater size and weight, but they are useful nonetheless.

1

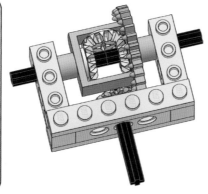

2

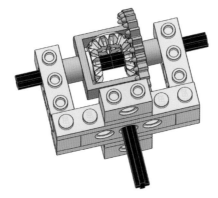

3

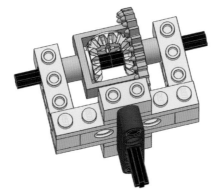

1

1x
6 1x
1x
5x
1x 4
2x 3x
2x 1x

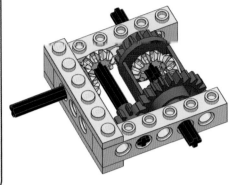

2

2x
2x

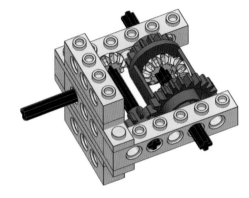

3

4x
5
2x

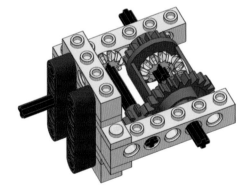

1

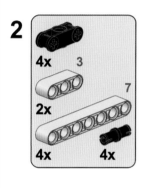

4
3x

3x

4x

7

1x   1x

2x   4x   2x

2

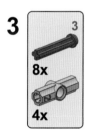

4x   3

2x   7

4x   4x

3

3

8x

4x

1

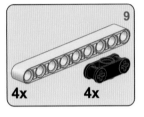

4
4x

3x

1x

5

1x

3

1x

4x

3x

2x

2x

4x

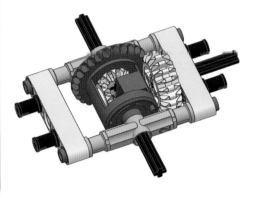

2

9

4x

4x

3

6

4x

4x

reinforced worm gear casings

Because of their unique design, worm gears need particularly solid reinforcement. As Figure 11-26 shows, apart from pushing the follower gear away, worm gears have a strong tendency to slide along the axle they're sitting on. This is a result of worm gears' enlarged axle holes, which allow them to slide along axles. This lateral force can be strong enough to make a worm gear drill through adjacent pieces if sufficiently high torque is applied to it for a prolonged time!

LEGO released special casings for worm gears, but they are relatively large and work only with 24-tooth follower gears, as shown in Figures 11-27 and 11-28.

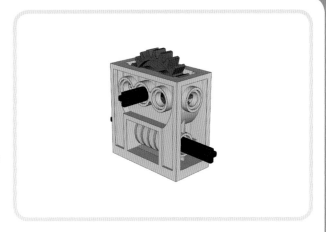

Figure 11-27: The LEGO casing for the worm gear is very sturdy and quite common, but it works only with a 24-tooth follower gear. It's also better suited for studfull structures than for studless ones.

Figure 11-26: The directions of forces exerted by a worm gear. Unlike regular gears, a worm gear doesn't push the follower gear to the side; instead, it pushes itself against the follower gear along its axle.

Figure 11-28: A gearbox with a worm gear and 24-tooth follower gear closed inside. It's even sturdier than the regular casing, but it's very rare.

three reinforced worm gear casings

Thankfully, if you have neither a casing piece nor a gearbox piece, you can easily build your own. Three designs for worm gear casings (using various follower gears) are shown here.

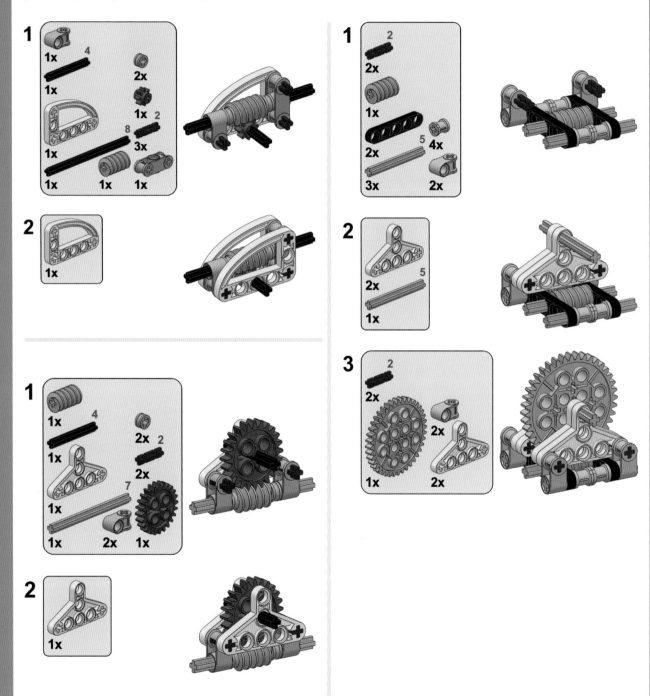

load-bearing structures

Load-bearing structures are the "skeletons" within our models. You might think of these structures as the framing of a house, the pylons of a suspension bridge, the chassis of a car, or even the bones within the human body. They support a construction's weight and maintain its rigidity, and they may have no other purpose beyond structural reinforcement.

rails, chassis, and body frames

A chassis is the type of a load-bearing structure most commonly used in vehicular models. A properly built chassis is sturdy enough to support the weight of the vehicle and rigid enough to maintain its shape as the vehicle negotiates obstacles and carries loads.

We're going to focus on the most convenient and commonly used way to build a chassis: *rails*, also called *stringers*. Almost all LEGO Technic sets use this method.

Rails are longitudinal members that span most or the entire length of the vehicle. Since one rail is not rigid enough to support a vehicle's weight, most body frames have two parallel rails, which are joined together with crossbeams so they act as one element. You can add other elements of the construction both in the gap between the rails and in the space around them.

Figure 11-29 shows a small, lightweight studless LEGO truck with two rails visible from the bottom. Note that elements are placed both on the sides of the rails (wheels, bumpers, side curtains) and between them (differential, piston engine).

Figures 11-30 and 11-31 show examples of simple studless and studfull rail/crossbeam configurations.

Configurations like these, which form a "skeleton" that supports other parts of the model, are called *body frames*. If you expect particularly large stress to be exerted on your model's chassis, you can add another pair of rails above the first one and connect the two pairs. Figures 11-32 and 11-33 show examples of a studless and studfull body frame, and Figure 11-34 shows a studfull body frame at work in my Tow Truck 2 model.

The most common gap size between rails is between 3 and 6 studs. A gap this size is big enough for most of the heavy elements you may want to place in the center of your model, such as big motors and power supplies, but not so wide as to affect the frame's rigidity.

Finally, we can build rails with more complex shapes to accommodate elements like pendular suspension components. Figure 11-35 shows examples of body frames with irregularly shaped rails.

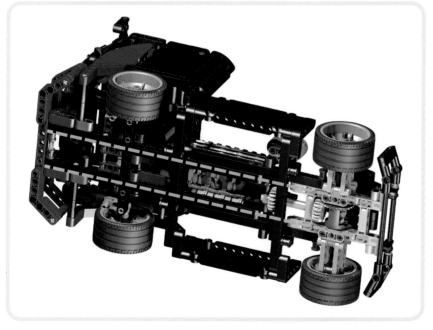

Figure 11-29: The LEGO 8041 set, a small racing truck, is a good example of a model built around two parallel rails.

Figure 11-30: A simple combination of rails made of studless beams, with extended body frames working as crossbars. The frames provide space for differentials for front and rear axles, and there is plenty of space between the rails for a propulsion system or a power supply.

Figure 11-31: A simple studfull chassis combining bricks, pins, and plates

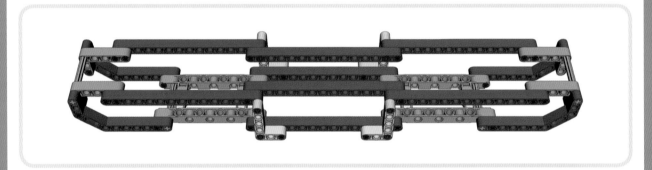

Figure 11-32: A studless body frame with two pairs of rails, one above the other. The upper pair is supported at the ends and in the middle. Studless frames work well with smaller, compact models where adding many elements to the chassis is more important than its rigidity.

Figure 11-33: A typical studfull body frame, reinforced with vertical beams. This kind of frame works well for big, heavy models where rigidity is of primary importance.

Figure 11-34: My Tow Truck 2 model was very heavy and almost 0.8 m long. It was held together by a massive studfull body frame with two pairs of rails, rigid enough to allow the model to be lifted by hand without any problems. The boom of the truck had its own frame of four studless rails, with the extendable section placed in the middle. It was covered with a studfull shell, which not only made it look better but also improved its rigidity.

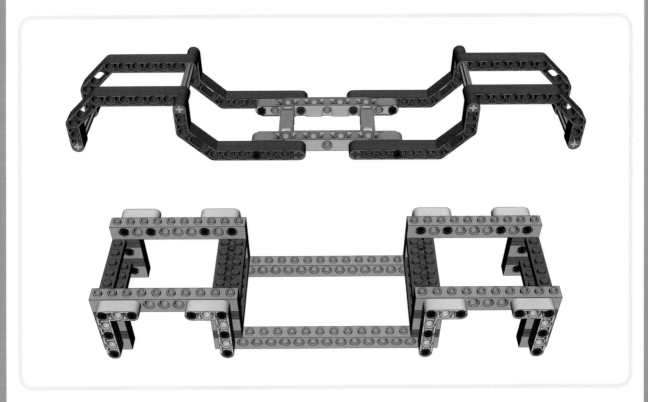

Figure 11-35: Examples of studless and studfull body frames with rails of complex shapes

trusses

A truss is a particular type of load-bearing structure that consists of beams that form repeated triangles, as shown in Figure 11-36. The triangles are often identical in size, but they don't have to be. The joints connecting these elements in a truss are often called *nodes*. Trusses are ubiquitous in the construction of buildings and machines—for example, tower cranes are built almost entirely with trusses. The advantage of trusses is that they can form large, lightweight, and very sturdy structures while using only a handful of basic pieces to build. Figure 11-37 shows a LEGO set that makes use of simple trusses.

Figure 11-37: The LEGO 8288 Crawler Crane set comes with two booms (greyish in this image) made entirely of simple trusses.

Figure 11-36: A simple truss

Trusses can be divided into two categories: *planar trusses*, with all nodes within a single plane (like the truss in Figure 11-36), and *space trusses*, in which nodes extend in all three dimensions (like the truss in Figure 11-38). Space trusses are generally sturdier than planar trusses, and their simple construction allows for modular building. As Figure 11-38 shows, a simple space truss can actually be a combination of two or more planar trusses.

Just like any other load-bearing structures, trusses can be subjected to as many as four types of stress: *compression*, *tension*, *bending*, and *torsion*, as shown in Figure 11-39. It's possible to build a truss that can resist all four types of stress, but such a truss is heavy, complex, and takes lots of pieces to build. A more "economical" approach is to choose the type of truss that can handle only the kinds of stress we expect it to experience.

There are more than 20 types of trusses in the world. However, their complex geometry makes many of them difficult to reproduce with LEGO pieces, so we'll limit our discussion to three practical designs.

Figure 11-38: Two planar trusses, connected using axles and pins with bushes, create a basic space truss.

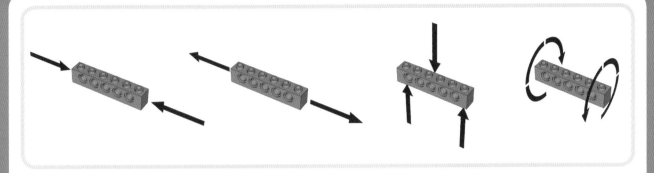

Figure 11-39: From left to right: compression, tension, bending, and torsion

Brown truss

Figure 11-40: Planar combinations of the Brown truss module

The Brown truss uses an X-shaped reinforcement between two horizontal members. If there is only one reinforcement between these members, its slant beams must be connected in the middle. If there are multiple Xs, this connection is not needed, as shown in Figure 11-40.

The length and angle of beams in the Brown truss module can be adjusted as needed, but the module is strongest with crossbeams exactly perpendicular to each other. Our example above, with 12-stud-long horizontal beams and 13-stud-long crossbeams, is of a convenient size: The gap between the pin holes of the upper and lower horizontal beams is exactly 10 studs tall.

The basic building block of the Brown truss, the planar X, can be combined into planar trusses similar in construction to a scissor mechanism, as shown in Figure 11-40. A more interesting solution is to combine the planar X into a space truss, as shown in Figure 11-41. The space combination can also be used to build modules that can easily be stacked on top of one another, as shown in Figure 11-42.

Figure 11-41: Space combination of the Brown truss module. Note that vertical beams (red) can be added for further reinforcement.

Figure 11-42: The Brown module is shown here combined into space modules that can be stacked on top of one another. This arrangement allows you to easily adjust the height of the resulting structure.

The Brown truss is resistant to compression and torsion. Its resistance to tension and bending depends on the strength of connections between its modules.

Warren truss

The Warren truss combines two simple planar trusses. The length and angle of the slanted beams (light grey) can be adjusted as needed. The slanted beams also don't have to be adjacent—small gaps between them are acceptable. The horizontal beams (dark grey) can be studless, as in Figure 11-38, or studfull, as shown above (in which case they can be further reinforced with plates).

The Warren truss is resistant to compression, tension, and bending. Torsion affects connections between its planar trusses and can lead to disintegration.

triangular Warren truss

The triangular Warren truss, shown in Figures 11-43 and 11-44, combines two simple planar trusses to form the shape of a triangular prism. The truss has two lower beams but only one upper beam, which makes it weigh less than the regular Warren truss, though its construction requires additional connectors (red in the illustration and in Figures 11-43 and 11-44). This variant is nearly as robust as the regular Warren truss, except that its lower beams are subjected to more stress than the upper beam. Also, pressure on the upper beam can push the two lower beams apart unless they are connected (by perpendicular plates, for example).

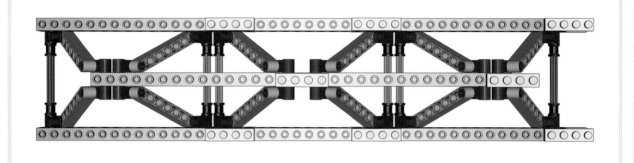

Figure 11-43: Top view of the triangular Warren truss

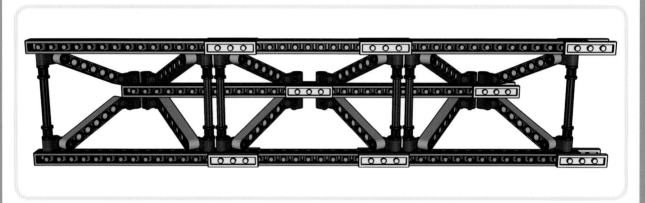

Figure 11-44: The bottom view of the triangular Warren truss shows that the lower beams (horizontal, top and bottom) are held together only from the inside of the truss. This means that they can be pushed apart by a sufficiently high load on the top beam (horizontal, middle).

The triangular Warren truss is resistant to compression, tension, and bending. With lower beams firmly connected by crossbeams, it is also considerably resistant to torsion.

choosing the right truss

A truss made of firmly connected Brown modules can withstand all types of stress. It is, however, complex and heavy, so we'll only want to use it if it's absolutely necessary. This section explores how to determine which truss will work best for various vehicles.

Let's first consider a bus, which has a large gap between its front and rear axle. Its axles support it from the bottom, while its weight presses from the top on the middle of its chassis, as shown in Figure 11-45. This means that the chassis is subjected to bending. A regular Warren truss will easily handle that stress while also resisting the minor compression and tension that occur when the bus starts and stops.

An off-road truck, on the other hand, is less subject to bending due to its shorter length. But such a truck is designed to negotiate difficult obstacles, which will make its suspension work hard, making the wheels go up and down. It's very likely that the front and rear axles of our truck will oscillate in opposite directions while traversing an obstacle, which will exert torsion on the chassis, as shown in Figure 11-46.

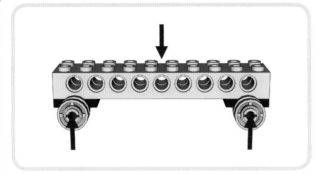

Figure 11-45: Forces exerted on the chassis of a bus. The chassis is primarily subjected to bending.

Figure 11-47: Forces exerted on various parts of a tower crane

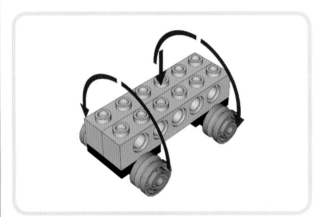

Figure 11-46: Forces exerted on the chassis of an off-road truck. The chassis is subjected primarily to torsion but also to bending.

We can use Brown modules in our truck's chassis if we want it to be extremely sturdy, but we can also use the triangular Warren truss to save some weight and space. With its lower beams held together, the triangular Warren truss will handle both torsion and bending.

Our last example is a *tower crane*, which has several elements that could use reinforcing. We'll see how different sections of the crane will benefit from using different kinds of trusses.

As Figure 11-47 shows, we can break our crane into four parts. First is the part that supports the entire crane, called the *tower mast* (yellow). As the weight of the crane rests on it, the tower mast is subjected to compression. Lifting loads also makes the crane tip a bit, so the structure is subject to some bending. Finally, the upper portion of the crane can rotate while the yellow truss remains fixed to the ground—this exerts torsion when rotation starts and stops. So we know our yellow tower mast truss must withstand all types of stress except tension. A truss made of space Brown modules will be a good choice.

Our second truss (blue) is called the *jib*. It's the part directly responsible for moving loads. As one end is fixed to the center of the crane, the other has loads suspended on it and is supported by a cable called the *jib tie*, which exerts some compression on it. As the crane rotates, the loads swing a little below the jib, exerting some torsion on it as well. Note that the jib is the second-largest part of the crane, and it can add a lot of weight. We want the jib to weigh as little as possible, so the triangular Warren truss will be a good choice here, resisting both compression and torsion while adding less weight than other options.

The third part (green) is called the *counterjib*. The counterjib is fixed to the center of the crane at one end and supports the crane's counterweight at its other end. It is therefore subjected to bending, just like the jib, but to a smaller degree because of its shorter length. Its counterweight doesn't swing during rotation, so it isn't subjected to torsion. We can use the triangular Warren truss here as well, or we can instead choose the simpler regular Warren truss—the counterjib is so short that the difference in weight will be minimal.

Finally, the grey part, called the *top mast*, simply supports the cable that connects opposite tips of the jib and counterjib. The jib tie exerts compression on the top mast and slight bending on the counterjib, which we've already accounted for. The top mast is small and little stress is involved, so we can use a small section of the Warren truss; alternatively, we can give up on trusses and use any structure capable of supporting some weight put directly on top of it. Figure 11-48 shows an example of a real tower crane built the same way as our model.

Figure 11-49: A bush: roughly 20 years old (left) and 1 year old (right). Note the crack in the old bush's side; under torque, this crack will soon lead to the bush's disintegration.

Figure 11-48: A real tower crane at work. As you can see, its tower mast is built with a Brown truss, and its jib is built with a triangular Warren truss, just like in our model.

choosing the strongest pieces

Although LEGO pieces are known for their lasting quality, they are prone to *aging* and *wear*. This means there are two things you should avoid when picking pieces for a tough job: aged pieces and physically worn pieces.

It's safe to assume that LEGO pieces fully maintain their quality for at least 5 to 10 years, unless damaged. As your collection ages, or is supplemented with older pieces and garage sale treasures, you should carefully select the pieces that will handle high stress. The easiest way to determine a piece's age is to keep a few new pieces for comparison. LEGO pieces, particularly white and grey pieces, *yellow* over time. Figures 11-49 to 11-51 show the difference.

Figure 11-50: A connector: old (left) and new (right). Even though the old piece is free from damage or visible wear, the difference is obvious.

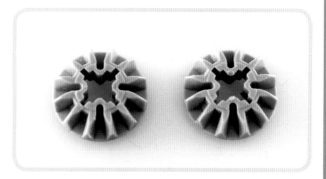

Figure 11-51: Two gears of the same type made roughly 10 years apart

Pieces that are physically worn aren't too difficult to spot. The wear can vary from very subtle—negligible for our purposes—to obvious damage. You should look for wear on the surfaces that contact other pieces, such as the teeth of gears or the area around the pin hole in a brick. Wear occurs more often on pieces that are subjected to high stress, such as knobs, small gears that are crucial for high gear reduction, or various pieces that work with worm gears. Figures 11-52 to 11-54 show typical examples of wear.

Figure 11-54: This visibly worn knob has polished edges where the material has been rubbed away. Knobs transfer high torque over very small areas of contact, resulting in intense wear. Worn knobs produce a distinctive squeaking when working under stress.

Figure 11-52: A close-up view showing the inside of a LEGO casing for a worm gear. Here, a worm gear has partially drilled into one of the casing sides.

Finally, note that differently colored pieces actually have different properties. The exact variations are difficult to measure, but I have observed that red pieces are particularly weak while yellow pieces are particularly strong. The difference isn't big, but it can manifest when pieces are subjected to prolonged stress.

Figure 11-53: This gear's teeth were ground away when it was misaligned to a larger, stronger gear. While the piece itself is new and most of it remains intact, this kind of wear makes the gear unusable.

motors

12

an inventory of LEGO motors

Electric motors are the muscle of most Technic creations. While it's perfectly fine to build mechanisms driven by hand, and some builders actually specialize in human-powered models, the most impressive constructions are motorized. Motors can be used for almost anything, from driving and steering to rotating, elevating, extending, and even controlling other electric components. In this chapter, we'll explore which LEGO motors are best suited for which purposes.

LEGO has been making electric motors since 1965, and they can be classified into three general categories. The first motors were 4.5V motors, but they're rare, old, and inferior when compared to the newer motors, so let's move straight to the next category.

In 1990, LEGO introduced a second line of motors, running at 9V on six AA batteries (shown in Figure 12-1). These motors are considerably more powerful and convenient to use than their predecessors. The 9V line also has greater variation, including motors for boats with propellers and watertight housings. The 9V motors are widely available and highly popular. We'll discuss this line of motors in this chapter, with the exception of some specialized ones, such as the Trains and Monorail motors, which are very difficult (or downright impossible) to use outside their intended applications.

The third category of motors is the *Power Functions (PF)* line, introduced in 2007 (shown in Figure 12-2). These motors are designed to use a 9V power supply as well, but unlike the previous category, they are part of a carefully planned and currently developed system of motors and specialized parts. The Power Functions line includes just a few motors, which are designed to complement each other. Each motor is suited for different tasks, and the characteristics of the motors vary considerably. PF motors are well suited to studless building because they have odd widths and pin holes, and their torque is optimized for high-load applications. Additionally, they can be controlled remotely, while the

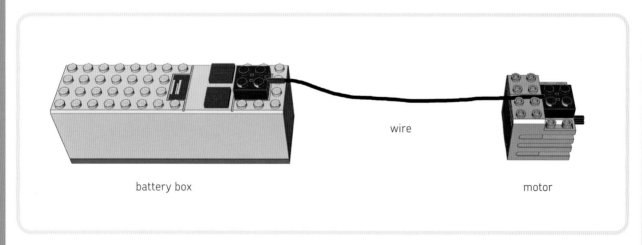

battery box   wire   motor

Figure 12-1: The 9V line is powered by a battery box, which also functions as a basic switch.

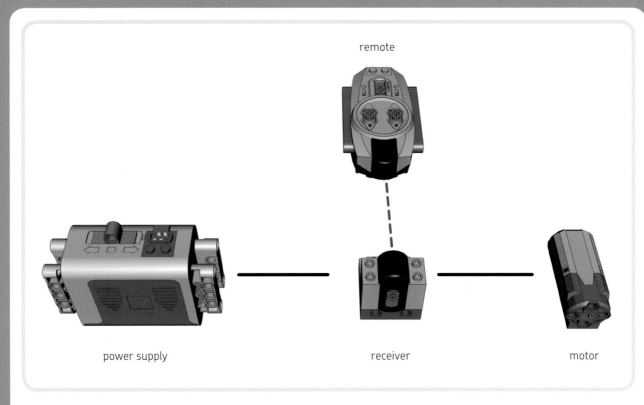

remote

power supply   receiver   motor

Figure 12-2: The Power Functions motor system can be controlled remotely.

motors in the other two categories can be controlled only with a wire connected to the power supply, which acts as a controller. Power Functions motors also allow more fine-grained control, with more options than simply *forward* and *reverse*. We'll explore the Power Functions system and its controls in Chapter 13.

The following list includes speeds of motors at both 9V and 7V whenever such data is available. (Rechargeable AA batteries and the rechargeable Power Functions battery provide a 7V power supply.) Also, note that motors are prone to wearing down over time; thus, the exact characteristics of any two motors of the same type can vary.

While there is no official technical specification for the LEGO motors, LEGO enthusiast Philippe "Philo" Hurbain has spent a lot of time performing many complex measures on these motors. This chapter's measurements are derived from his work and used with his kind permission. (Read more about Philippe's work at his site, *http://www.philohome.com/motors/motorcomp.htm*.)

2838, the first 9V motor

Torque: 0.45 N•cm
No-load speed at 7V: 2000 RPM
No-load speed at 9V: 3300 RPM

The first motor in the 9V line, the 2838, is relatively large and has no internal gearing, which results in very high speed and low torque. It's ineffective in high-load applications where it requires substantial gear reduction, often including one or more worm gears. This motor is also prone to overheating. The motor has a 1L axle protruding out of it and connects to the power supply through a 2×5 contact area in the middle of its bottom surface.

71427, a popular and powerful 9V motor

Torque: 2.25 N•cm
No-load speed at 7V: 160 RPM
No-load speed at 9V: 250 RPM

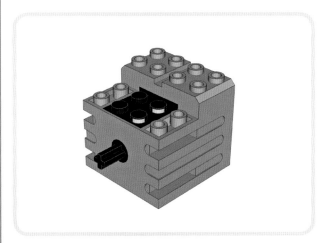

This 9V motor is popular due to its reasonable size and favorable characteristics. It's a very quiet motor with substantial internal gearing, which creates noticeable inertia when the motor is stopped. The motor has a 1L axle and connects to the power supply through a 2×2 contact area on its top. Its upper surface is conveniently shaped, with one recess for the power plug and another for routing the wire backward. Its lower surface has a 1-plate-tall 2×2 bulge in the back.

43362, a lighter 9V motor

Torque: 2.25 N•cm
No-load speed at 7V: 140 RPM
No-load speed at 9V: 219 RPM

Externally identical to the 9V 71427 motor (shown previously), this motor is almost one-third lighter at the expense of slightly reduced speed. The difference in weight makes it more sought after than the original 71427 motor, so it sells for significantly higher prices. The motor has a 1L axle and connects to the power supply through a 2×2 contact area on its top. Its upper surface is conveniently shaped with one recess for the power plug and another for routing the wire backward. Its lower surface has a one-plate-tall 2×2 bulge in the back. Just like the 71427 motor, this motor can be mounted on rails using the two slots on its sides (shown in Figure 12-3).

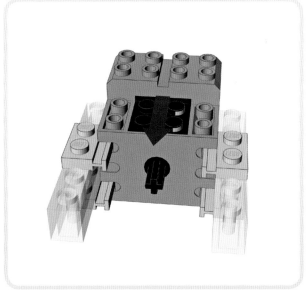

Figure 12-3: The slots on the sides of the 43362 motor fit plates with rails. The motor can be firmly secured using two of these (or more). As shown by the red arrow, the motor must be slid onto these plates with rails.

47154, a 9V motor in a semitransparent housing

Torque: 2.25 N•cm
No-load speed at 7V: 210 RPM
No-load speed at 9V: 315 RPM

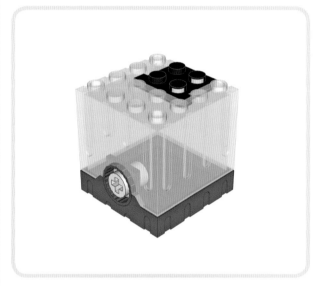

This motor is similar to the 71427 motor, except that it has a higher speed and is louder. It's 1 plate taller than the 71427 motor and comes with a completely flat bottom. The motor has a 1-stud-deep axle hole and connects to the power supply through a 2×2 contact area on its top.

Micromotor

Torque: 1.28 N•cm
No-load speed at 9V: 16 RPM

This 9V motor is exceptional for its small size. It's rare, highly sought after, and expensive. Its speed is so slow that it doesn't usually need external gear reduction, while its torque is quite high for a motor this size (higher than the 2838 motor's torque, for example). A complete Micromotor consists of four individual pieces: an upper and lower brace, a "Micromotor pulley," and the motor itself. The motor is rarely used without these pieces, although it can be operated without the braces if it is connected to something by its power plug. The motor connects to the power supply through a 2×2 contact area at its back. Figure 12-4 shows an exploded view of the Micromotor and its parts.

Figure 12-4: An exploded view of the Micromotor, showing its upper and lower brackets, pulley, and motor

The Micromotor's specially designed pulley has a 1-stud-deep axle hole and a belt groove for a rubber band. The pulley allows the motor to be connected to an axle. The pulley also works like a slip clutch, preventing the motor from stalling.

NXT motor

Torque: 16.7 N•cm
No-load speed at 7V: 82 RPM
No-load speed at 9V: 117 RPM

This motor was designed specifically for the MINDSTORMS NXT set. It has the highest torque of all existing electric LEGO motors and high power consumption. It includes a rotation sensor with a one-degree resolution, which is useful when designing robots that require precise control.

However, its shape and size are a disadvantage when one is using it outside MINDSTORMS constructions, and it connects to the power supply through a MINDSTORMS-type plug, which means that a special converter cable is required to connect it to regular 9V or Power Functions power supplies. Unlike other motors, its output is a 3-stud-wide ring (orange in the figure above) with four 1-stud-deep pin holes around the center. It also has an empty axle hole in the center through which any axle longer than 3 studs can be inserted.

Power Functions E motor

Torque: 1.32 N•cm
No-load speed at 7V: 300 RPM
No-load speed at 9V: 420 RPM

This unusual Power Functions motor was designed for LEGO Education sets. It has low internal gearing, which allows it to be easily driven and to act as a power generator. However, its large size and poor speed and torque performance make it practically useless when compared to other Power Functions motors. The motor has a 1-stud-deep axle hole and an integral wire.

Power Functions Medium (M) motor

Torque: 3.63 N•cm
No-load speed at 7V: 185 RPM
No-load speed at 9V: 275 RPM

With a diameter of only 3 studs, this popular Power Functions motor takes up little space and fits studless constructions exceptionally well while offering very good torque. The only downside to this motor is that it's 6 studs long; other than that, it's easy to use, powerful, and versatile. This motor has a 1-stud-deep axle hole and an integral wire. It can be mounted either from the front using some of its four pin holes or from the bottom using studs.

Power Functions L motor

Torque: approx. 6.48 N•cm
No-load speed at 7V: 203 RPM
No-load speed at 9V: 272 RPM

Introduced in 2012, the L motor works where the Medium motor is too weak and the XL motor is too big. At 3×4×7 studs it's only slightly larger than the Medium motor, while delivering nearly 180 percent of Medium's torque. It's a little slower than Medium motor though, and its power consumption is higher (see "Understanding the Speed Control Feature" on page 177 for details). This motor has a 1-stud-deep axle hole and an integral wire. It can be mounted from the front or back, or from two of its sides using pin holes—it has 14 of those, including 2 at the back.

Power Functions XL motor

Torque: 14.5 N•cm
No-load speed at 7V: 100 RPM
No-load speed at 9V: 146 RPM

This is the most powerful Power Functions motor. It shares some essential internal parts with the NXT motor but has lower torque and higher speed. The XL motor is popular because it's extremely powerful, and it's more prevalent and easier to use than the NXT motor. Still, its large size makes coupled Medium motors a better choice in many cases. This motor has a 1-stud-deep axle hole and an integral wire.

This motor cannot be connected via studs. It has six axle holes on its front and four on its sides, which allow it to be firmly braced in a construction against considerable output torque.

Power Functions Servo motor

Introduced in 2012, the Servo motor is designed for steering systems. It can't rotate continuously—instead, it rotates 90 degrees clockwise or counterclockwise from its central position. Its low speed allows it to be used with most steering systems directly, with no gearing in between, while its huge torque makes sure it won't be easily stalled.

When used with a basic PF remote, the Servo motor rotates 90 degrees in one direction or the other when the remote's lever is pushed, and it returns to the central position when the lever is released. When used with the speed control PF remote or directly with the rechargeable PF battery, the motor follows the rotation of the speed dial, meaning that it provides proportional steering with 7 steps in either direction and 1 neutral position (which it returns to after the remote's stop button is pressed). In other words, it uses the PF speed control feature to break its 180 degrees of total rotation range into 15 steps, 12 degrees each, while its speed remains constant at all times.

This motor measures 3×5×7 studs, and it has a bulge on its bottom with a 1-stud-deep axle hole on the front and another on the back. Thus, the motor can be inserted between two axles; it will keep them 1 stud apart and rotate them as one in the same direction. It also has an integral wire and can be mounted from the front or from two of its sides using pin holes.

RC motor

Torque (inner output/outer output): 1.83 N•cm/2.48 N•cm
No-load speed at 7V (inner output/outer output):
    906 RPM/670 RPM
No-load speed at 9V (inner output/outer output):
    1245 RPM/920 RPM

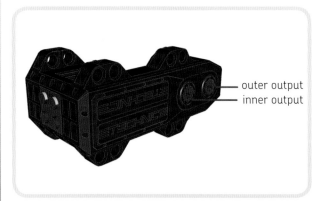

— outer output
— inner output

This 9V motor was originally designed for a discontinued series of fast radio-controlled cars. As such, it has an unusual shape, good torque, and very high speed. Unfortunately, it is also very noisy and has extremely high power consumption; in fact, some power supplies can't even let it run at full power. In theory, its speed and torque make it the most powerful electric LEGO motor, and with efficient external gearing, it can perform better than XL or NXT motors. It does, however, tend to become overheated under high loads, which causes its internal electronic protection to shut the power off until the motor cools down.

The RC motor is unique because it has two outputs. Both are empty axle holes running in the same direction, but the motor's internal gear ratio is different for each of them. Because of this, the inner output runs faster at lower torque than the outer one.

13

LEGO Power Functions system

The LEGO Power Functions system (or PF for short), introduced in 2007, is a combination of LEGO elements that
allows you to motorize your constructions, to equip them
with lights, to move them with linear actuators, and, above
all, to control them remotely. In this chapter, we will learn
how this system works and how its elements can be
combined.

The core parts of the Power Functions system can be
divided into three groups: power supplies, control elements,
and motors. There are several types of motors in the Power
Functions system, and all of them are described in the previous chapter. The Power Functions system allows us to control motors with more flexibility, offering fine-grained control
of speed and the ability to control multiple elements at once.

NOTE One of the novelties of the Power Functions
system is that the majority of its elements have been
released as stand-alone, separate LEGO sets. A list of
these sets can be found at the end of this chapter.

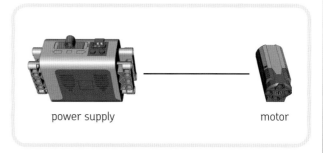

power supply   motor

Figure 13-1: The simplest Power Functions motor configuration

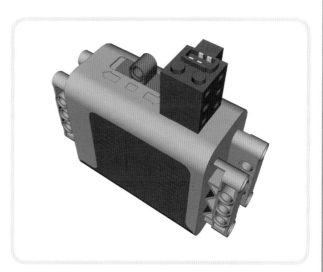

Figure 13-2: A regular Power Functions battery box with three plugs stacked
on its outlet. Three elements can now be powered and controlled from this
box at the same time.

manually controlling motors

To control a motor by hand with Power Functions system,
you need only two elements: a power supply and a motor, as
shown in Figure 13-1. All Power Functions power supplies
come with controls on them, some basic and some advanced,
and these controls affect any and all motors directly connected to the power supply.

Note that the plugs of the Power Functions wires are
stackable, and we can connect many wires to a single outlet,
as shown in Figure 13-2.

The simple *power supply and motor* configuration has
one serious disadvantage: If many motors are connected
to one power supply, they will all work as one. This is inevi-
table when using the power supply as a control mechanism,

which is why the Power Functions system includes a separate group of control elements. The simplest element from this group is a switch, shown in Figure 13-3.

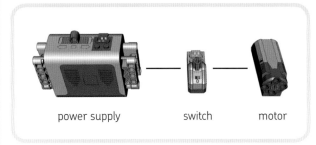

power supply   switch   motor

Figure 13-3: A slightly more complicated configuration for the Power Functions system

Just like all control elements, the switch is connected between the power supply and the element we want to control. It has three positions—forward, stop, and reverse—and they affect all elements connected to the switch.

Note that in this configuration, the controls of a switch and the regular battery box can work at the same time, so either can be used to control the motor. (But if the power supply is set to off, obviously, the setting of the switch won't affect the motor.)

remotely controlling motors

While direct manual control is a nice option, the key advantage of the Power Functions system is the ability to control motors remotely. This is done by a pair of elements: a remote and a receiver (see Figure 12-2 on page 164).

You can think of the remote and receiver as a switch split into two parts. One part, the receiver, is between the power supply and the elements we want to control, just like a switch. It also has a wire just as a switch does. The other part, the remote, has no wires and isn't physically connected to anything. It sends commands to the receiver using an invisible infrared link, just as most TV remotes do. It also houses batteries, just as TV remotes do, so it needs no external power supply. Your construction, with the receiver integrated into it, can be controlled from a distance using the remote.

It's important to remember that the infrared link between remote and receiver has its limitations. The black, semitransparent parts of both remote and receiver house infrared sensors that need to be exposed and within a line of sight of each other to maintain a link. The remote is actually sending out invisible light signals, and they won't reach the receiver if something blocks their way or if they are sent in the wrong direction. They can, however, bounce off walls and ceilings; so as long as you remain indoors, pointing the remote in the receiver's general direction is sufficient. You can also cover up the receiver almost entirely in constructions intended for indoor use, as Figure 13-4 shows. A 2×2 opening around or slightly above the receiver's top will do the job. Outdoors, maintaining the link between remote and receiver is more difficult: The remote has to be aimed with good precision, and its range can drop to as little as 1 m if the receiver's sensor is exposed to strong sunlight.

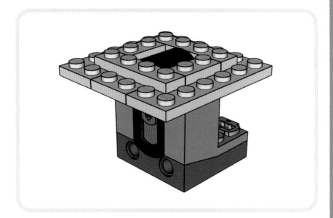

Figure 13-4: An IR receiver doesn't have to make your construction ugly. You can cover it up almost completely, leaving only the 2×2 opening around the sensor. The cover can end up level with the sensor or even slightly above it and still work, as long as you hold the remote higher than the receiver.

As Figure 13-5 shows, a receiver has two levers, one blue and one red, along with two outlets colored the same way. The levers and outlets correspond—the blue lever controls everything connected to the blue outlet, while the red lever controls everything connected to the red outlet. The remote comes with two pole reversers, one for each outlet/lever. The reversers' function is simple: They determine whether pushing a lever forward makes a motor connected to the corresponding outlet rotate forward or in reverse. The blue/red elements are independent and can work at the same time. In other words, the blue lever doesn't interfere with the red lever, and the blue pole reverser doesn't interfere with the red pole reverser.

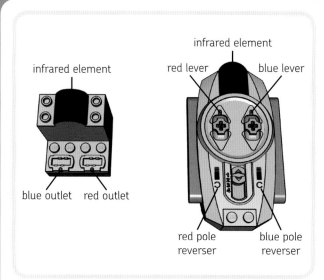

Figure 13-5: The receiver and basic remote

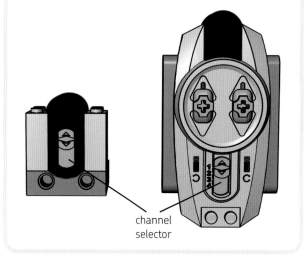

Figure 13-6: The channel selectors on a receiver and basic remote

There is a reason why we said that a lever controls *everything* connected to its corresponding outlet. Since the Power Functions plugs are stackable, you can connect as many motors or other elements to an outlet as you want—all of them will be controlled simultaneously by the corresponding lever. This means that you can control more than two motors using a single receiver, and the motors connected to the same outlet will work as one. For example, you can drive your vehicle with two motors together when one is too weak, or you can have the headlights in your vehicle turn on as it drives.

NOTE The actual number of elements that can run off a single power supply simultaneously is limited by their total power consumption. If it becomes too high, the power supply shuts down. This is most likely to happen with motors and least likely to happen with LEDs.

This limits us to controlling two functions independently per one individual receiver. We can, however, control more functions using many receivers and just a single remote. As Figure 13-6 shows, both receiver and remote come with a simple orange switch called a *channel selector*. It has four positions numbered from 1 to 4. With a channel selector, we can use a single remote with up to four receivers.

Imagine that we have four receivers, each set to a different channel: the first receiver set to channel 1, the second to channel 2, and so on. If you set the channel selector on the remote to 1, only the first receiver will react to the remote and the other three will not. Similarly, if you set the remote's selector to 2, only the second receiver will react to it; if you

set it to 3, only the third one will react; and if you set it to 4, only the fourth one will react. This way you can control up to eight functions independently with a single remote, but since the remote can only be set to one channel at a time, you can control only two functions at the same time. Controlling another two functions requires switching the remote's channel selector to a different position. Figure 13-7 shows the 1 remote / 4 receivers / 8 motors arrangement.

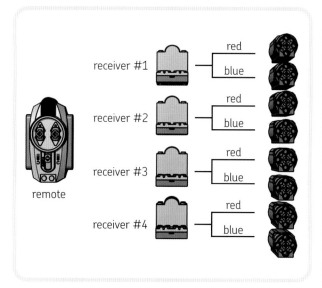

Figure 13-7: Each receiver is set to a different channel and has one motor connected to each of its outlets. In this way, eight motors can be controlled independently.

Controlling just two functions simultaneously is clearly a limitation—but one that can be overcome with additional remotes. You can use many remotes at the same time, even four, each tuned to a different channel. Many builders prefer to use several remotes at once rather than a single remote that needs switching between channels. It's even possible to use many remotes set on the same channel with a single receiver, for example, to let several people control the same construction.

Note that when many remotes are sending commands at various channels at the same time, receivers react more slowly. This is because each receiver reads commands from all four channels all the time, and its channel selector tells it only which to ignore and which to accept. When there are many commands to read simultaneously, the receiver is slowed down.

Now that we know how the Power Functions system works, let's take a look at its individual elements.

power supplies

The power supplies of the Power Functions system come in several variants, allowing us to choose between two types of batteries or even freeing us from the need for regular batteries at all. Every power supply can have many elements connected to it, but if too many elements are running off a single supply simultaneously, the electronic counter-measures in it will shut it down. This is most likely to happen with power-costly elements, such as motors. When it does, simply turn the supply off and on again.

AA battery box

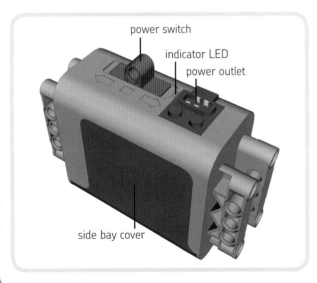

power switch

indicator LED

power outlet

side bay cover

This simple box contains six AA batteries, with two side bays for three batteries each. The box is 11×4×7 studs, with an orange power switch protruding by 1 stud on top of it. The switch has three positions—forward, stop, and backward—and the indicator LED adjacent to the switch shines green on the first and last position. The box is completely studless and connects by pin holes on its sides.

AAA battery box

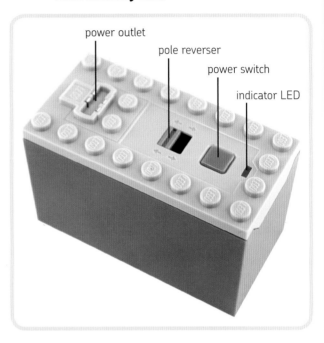

power outlet

pole reverser

power switch

indicator LED

The box contains six AAA batteries, which are inserted by unscrewing the box's bottom. The box is 8×4×5 studs, with a studfull bottom and top. Its power switch has the form of a simple green button. Pushing the button toggles the box between *on* and *off*. The box also has an indicator LED that shines green when the box is on and a simple orange pole reverser that determines whether turning the box on makes motors connected to it run forward or backward. The AAA batteries are smaller and lighter than AA ones; they can't power as many elements simultaneously, and they last roughly a third as long.

NOTE This box comes with a timer: Once turned on, it will turn itself off after 2 hours. You can stop the timer by holding the power switch down for 3 seconds. Turning the box off and on again resets the timer. This feature, intended to prevent the batteries from running dry if we forget to turn the box off, can be mistaken for a malfunction or battery failure.

rechargeable battery

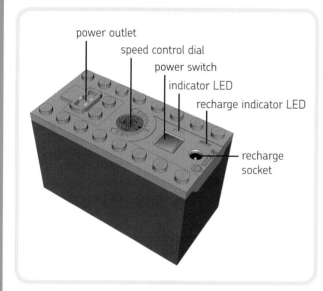

- power outlet
- speed control dial
- power switch
- indicator LED
- recharge indicator LED
- recharge socket

This self-contained battery with rechargeable power cells can be recharged using a transformer, without the need for replaceable batteries of any type. It's 8×4×5 studs, with a studfull bottom and top. Unlike regular battery boxes, it does not open. Its power switch has the form of a simple green button, and pushing it toggles the battery between *on* and *off*. Next to the power switch, there is an indicator LED that shines green when the battery is on and an orange speed dial with 15 positions: 7 forward, 7 backward, and 1 stop position. Turning the dial controls the speed of all motors and the brightness of all lights connected to the battery. It does not affect receivers connected to it. On the other side of the power switch, there is a recharge socket for the transformer, and an adjacent indicator LED blinks red during recharging and shines red when recharging is complete.

The battery houses two lithium ion polymer cells with a total capacity of 1100 mAh, providing a constant voltage of 7.4 V. The LEGO Group recommends recharging it with a dedicated transformer, sold separately, and defines the full recharge time as 4 hours.

While costly, the battery can be attractive to builders who use plenty of standard batteries. It allows them to build lighter and simpler because it weighs under 80 g (the AA battery box can weigh over 200 g, depending on the batteries' make). This battery can also be integrated into your construction permanently, with only a 2×2-stud opening to access its power switch and recharge socket. It provides lower voltage than standard batteries do (9 V) but higher voltage than rechargeable AA batteries do (7.2 V). Its capacity is smaller than that of most AA batteries, meaning

that it runs dry more quickly, but it makes up for this by never needing a battery replacement. When empty, it can be recharged inside your construction by simply connecting the transformer to it, while the battery boxes usually need to be taken out of your construction to replace batteries.

NOTE This battery also comes with a timer: Once turned on, it will turn itself off after 2 hours. Unlike the timer in the AAA battery box, this timer can't be stopped. Turning the battery off and on again resets the timer.

receiver

The Power Functions receiver, shown in Figure 13-8, is 4×4×5 studs and requires at least a half stud of space at the back for plugs connected to it. It has a studfull bottom and top and two pin holes in front. It also has a four-position channel selector in front and an indicator LED adjacent to it, which shines green when the receiver is under power and blinks when the receiver accepts commands from its selected channel.

In 2012, a version with upgraded electronic components was released. This version is distinguished by the *V2* printed on the front (see Figure 13-9) and is otherwise identical externally. It delivers more power to the motors, meaning that it can fully power two PF L motors through a single outlet. You can connect two L motors to a single outlet of the older version, too—they just won't run at full power.

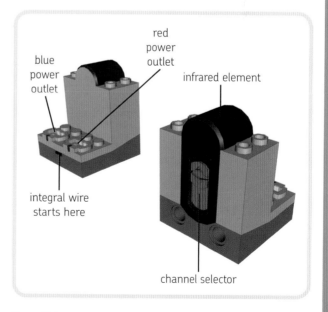

- blue power outlet
- red power outlet
- infrared element
- integral wire starts here
- channel selector

Figure 13-8: A front and back view of the Power Functions receiver

Figure 13-9: The V2 Power Functions receiver. Note the shining indicator LED.

remotes

As shown in Figure 13-10, there are two types of Power Functions remotes: a basic remote and a less common speed control remote. They work in a slightly different ways:

basic remote   The *go* command makes motors run until the *go* command is no longer received.

speed control remote   The *go* command makes motors run until the *stop* command is received.

The key difference is that when the basic remote stops sending the *go* command, the motors stop. This means that we must maintain an infrared link between remote and receiver as long as we want the motors to go. Note that while moving the remote's lever to the stop position stops motors immediately, breaking the infrared link means losing control over motors. With the link broken, they carry on the last received command for 2 seconds and then stop—unless we manage to reestablish the link during these 2 seconds.

With a speed control remote, we just have to send the *go* command to start motors and the *stop* command to stop them. There is no need to maintain a constant infrared link between sending these two commands.

Another difference is in how the remotes send commands. The basic remote keeps sending a command continuously for as long as you keep its lever in forward or reverse position. The speed control remote sends a command just once for every turn of a dial and once for pressing the stop button.

NOTE   It's not recommended to use both types of remotes with the same receiver simultaneously. They will interfere with each other, causing all motors connected to the receiver to stop or to behave erratically.

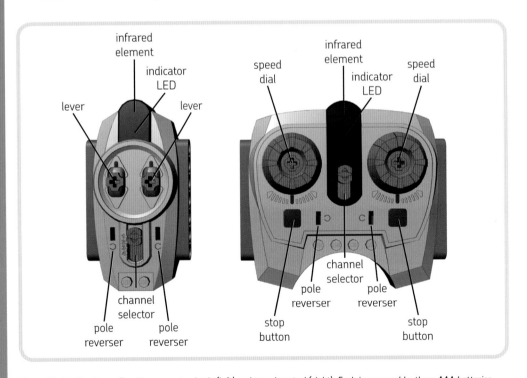

Figure 13-10: The Power Functions remotes: basic (left) and speed control (right). Each is powered by three AAA batteries.

This limitation becomes complicated when we want to drive and steer a model with a speed control remote, which is well suited for controlling drive but ill suited for controlling steering (unless you're using the Power Functions Servo motor, as explained in "Understanding the Speed Control Feature"). The best solution, then, is to control steering with the basic remote on another channel by connecting the steering and driving motors to two separate receivers set to two different channels. The steering can be controlled by one receiver set to channel 1, and the drive can be controlled by a second receiver set to channel 2. There will be no interference as long as the remotes are set on proper channels.

basic remote

The basic remote comes with two levers: red and blue, each with forward, stop, and reverse positions. The levers return to the stop position when released. The basic remote also has two pole reversers, one for each lever. The remote is 10×6×4 studs and has a channel selector and an indicator LED that shines green for as long as a command is being sent. The remote is powered by three AAA batteries inserted by unscrewing a cover on its bottom. Both its sides have seven pin holes each, allowing you to connect several remotes side to side with pins.

speed control remote

The speed control remote comes with two dials: red and blue. The dials have no definite positions and stay in place when released. This remote, too, has two pole reversers (one for each dial), two red stop buttons (one for each dial), a channel selector, and an indicator LED that blinks green when a command is sent. The remote is 10×12×4 studs and powered by three AAA batteries inserted by unscrewing a cover on its bottom. Both its sides have seven pin holes each, allowing you to connect several remotes side to side with pins.

Note that this remote works in a special way with the Power Functions Servo motor: Instead of controlling the motor's speed, the speed control remote controls the angle of its output. So rotating the dial 30 degrees right makes the Servo motor's output rotate 30 degrees right, too—or left, depending on how you set the remote's pole reverser.

understanding the speed control feature

There are 15 possible speeds in the Power Functions system: 7 forward, 7 reverse, and 1 "zero" speed, which stops the motors. Speed control is carried out by changing the voltage, meaning that speed control can affect not only a motor's speed but also the brightness of the lights.

The basic Power Functions remote uses only three speeds: top speed forward, zero speed, and top speed reverse. The speed control Power Functions remote, on the other hand, comes with dials that can be rotated in one direction or another. Rotating a dial in one direction sends a *speed +1* command; rotating it in another sends a *speed -1* command, but the rotation has to stop for a moment for the remote to finish sending the command. This means that the dials' rotation is intermittent, not continuous.

You can rotate a dial through all speeds, from +7 to –7, but note that dials don't stop even when maximum speed is reached. Since dials have no definite positions and can rotate infinitely, sending one command after another, it's impossible to change speed very quickly or to tell the current speed from the dials' position. This is why the speed control remote comes with separate stop buttons, one for each dial. While it's possible to rotate a dial to stop a vehicle, it takes some time and precision; you have to watch the vehicle itself to know when you're changing the speed to zero, for example, and not to -1. The stop buttons are the quick and sure way to go—you'll see why when your model is heading fast toward the edge of a cliff!

Note that the rechargeable Power Functions battery has a dial that does have definite speed positions. This control affects all motors and lights connected to the battery directly or through a switch but not through a receiver, as the receiver ignores the battery's dial.

modifying the remotes

Many possible modifications can make the remotes better suited for our needs. Let's look at three of them.

a basic remote with steering wheel

This simple, robust modification is suitable for driving and steering.

1

2

3

4

a basic remote with sideways lever

This more complex and less robust modification uses links.

1

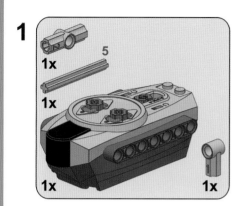

1x
5 1x
1x 1x

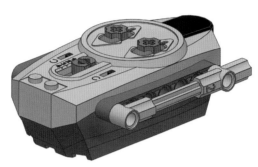

2

2x

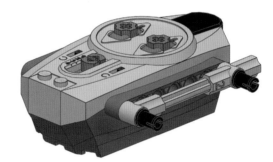

3

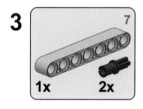

7
1x 2x

4

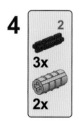

2
3x
2x

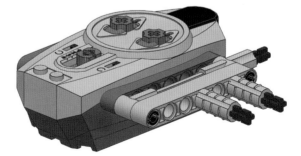

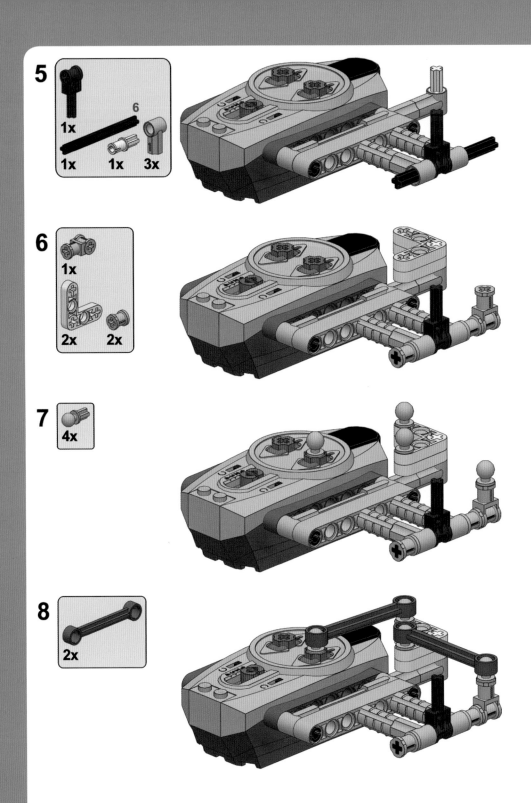

a speed control remote with central steering wheel

This modification is designed to control tracked vehicles, with each speed dial controlling a single track. Two speed dials are connected by a central steering wheel, which can be rotated as well as tilted forward and backward. With properly switched pole reversers, the steering wheel tilt controls drive, and the steering wheel rotation controls steering. To make the vehicle drive forward and then turn

right, for instance, you would tilt the steering wheel forward and then rotate it right.

Note that this modification is subject to the disadvantages of the speed control remote—that is, it is limited to sending no more than two commands per second. It works best when operated carefully and not too fast.

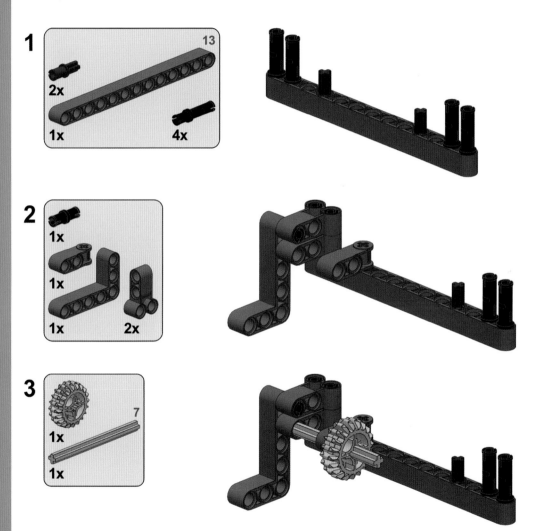

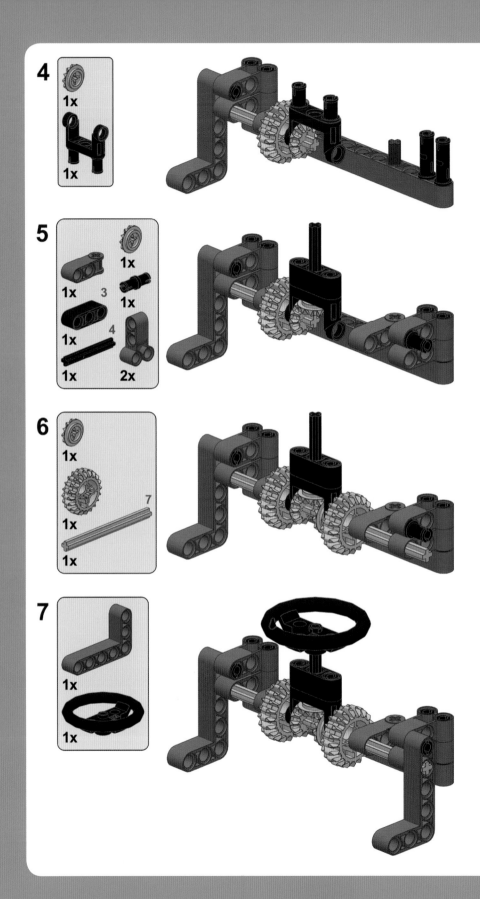

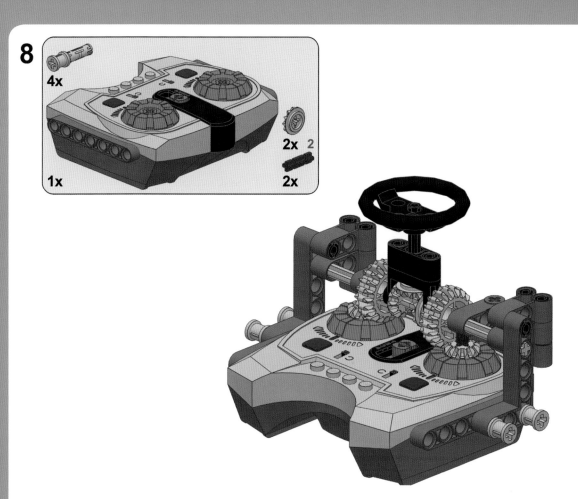

linear actuators

Linear actuators, designed as supplementary parts of the Power Functions system, are an interesting alternative to the LEGO pneumatics. They come in two variants, large and small, and both work thanks to inner screws. Each actuator has an input whose rotation makes the actuator extend or retract, depending on direction. When an actuator is extended or retracted to maximum, its inner clutch engages, allowing the input to continue rotating without damaging the actuator.

The actuators can thus be motorized without external clutches, and their inner gear ratio makes them work well with Power Functions motors without the need for external gearing. Their performance differs from that of LEGO pneumatics, so they can replace LEGO pneumatics in some applications and complement them in others. Let's have a look at linear actuators and then compare them to pneumatics.

large linear actuator

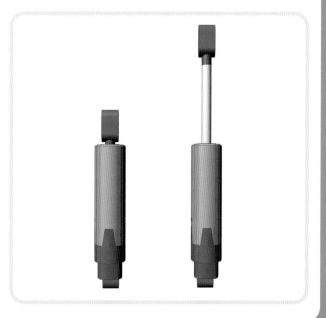

A large linear actuator is 11 studs long when fully retracted and 16 studs long when fully extended. It has a diameter of 2 studs, and it comes with two types of brackets (shown in Figure 13-11) that increase the diameter to 3 studs. One bracket provides an articulated mounting for the actuator, and the other provides a fixed one. It takes one or two 2L axles to firmly attach a bracket to the actuator. Examples of driving an actuator are shown in Figures 13-12 and 13-13.

Figure 13-13: The bracket with fixed mounting can connect a motor and actuator as a single unit that can pivot around one of the mounting axles (light grey).

Figure 13-11: A large linear actuator plus bracket with articulated (left) and fixed (right) mounting

In 2010, LEGO announced that the actuators released earlier had a design flaw that could result in high friction occurring inside them when under load and lead to slow and coarse operation. The new design was introduced in September 2010. Actuators produced after this date are externally identical to the older ones, so the easiest way to distinguish them is by checking the production code on each actuator, shown in Figures 13-14 and 13-15.

Figure 13-14: The location of the production code on the actuator is shown by the red arrow. Look for three digits and the letter X minted on the flat dark grey surface.

Figure 13-12: Three examples of transferring drive to the small linear actuator. Note that all three have a 1:1 gear ratio.

The production code consists of three digits and the letter X—for example, 36X0. The first two digits mark the week of the actuator's year of production, and the last digit is the ending digit of the year of production. So the

Figure 13-15: A close-up view of a linear actuator. The production code is 40X0, which means the 40th week of 2010, or four weeks after the improved design was introduced.

36X0 production code means the 36th week of 2010; this is exactly when the new design was introduced. Actuators produced before this date—for example, 29X0—are of earlier design; actuators produced after this date—for example, 40X0—are of improved design. Keep in mind that even if you have "flawed" actuators, it doesn't necessarily mean that failure will occur.

The large linear actuators can handle impressive loads. Their disadvantage, however, is their inner clutch, which creates significant noise and vibrations when engaged.

small linear actuator

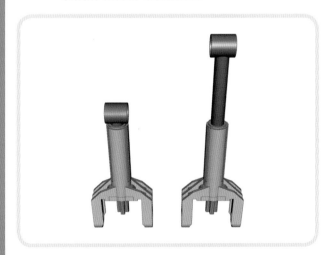

A small linear actuator is 7 studs long when fully retracted and 10 studs long when fully extended. It has a diameter of a single stud and a fixed bracket that is 3 studs wide.

Instead of an axle hole, it has input in the form of a 1L axle. Figure 13-16 shows simple ways of driving a small linear actuator.

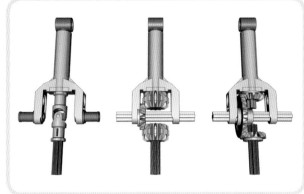

Figure 13-16: Three examples of transferring drive to the small linear actuator. Note that all three have a 1:1 gear ratio.

The load capacity of the small linear actuator is much smaller than that of its larger variant but still impressively useful given its size. Unlike the large actuator, the small one comes with a plastic internal shaft, which is less robust than the large actuator's metal one. The clutch in the small linear actuator works very smoothly and engages almost seamlessly. The small actuator can be very space efficient when combined with the Medium motor.

linear actuators vs. pneumatics

Linear actuators can do most of the tasks that pneumatic cylinders can, but they were not designed to replace them. The two systems differ in many areas, and the best results can be achieved by combining them so that they complement each other's advantages. Here's what linear actuators look like when compared to pneumatics.

Advantages:

* Have a higher load capacity
* Can be motorized directly, without the need for compressors or valves
* Maintain better accuracy in all positions, as they don't depend on air pressure
* Maintain their position under any load; their inner screws lock them once stopped so they can't be moved by the weight of the load
* Don't have pneumatic hoses, just driveshafts

Disadvantages:

* Can be difficult to transfer drive to, as driveshafts are less versatile than pneumatic hoses; this disadvantage grows with more complex systems and with the number of actuators
* Move with constant speed, lacking the smoothness of movements that can be achieved with pressure-dependent pneumatics
* Are generally larger in size
* Large actuators can cause problems when their inner clutches engage, as they produce lots of vibrations
* Are much more difficult to pair
* Resemble real-life hydraulic systems significantly less than pneumatics do

extension wires

We already know that the vast majority of the Power Functions electric components come with integral wires that are permanently attached to them on one end and have a plug on the other. These wires are obviously limited in length, which is why two kinds of extension wires were introduced: a 20 cm wire and a 50 cm wire (see Figure 13-17).

Beyond the obvious goal of adding extra length to any PF electrical connection, the extension wires have one very important feature: Each comes with one *adapter plug*. An adapter plug is a special variant of the Power Functions plug that can have regular PF plugs attached on top of it and old 9V system plugs attached to the bottom of it (see Figures 13-18 and 13-19). This way, each extension wire allows you to connect elements of the Power Functions and old 9V systems together.

A variety of 9V elements can be controlled with the Power Functions system, including all motors (the speed control feature works with them as well) and all types of lights. It is also possible to integrate PF elements into the 9V system to a limited degree. For example, the PF motors can be controlled with 9V battery boxes and switches, but PF receivers work only with PF power supplies.

Figure 13-17: Power Functions extension wires: 50 cm long (top) and 20 cm long (bottom)

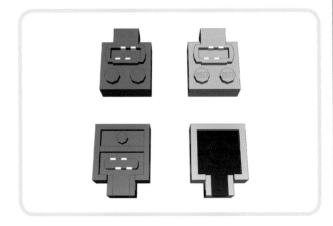

Figure 13-18: Top and bottom view of a regular Power Functions plug (left) and the adapter plug (right). Each extension wire comes with one plug of each type.

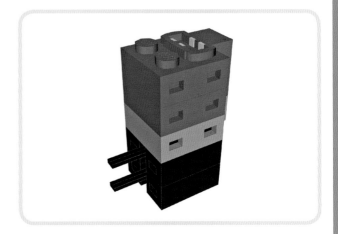

Figure 13-19: The Power Functions adapter plug (light grey) can have an unlimited number of Power Functions plugs (dark grey) attached on top of it and an unlimited number of 9V plugs (black) attached to its bottom.

POWER FUNCTIONS ELEMENTS AS LEGO SETS

The following Power Functions elements have been released as separate LEGO sets:

* 8869: switch
* 8870: LED lights
* 8871: extension wire, long
* 8878: rechargeable battery
* 8879: speed control remote
* 8881: AA battery box
* 8882: XL motor
* 8883: Medium motor
* 8884: receiver
* 8885: basic remote
* 8886: extension wire, short
* 8887: rechargeable battery transformer
* 88000: AAA battery box

miscellaneous elements

There are just a few more elements of the Power Functions system, and most of them are highly specialized—for example, train sets—so we will omit them here. That leaves just two elements so universal that they deserve to be described.

switch

As mentioned earlier, the switch is the simplest control element. It is 5×2 studs and has a 1-brick-tall base, and it comes with an integral wire, one power outlet, one pole reverser, and an orange lever. The lever is identical to the one on the basic remote, with three positions—forward, stop, and backward—except that it doesn't return to the central position. It also has an axle hole through which any axle can be put—this comes in handy, for example, when we want to motorize the switch.

LED lights

The PF system's lights, shown in Figures 13-20 to 13-22, are a pair of LEDs with a piece of wire and a regular Power Functions plug. At half of its length, the wire enters a black 2×2×1 brick that separates in two, so the two LEDs can be placed relatively far from each other. Note that the black brick is not a plug of any kind: It's fully closed, just like a standard LEGO brick. The LEDs are enclosed in transparent housings that are less than 2 studs tall and less than 1 stud

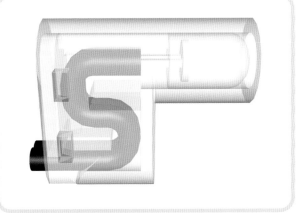

Figure 13-20: The Power Functions LEDs with a hamster provided for scale

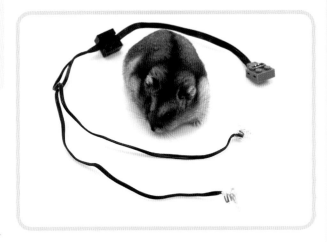

Figure 13-21: Side view of the LEGO LED. You can see part of the wire tucked in to prevent it from being ripped off. The actual LED is located in a protruding tube that fits into a pin hole and is slightly less than a single stud long.

Figure 13-22: The most common examples of installing LEDs in other LEGO pieces. The LEDs fit perfectly into a pin hole. Since their protruding part is less than a stud long, there is still enough room to put in, for example, semitransparent round plates from the other side, creating lights in various colors.

wide and that have protruding tubes with LEDs inside that fit perfectly into a pin hole.

The LEDs provide bright white light, directed only forward. Their power consumption is minimal, and their brightness can be controlled with the Power Functions speed control feature. Note that the type of LEDs used by LEGO has changed over time: The glow of older batches is slightly yellowish, while the glow of newer batches is bluish.

PART IV

advanced mechanics

14

wheeled steering systems

The steering of wheeled vehicles is a complex subject in automobile design. While some real-life issues are of lesser importance in LEGO models because of their limited size and weight, it still pays to understand the principles at play.

In this chapter, we're going to learn how to build typical LEGO steering systems as well as how to implement optional features, such as return-to-center steering. We'll also explore issues of steering geometry and multi-axle steering.

Note that this chapter omits vehicles with fewer than four wheels. Steering bikes or trikes is elementary, so we are moving straight to where the real challenges begin.

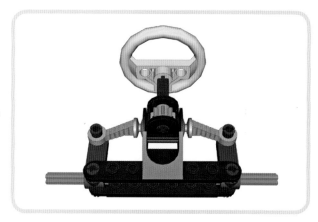

Figure 14-1: A typical LEGO steering mechanism

basic LEGO steering systems

The steering systems in LEGO constructions can be built with a number of specialized pieces, but it's also perfectly possible to rely only on common pieces. Let's start our exploration of steering by examining a typical steering mechanism, shown in Figure 14-1.

Note that we will be using colors consistently throughout this chapter: The black pieces are parts of the chassis, and the yellow one is obviously a steering wheel. That leaves four other important parts:

a steering shaft (red)　This is an axle that connects a steering wheel or a motor to the pinion of the rack-and-pinion gearset.

a rack-and-pinion gearset (grey)　This gearset consists of a pinion (here, an 8-tooth gear) and a rack, which is a toothed plate, below it (see Figure 14-4); when the pinion rotates left or right, it makes the rack slide.

steering arms (blue)　These arms rotate around the connection to the chassis, and their rotation is controlled by the rack.

spindles (green)　These are the axles in the steering arms on which the wheels are mounted.

Figure 14-2 shows our mechanism in action. Rotating the steering arms makes the entire vehicle turn. And obviously, to turn, the vehicle needs at least one more axle, as Figure 14-3 shows.

In Figure 14-2, the rack gear is a specialized piece (#2791) that is slightly elastic, allowing it to bend to stay mated with the round pinion gear as the steering wheel turns. The pinion gear can be used with other gears, but we'd have to compensate for the rotation of the steering arms. Figure 14-4 illustrates the problem.

When the steering arms are turned, the pins that connect them to the rack actually trace part of a circle. This causes the rack to move in two dimensions: not only left and right but also forward and backward. Only the lateral movement is desired, as the forward-and-backward displacement

Figure 14-3: A LEGO vehicle with two axles: one fixed and one steered

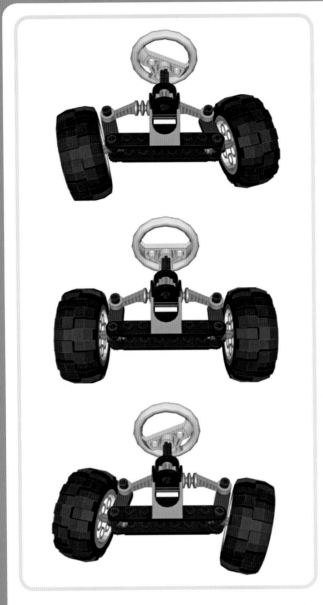

Figure 14-2: Our simple steering mechanism in extreme left, straight, and extreme right positions

Figure 14-4: The rotation of the steering arms (blue) makes the rack (light grey) move not only side to side but also forward and backward.

can disengage the rack from the pinion. Figure 14-5 shows the simplest solution to the problem: adding an extra pinion.

Another solution is to place the pinion in the middle of the rack's path of forward-and-backward motion, as shown in Figures 14-6 and 14-7.

These figures also introduce a new, simple element of the steering system. When we use nonspecialized pieces to build a steering system, we'll use two pieces: a *rack gear* (shown in light grey under the pinion), which is a 1×4-stud plate with teeth on top of it, and a *tie rod* (shown in light blue). A tie rod connects the ends of the steering arms to the rack gear.

As you can see, the tie rod travels forward and backward, requiring a margin of free space—the 2-stud-wide gap around it. But we may not want to waste space for such a gap; another solution is to make the rod more complex, as shown in Figure 14-8.

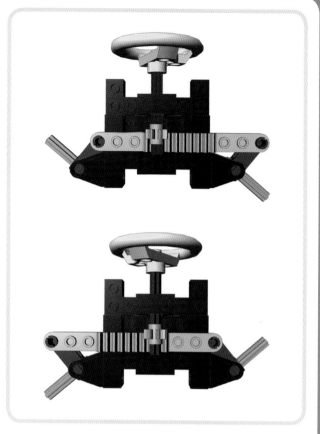

Figure 14-5: The simplest solution to the problem of an "escaping" rack is using two pinions so that when the rack moves away from one, it will be meshed with the other.

Figure 14-7: A steering mechanism in extreme right and extreme left positions. Note that the tie rod moves forward inside the 2-stud-wide gap around the pinion.

Figure 14-6: A steering mechanism in straight position. Note that the light blue tie rod is located in the center of the 2-stud-wide gap around the pinion.

Figure 14-8: A steering mechanism with a three-piece tie rod. The short, articulated sections on the sides pivot to accommodate the rotation of the steering arms.

Here the tie rod consists of three sections: a long central one (with the rack) and two short ones on its sides, connected by pins. These short sections pivot to accommodate the rotation of the steering arms and reduce the central section's forward-and-backward travel to zero, as Figure 14-9 shows.

The three-piece tie rod is a reliable and popular solution, but its side sections must be shorter than the central one. The whole assembly is rather wide and thus not suited for narrow vehicles. We can solve this by building a very simple steering system in which the rack gear is replaced by a lever, as Figure 14-10 shows.

You now know three solutions to the problem of a tie rod's travel, and you have seen examples of simple steering systems built with a handful of common pieces. Now that your steering system is working, you may want to add features to it.

Figure 14-10: A steering mechanism without a rack. Instead, it uses two knob wheels and a short lever (grey) to transfer movement from the steering shaft to the tie rod.

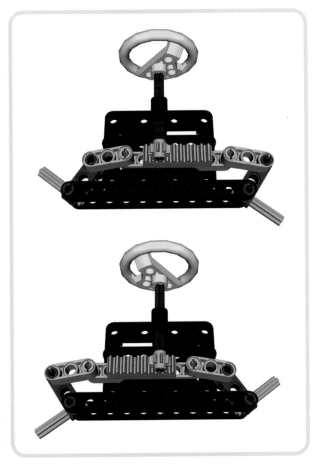

Figure 14-9: A steering mechanism with a three-piece tie rod in extreme left and right positions. Note that the longitudinal travel of the central section is zero.

return-to-center steering

Return-to-center steering is just what the name implies: a mechanism that returns the steering system to the center (straight) position when the system is released. Such a mechanism is best placed between the steering system and a motor controlling it, and such a "self-centering" design complements the use of remote controls. It allows you to build a steering system that steers to extreme left or extreme right when you push levers on your remote and that returns to center when you release it.

The easiest way to build a self-centering steering system with LEGO pieces is to use a rare specialized piece, #x928cx1, often called a *hockey spring*. It comes with a spring inside and can be attached to a PF Medium motor (as shown in Figure 14-11). In such a configuration, it will backdrive the motor to the central position every time the motor stops.

If you cannot find this specialized piece, you can use a rubber band for a simple centering mechanism. Shown in Figure 14-12, the mechanism consists of the band (white), which squeezes two beams (yellow) together to the sides of a connector sitting on the steering shaft (red). As the motor starts to rotate the shaft, the connector pushes the beams apart. If the rubber band is strained enough, it will stop the connector quickly, and when the motor stops, it will squeeze the beams back together, returning the connector and the shaft to the central position. Note that you have to find a rubber band providing just the right tension for this mechanism to operate smoothly.

As with any mechanism, return-to-center steering has its pros and cons. It works fast and simplifies the control of a model, but it doesn't allow accurate maneuvering because it only has three possible positions. This makes it better suited for fast models where a steering system has to react quickly, rather than for slower ones that benefit from a steering system that allows for greater accuracy. It's also risky to use return-to-center steering with a large steering lock because rapid wide turns can make a vehicle unstable. (Steering lock is the maximum angle that wheels on a steered axle can be turned, as described in Chapter 1.) In my experience, any model that isn't built specifically for speeding will be better off with a regular steering system that allows you to adjust the driving direction accurately. In most cases, the PF Medium motor geared down to a 9:1 gear ratio provides optimum speed/accuracy balance for a regular steering system.

Ackermann steering geometry

When a wheeled vehicle makes a turn, its inner and outer wheels follow circles of different radii because the width of the vehicle separates them. If the inner wheels follow a circle of radius r_1, then the outer wheels follow a circle of radius r_2 (equal to r_1 plus the width of the vehicle), as Figure 14-13 shows.

A regular steered axle turns both left and right wheels at exactly the same angle, which means that none of the wheels follows exactly its proper radius. This creates additional friction and tire wear. Ackermann steering geometry corrects that by turning wheels at different angles. More

Figure 14-11: The hockey spring (yellow) and a schematic for attaching it to a PF Medium motor

Figure 14-12: The rubber band–based return-to-center steering attachment for a PF Medium motor

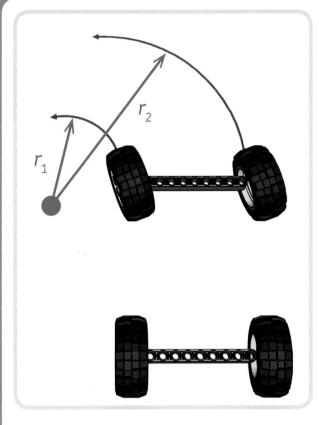

specifically, it turns them so that they are perpendicular to the center of the vehicle's turning radius, as shown in Figure 14-14.

This geometry, which makes the wheels follow correct radii, is achieved by modifying the steering arms so that they point at the middle of the rear axle, as Figure 14-15 shows.

When it comes to LEGO vehicles, this additional friction and the tire wear are negligible, except for very heavy and large models. The improved handling that comes with Ackermann geometry is advantageous but only noticeable with large vehicles with significant steering lock. Ackermann geometry is important enough to be used in many high-end RC cars, and two official LEGO Technic supercars use it: the 8865 and 8880 sets (shown in Figure 14-16). Both use independent steered suspension, which is also driven in the 8880 set.

Both the 8865 and 8880 sets use special steering arms with shifted pivot points, shown in Figure 14-17. Both are rare pieces by now, but we can build our own custom steering arm using other pieces, as shown in the building instructions on page 198.

There is one more way to achieve Ackermann geometry: We can use a three-piece tie rod with a longer central section and with the two side sections set at an angle, as shown in Figure 14-18. Such a tie rod has little travel, and it should be placed in front of the front axle. Note that with this solution, the steering arms don't point at the middle of the rear axle, so it's difficult to see whether the proper geometry is

Figure 14-13: The inner and outer wheels of a steered vehicle follow circles of different radii: r_2 is equal to r_1 plus the width of the vehicle.

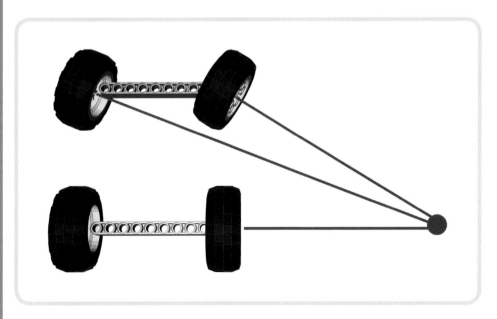

Figure 14-14: Ackermann steering geometry keeps the wheels on the steered axle perpendicular to the center of the turning radius when making a turn.

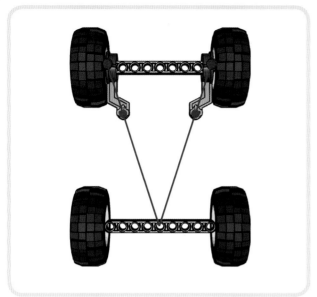

Figure 14-15: A proper Ackermann geometry: The front axle's steering arms point at the center of the rear axle.

Figure 14-17: Steering arms from the 8865 (left) and 8880 (right) sets, mounted in suspension arms (blue). Both have shifted pivot points to allow Ackermann geometry; the 8880 arm also allows the wheels to be driven.

Figure 14-18: Ackermann steering geometry achieved by using a three-piece tie rod with a longer central section

Figure 14-16: The LEGO 8865 and 8880 sets are designed with Ackermann geometry in mind.

achieved. This solution puts very high forces in the tie rods. Note that the central gear rack needs to be guided to keep it perpendicular to the chassis.

Ackermann steering geometry was included in the official LEGO sets as an additional technical highlight rather than for its actual advantages. Given the weights and sizes of most LEGO models, the benefits of such a sophisticated solution are negligible. Still, many builders consider including it in a model a great display of skill.

a simple steering arm
with Ackermann geometry

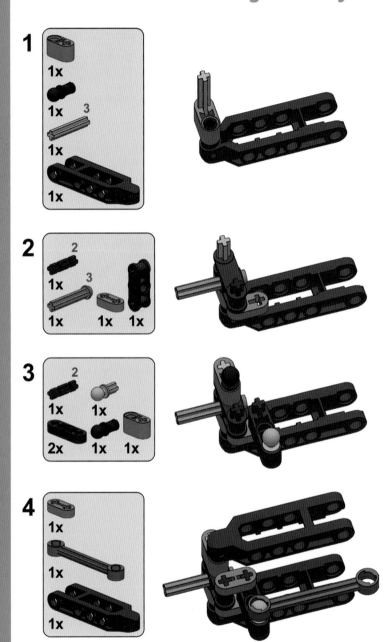

convergence of axles

While discussing Ackermann steering geometry, we learned that every vehicle has its *center of turning radius*. When the wheels are turned, the center is where lines perpendicular to each wheel meet (ignore the outer steered wheels if you use a regular steering geometry), as shown in Figures 14-19 and 14-20. The center can be closer or farther from the vehicle, depending on how much the wheels are turned.

Now, consider a line that points at the center and at the same time is perpendicular to the chassis of the vehicle. In Figure 14-21, that line goes exactly through the rear, fixed axle. No matter how much the steered wheels are turned, this line will always cross the chassis in the same place. We call it *the convergence line*.

When the axles of a vehicle are convergent, the vehicle turns easily and with little friction. The exact placement of the convergence line depends on the nonsteered axles. For example, when there is one such axle, the convergence line agrees with it; when there are two such axles, the convergence line is exactly between them (as shown in Figure 14-22). When there are three such axles at equal intervals, the convergence line agrees with the middle one, and so on.

When we have more than one steered axle, the convergence line helps to determine the proper spacing between them and the difference in their steering locks. For example, if we have steered axles in the front and rear of the vehicle, they should be symmetrical to the convergence line, which

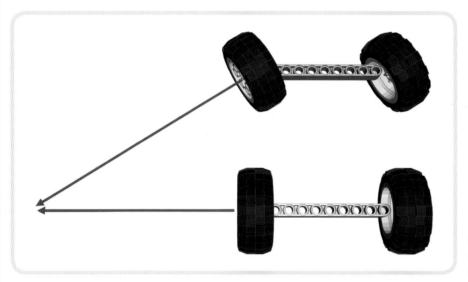

Figure 14-19: The center of turning for a vehicle with regular steering geometry: The outer steered wheel is ignored.

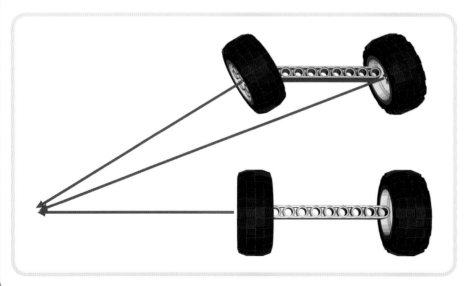

Figure 14-20: The center of turning for a vehicle with Ackermann steering geometry: All wheels "point" at it.

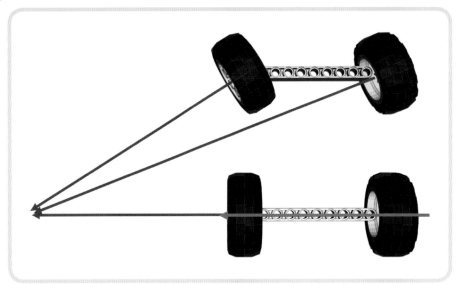

Figure 14-21: Blue marks the convergence line—the line that is perpendicular to the chassis while pointing at the center of turning.

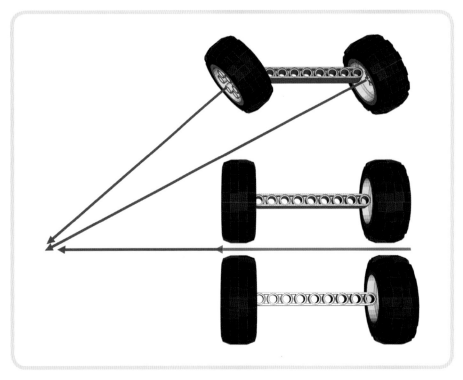

Figure 14-22: For a chassis with a single steered axle and two rear nonsteered ones, the convergence line lies exactly between the rear axles. In this example, since the rear wheels do not point at the rotation center, they will scrub in a turn. This is a big problem for vehicles and trailers with many nonsteered axles. It's also a big problem for airplanes, which turn very tightly.

means that the front axle should steer in the opposite direction of the rear axle, as shown in Figure 14-23.

The most complex case is when we have two or more steered axles next to one another; to maintain convergence, they need different steering locks. It is possible to calculate this difference, but it involves using trigonometry to calculate an inverse tangent.

Figure 14-24 shows a chassis with two steered axles and one nonsteered axle. We know that in this case the convergence line agrees with the only nonsteered axle. We need to calculate the relationship between the angles of both steered axles, and to do this, we need to know these angles. This can be done by comparing distances between the steered axles and the convergence line for a given angle

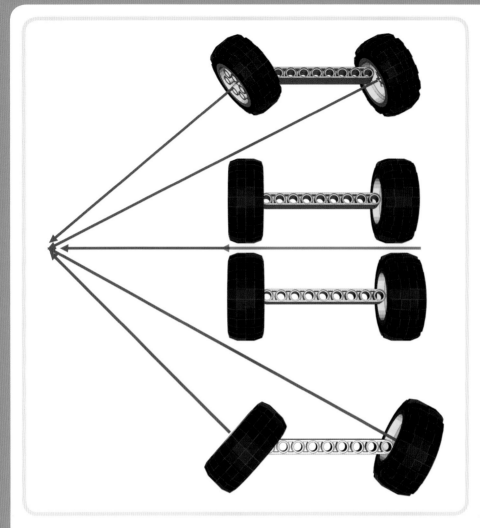

Figure 14-23: If there are steered axles in the front and rear, they should be symmetrical to the convergence line.

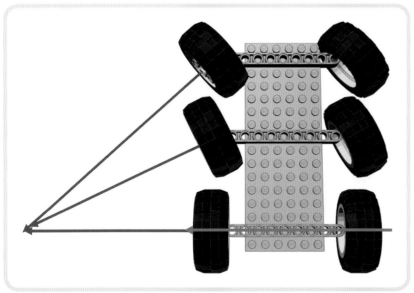

Figure 14-24: The steering locks of the two front axles of this chassis should differ to maintain convergence.

of the front wheels. In this example, let's assume the angle is 45 degrees. As we can see, the front axle is 13 studs away and the middle one is 7 studs away from the convergence line. We need to calculate the relationship between the shorter and longer distances:

$$\frac{7 \text{ studs}}{13 \text{ studs}} = 0.54$$

Next, we need to find the inverse tangent (arctangent) for this relationship.

$$\tan^{-1}(0.54) \approx 28 \text{ degrees}$$

We have just calculated the angle at which the middle axle should be steered, and we know that the angle of the front axle is 45 degrees. Now we need to compare these angles to know the difference between angles and translate it into gearing in the steering system.

$$\frac{28 \text{ degrees}}{45 \text{ degrees}} = 0.622$$

We can round the result to 0.6. This means that the middle axle should steer at 0.6, or about 60 percent of the front axle's angle. Therefore, the steering on the middle axle should be geared down to 0.6 as compared to the front axle. We can do this in two ways:

* Use a single steering shaft for both axles but with pinions of different sizes on each rack (see Figure 14-25).
* Use the same pinions on both axles but with two steering shafts with gearing between them (see Figure 14-26).

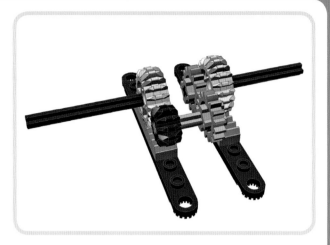

Figure 14-26: Second method for two axles with different steering locks: two identical pinions but two separate steering shafts with gearing between them

Whichever way we choose, it all comes down to the gear sizes. If we use a 20-tooth gear on the front axle, here's how we calculate the middle one:

$$20 \text{ teeth} \times 0.6 = 12 \text{ teeth}$$

As you see from the calculation, we need a 12-tooth gear. When assembling the model, we also need to make sure that the two steered axles are aligned.

Finally, a simple (and math-free!) alternative is to make a simple mock-up of the chassis showing just the distances between axles. You place the mock-up on a sheet of paper, turn the wheels so that they point at the center of the turning radius, and physically draw the lines and measure the angles. If you find any of these methods troublesome, you can always ignore convergence completely. It won't stop your models from driving or turning—they just won't handle as well as they would with convergent axles.

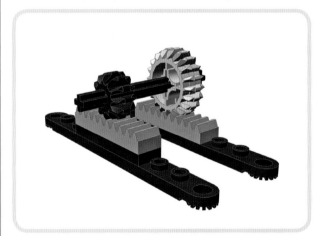

Figure 14-25: First method for two axles with different steering locks: a single steering shaft with two pinions of different size

15

wheeled suspension systems

The previous chapter introduced us to the principles of steering in wheeled vehicles. Now, we'll take a look at two topics that are inextricably linked to steering axles: suspending axles and driving them. These interrelated mechanisms are frequently "separate," yet because they affect the same final element, the wheels, they can be built only in a limited number of combinations. For example, a suspension of a given type will work only with certain steering and drive systems.

Any axle of a wheeled vehicle can be suspended, driven, and steered at the same time. An axle can, of course, do none of these things and merely hold wheels together, but since such an axle is very simple to build, this chapter will focus on axles that are at least driven. We're going to discuss axles in four groups of increasing complexity:

* Driven axles (those that receive power)
* Driven and suspended axles
* Steered and suspended axles
* Driven, steered, and suspended axles

After going through the first group, we'll focus on the concept of suspending wheels; we'll learn how suspension systems work, how they are categorized, and how to choose the suspension that best suits our needs.

driven axles

A driven axle is a mechanism that connects two wheels while transferring drive to them from the chassis. The power is usually received from a driveshaft that is longitudinal to the chassis and perpendicular to the axle. Connecting these two elements is necessary, and a pair of bevel gears is the simplest solution. But in practice, bevel gears are prone to skipping under high torque, and a driven axle is where we can expect high torque. This leaves us with two other options: a differential or a pair of knobs. A differential is less likely to

skip, especially if braced inside a proper structure (shown in Figure 15-1), and knobs are extremely unlikely to skip at all thanks to their design (shown in Figure 15-2).

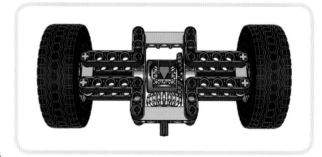

Figure 15-1: This is what a simple driven axle, also known as a live axle, can look like. The driveshaft (red) drives the 20-tooth double-bevel gear meshed with a differential case. The 5×7 studless frame braces the differential and prevents it from skipping. Note that there are two separate 7-stud-long axles connecting the differential to the wheels—axles used in this way are called halfshafts.

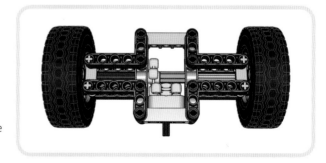

Figure 15-2: The same simple driven axle with a pair of knob wheels instead of a differential. The knob wheels are very unlikely to skip even if braced in a weak structure. Note that the two wheels' axles are now connected with an axle joiner (green), so they work like a single axle. For more information about using differentials, their pros and cons, and even ways of creating a custom differential, see Chapter 8.

suspension systems: concept and categories

A suspension is a system of linkages that connects the chassis of the vehicle to the wheels. Its primary purpose is to keep all wheels in constant contact with the ground, thus ensuring stability and proper traction of the vehicle. The suspension can also isolate the chassis from bumps and vibrations generated by the ground—but this is actually its secondary function, and it's not even present in all types of suspensions.

In order to maintain stability, a vehicle needs to be supported at no fewer than three points. For example, a bicycle is supported at just two points—where its wheels touch the ground—and it will fall over unless you support it at another point or drive it fast, in which case the stability comes from the gyroscopic effect of a wheel's rotation. So a vehicle needs at least three points of support, and we'll call these points *fulcrums* in our suspensions. Sometimes they are simply called *points*—hence the name *3-point suspension* for a suspension that provides three fulcrums for a vehicle and *4-point suspension* for one that provides four.

It's important to understand that with a suspension system, the number of wheels and the number of fulcrums differ. An unsuspended axle provides two fulcrums (one at each wheel), while a suspended axle provides just one, at the point of its attachment to the vehicle. For instance, a vehicle with four wheels can have one suspended and one unsuspended axle to get three fulcrums (Figure 15-3). A six-wheeled vehicle will also have three fulcrums if all three axles are suspended (Figure 15-5).

Consider a few simple examples in Figures 15-3 to 15-7 of chassis with various numbers of wheels and three (or more) fulcrums (fulcrums are marked with red arrows, chassis are black, and oscillating suspension parts are blue).

The way the wheels move in relation to each other is the first way to categorize a suspension:

* A suspension is *independent* when one wheel on a given axle can move without affecting the other one.
* A suspension is *dependent* when it's impossible to move one wheel on a given axle without affecting the other one.

In dependent suspensions, when one wheel of the axle goes up, the other one goes down, and vice versa. All the simple examples here are *dependent* (Figures 15-3 to 15-7).

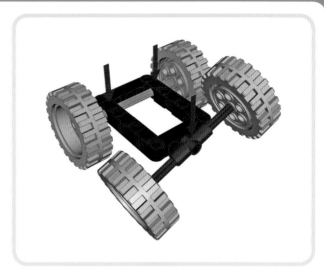

Figure 15-3: A simple chassis with four wheels, including two on a suspended axle

Figure 15-4: It's possible to build chassis with just two fulcrums, like this one with two suspended axles, but the chassis will need elastic elements supporting it against the axles to prevent it from falling to the side.

Also note that suspension types can vary between different axles. One vehicle can have, for example, an independent front suspension (on the front axle) and a dependent rear suspension (on the rear axle). Such a combination is actually quite popular because it allows you to build vehicles that are only as complex as necessary. In many cases, there is simply no need to use advanced suspension systems on all axles.

Figure 15-5: A chassis with six wheels, all suspended

Figure 15-6: A chassis with eight wheels and four fulcrums, meaning it has a 4-point suspension. Long, multiwheeled vehicles often have more than three fulcrums.

Secondly, we can categorize suspensions by how they transfer shock from the road surface:

* A suspension is *sprung* when the chassis is supported by elastic elements attached to the given axle so the shocks from the axle are partially absorbed.

Figure 15-7: Even with many wheels, the number of fulcrums can be reduced by using more complex suspension systems that oscillate around more than one axle. This allows the wheels to adapt to the shape of obstacles in more planes.

* A suspension is *unsprung* when the chassis is supported by the given axle directly so the shocks from the axle are fully transferred to the chassis.

The easiest way to tell a sprung suspension from an unsprung one is by trying to press the vehicle's body down on its wheels. A sprung suspension will make the body yield, while an unsprung suspension will not. This is because a vehicle with unsprung suspension maintains *constant ground clearance*, which means that the middle of the chassis always stays the same distance from the ground. That makes unsprung suspension commonly used in heavy machinery, as it does not yield under heavy loads.

types of suspensions

Of the many real-world suspension systems, we will learn to build four with LEGO pieces:

* Basic independent suspension
* Tatra-type suspension (a special kind of independent suspension developed and patented by the Tatra company)

* Pendular suspension (a very simple, dependent suspension based on a single axle's rotation)
* Floating axle (an axle with no rigid connections to the chassis whatsoever)

We will now discuss these suspension types using simple models of each. After that, we'll look at actual suspension designs.

double-wishbone independent suspension

Type: Independent, sprung

The chassis is black, the suspension arms are yellow, the steering arms (not steered in this case) are blue, and the spindles are green. As you see, each steering arm is suspended on four parallel levers that allow it to move up or down relative to the chassis while keeping the wheel in a vertical position. Consider the examples in Figures 15-8 and 15-9.

One element is missing from these images—the suspension arms need to be actually suspended. In other words, the chassis needs some elastic elements to support it against the suspension arms, or else the entire suspension will collapse. Shock absorbers are well suited and popular in this role (see Figure 15-10). Figure 15-11 provides an example of a model that uses independent suspension.

* **Advantages:** Best suspension type in terms of stability and traction; the orientation of the wheels is maintained at all times
* **Disadvantages:** Large width; relatively fragile construction

Note that it's possible to use the same elastic elements for the suspension arms for both wheels, but this will make the suspension dependent—causing one wheel to go up while the other one goes down (see Figure 15-12).

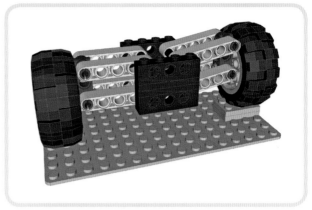

Figure 15-8: Independent suspension with one wheel on an obstacle. Note that the position of the other wheel is unaffected, as it should be with an independent suspension.

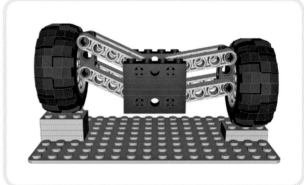

Figure 15-9: Independent suspension with both wheels on obstacles. Both wheels negotiate obstacles independently; hence the name of the suspension type.

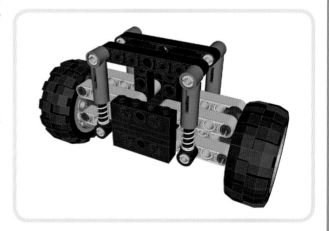

Figure 15-10: Independent suspension with four shock absorbers supporting the chassis against the suspension arms

Figure 15-11: My Monster Truck model was a good example of independent suspension. Note that the vertical orientation of both front wheels was identical despite the extreme difference in their heights.

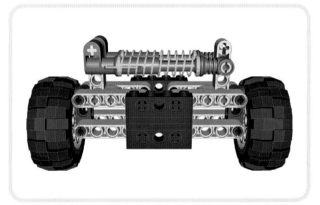

Figure 15-12: A suspension with shock absorbers supporting the suspension arms against each other (left and right). This solution will keep the chassis stable, but the suspension will become dependent.

Tatra-type suspension

Type: Independent, sprung

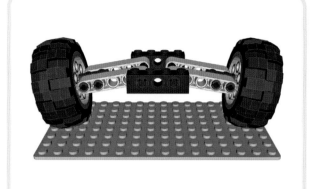

The Tatra-type suspension, also known as a swing-arm suspension, was developed and patented by the Tatra company, which uses it almost exclusively. The Tatra-type suspension is a simpler variant of the independent suspension that uses only two levers per wheel as suspension and keeps the spindles perpendicular to the suspension arms at all times. This means that the orientation of the wheels changes as they negotiate obstacles. By default, the wheels are tilted, as shown in Figure 15-13, a unique feature for this suspension type.

Figure 15-13: The default position of the Tatra-type suspension offers extra ground clearance. This "bowed" look can be mistaken for damage or warping.

Other than the tilting of the wheels, the Tatra suspension, shown in action in Figure 15-14, shares all the qualities and properties of a regular independent suspension. It is valued for the robustness coming from its simplicity, and it performs very well on rough terrain (Tatra off-road trucks are nothing short of legendary); its only downsides are inferior sideways stability and poor tire wear. Such a suspension is viable only for heavy off-road vehicles.

* **Advantages:** Simpler, more robust than a typical independent suspension
* **Disadvantages:** Slightly inferior traction because of the wheels' changing orientation; inferior sideways stability

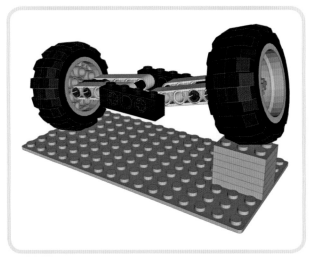

Figure 15-14: The Tatra-type suspension negotiating an obstacle with one wheel. Note that the orientation of the wheels changes in the process, which is why this suspension requires tires with a round profile (balloon tires) to maintain good traction.

pendular suspension

Type: Dependent, unsprung

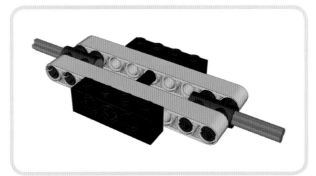

A pendular suspension is the simplest and the most robust kind of suspension: It allows the axle to swing back and forth on a single point just like a pendulum. As it's only one solid element, it can be very narrow and built with just a few pieces. Figure 15-15 shows a pendular suspension in action.

Figure 15-15: A pendular suspension negotiating an obstacle with one wheel. Note that the chassis, which is connected to the axle by the axle going through its center, is raised by 50 percent. This is generally bad for stability and for the driver's comfort.

On the downside, pendular suspension systems take a lot of space in the chassis, requiring the model to have a large gap in order for the suspension to fit. The pendular suspension system can't be sprung, but it often requires shock absorbers (see Figure 15-16) or other elastic elements to keep it stable—unless you arrange the suspended axles of your vehicle so as to provide three or more fulcrums. The longitudinal axle that goes through it is also the only way to transfer the drive to the suspension from the chassis. So the longitudinal axle is used as the driveshaft, which means that this suspension is mounted on the driveshaft and presses on it, creating extra friction.

* **Advantages:** Simplest and most robust suspension type; can be very narrow
* **Disadvantages:** Unsprung; takes a lot of space in the chassis; adds extra friction on the drivetrain (see "Pendular Suspension with Turntables" on page 210 for a means of mitigating this effect)

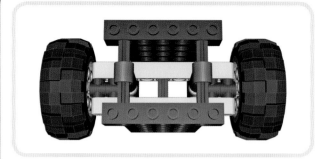

Figure 15-16: A pendular suspension stabilized with a pair of shock absorbers. Note that the shock absorbers work against each other and need to be half compressed when the suspension is level. When one wheel goes up, the absorber close to it is compressed more, and the other one is compressed less.

trailing arm suspension (floating axle suspension)

Type: Dependent, sprung

A floating axle suspension (or live axle) is a sprung variant of the pendular suspension. It's a single solid element that has no rigid connections to the chassis whatsoever; instead, it is connected to it by a number of links that form a linkage allowing it to move up and down and tilt to the sides. It can be just as narrow and robust as a regular pendular suspension, and it doesn't press on the driveshaft. However, it takes an extreme amount of space in the chassis because of the linkage that comes between it and the chassis.

Floating axles can be extremely complex. The variant we will focus on is a simple one (see Figure 15-17): It uses four links and two independent suspension arms above the actual axle that need to be supported by some elastic elements. It also uses a driveshaft with a single universal joint on it to keep the axle aligned with the chassis.

* **Advantages:** Combines all the advantages of pendular suspension with being sprung and usually more stable
* **Disadvantages:** Takes a lot of space in the chassis

Choosing the best type of suspension for the job is always a little tricky, but your decision can be made easier by considering what is used in real vehicles. For example, luxury cars usually have full independent suspension to improve passengers' comfort, while construction vehicles—such as front-end loaders, for instance—usually have pendular suspension because the heavy loads they are handling would affect a sprung suspension too much.

Figure 15-17: A floating axle negotiating an obstacle with one wheel. Note that the orientation of all four links is changed, while the chassis' orientation remains the same.

driven and suspended axles

Axles that are driven and suspended at the same time are relatively easy to build, and they're important as the vast majority of vehicles has at least one.

pendular suspension with turntables

As explained earlier, the pendular suspension has the disadvantage of being attached to the chassis by the driveshaft, which is subject to stress generated by the vehicle's weight. This single point of stress creates additional friction; however, this problem can be prevented almost completely by using a Technic turntable to attach the suspension to the chassis (see Figure 15-18), as an alternative to using ball joints. The turntable then supports the weight of the vehicle, while the driveshaft can go through the middle of the turntable nearly unburdened.

Note that the large diameter of the turntable is bad for ground clearance, so it's a good idea to use this design in concert with portal axles. Also note that the hole in the turntable is large enough to install a differential case in it, which can be used to transfer both drive and steering through a single turntable (see Figure 15-19).

Figure 15-19: As an empty differential case rotates freely on an axle, it can be used to transfer steering over the driveshaft. Here, red pieces are acting as a driveshaft and green pieces are acting as a steering shaft without interfering with each other. Note that the steering shaft is slightly affected when the suspension tilts and the turntable rotates. Still, it's a useful solution when the driveshaft and steering shaft need to be connected to the suspension from the same side.

Figure 15-18: The newer type of Technic turntable is used to attach the suspension (the light grey frame) to the chassis (the black L-shaped beams). A turntable is a very rigid structure capable of supporting huge loads while adding minimum friction to the driveshaft (red) that goes through it.

a stabilized pendular suspension

This is a simple, robust, and compact suspension kept stable by four shock absorbers. Keep in mind that absorbers of various length and hardness can be used.

1

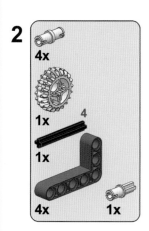

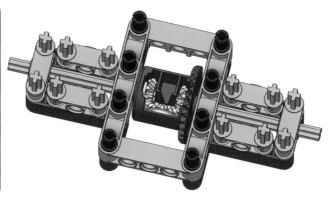

2

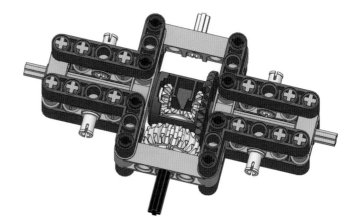

3

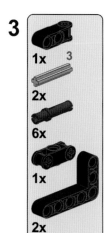

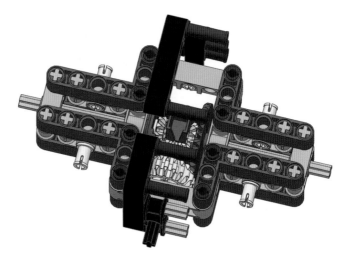

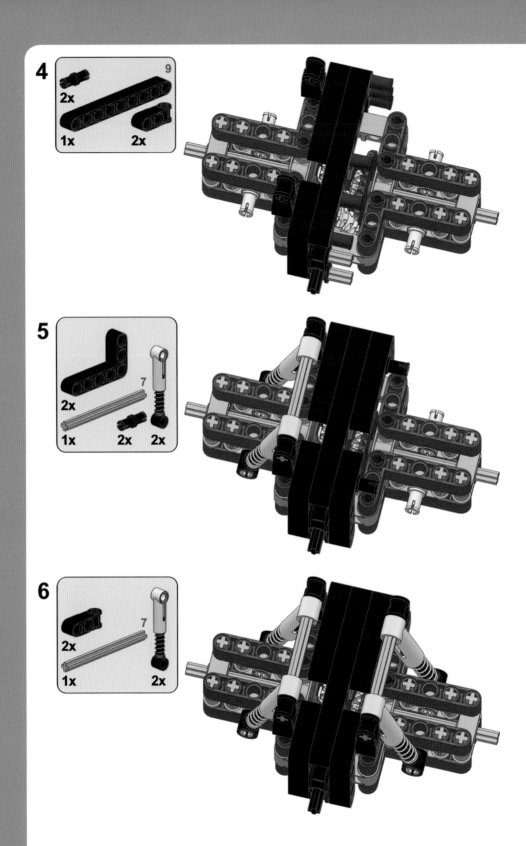

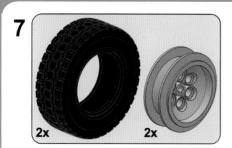

7

2x　2x

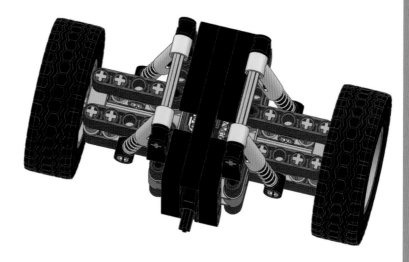

portal axles (geared hubs)

Portal axles are axles with gear hubs on the wheels that increase both ground clearance and the gear reduction of the drivetrain, as Figure 15-20 shows. Practically any axle, including a steered one, can have gear hubs and become a portal axle at the cost of increased width. The most popular are hubs with a 24-tooth and 8-tooth gear combination, providing a 3:1 gear reduction. The 3:1 gear reduction means not only that torque on the wheels is increased three times but also that other parts of the drivetrain handle only a

third of the overall load. This is very useful for steered axles because it allows us to use universal joints, which could otherwise be damaged by the load.

There are a number of ways to build narrow, strong gear hubs. The easiest one, however, involves a ready-made LEGO gear hub housing: a #92908 piece, into which a #92909 is inserted to support the wheel (see Figure 15-21). We will refer to this very convenient combination as a LEGO hub. Figure 15-22 shows a model that makes use of LEGO hubs.

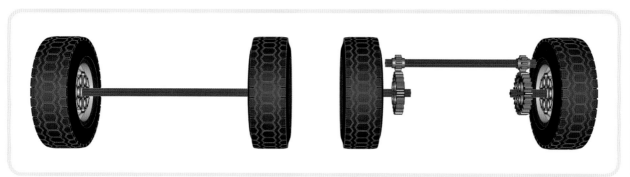

Figure 15-20: A regular axle (left) and portal axle (right)

Figure 15-21: Pieces #92909 (left) and #92908 (right) together form a so-called LEGO hub.

Figure 15-22: My model of the RG-35 4×4 MRAP vehicle made use of LEGO hubs to achieve an impressive ground clearance exceeding 6 studs.

a stabilized pendular suspension with a portal axle

This is a variant of the previous design with hubs added to make it a portal axle.

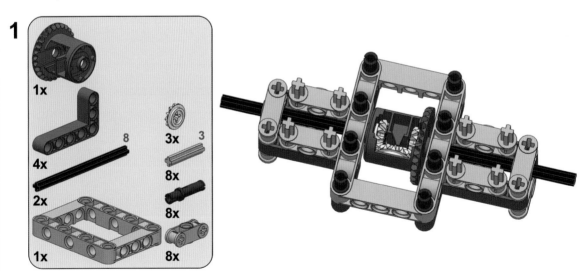

2

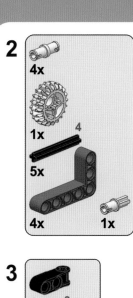

4x

1x   4

5x

4x   1x

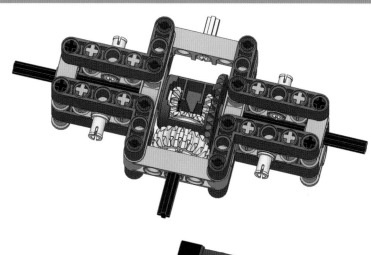

3

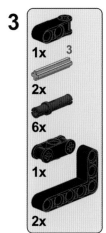

1x   3

2x

6x

1x

2x

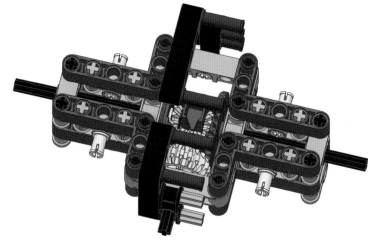

4

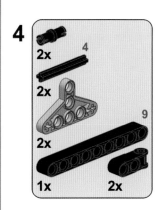

2x   4

2x

2x   9

1x   2x

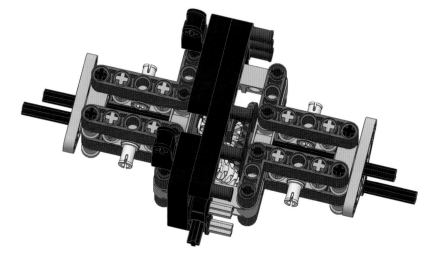

5

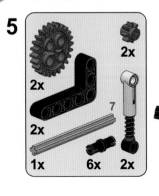

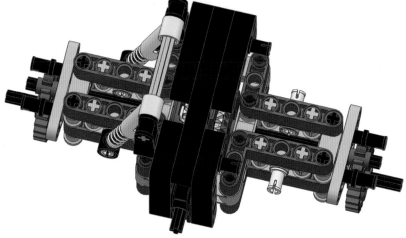

6

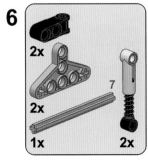

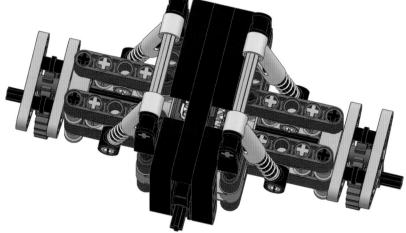

7

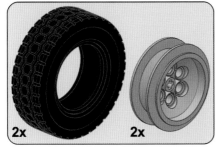

2x   2x

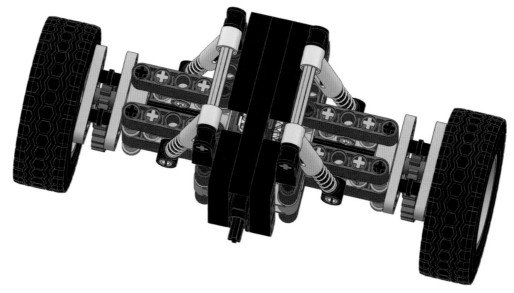

a Tatra-type suspension stabilized with four shock absorbers

This is a simple, robust suspension without a differential, well suited for rough terrain. Remember to set up the shock absorbers so that the wheels are tilted slightly downward when the suspension is unloaded.

NOTE It's possible to convert this design to use a portal axle, but it's not recommended with this suspension as doing so would decrease its sideways stability.

1

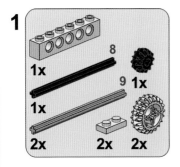

1x

1x

8

9   1x

2x   2x   2x

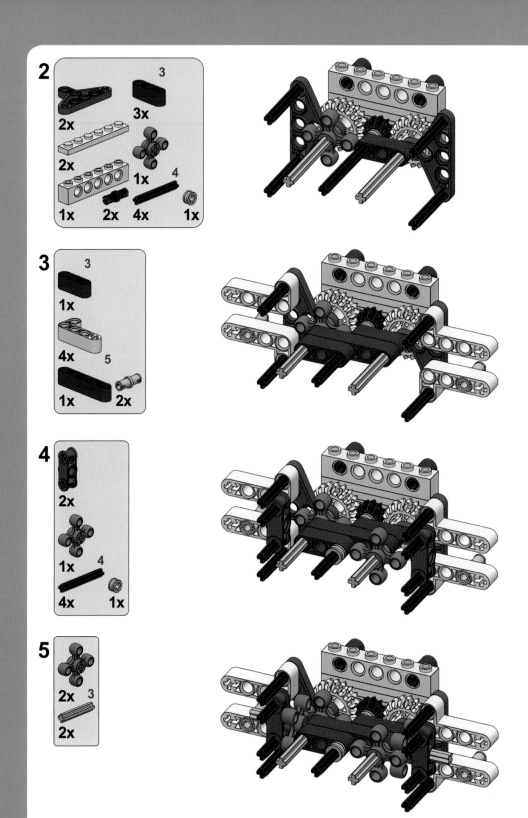

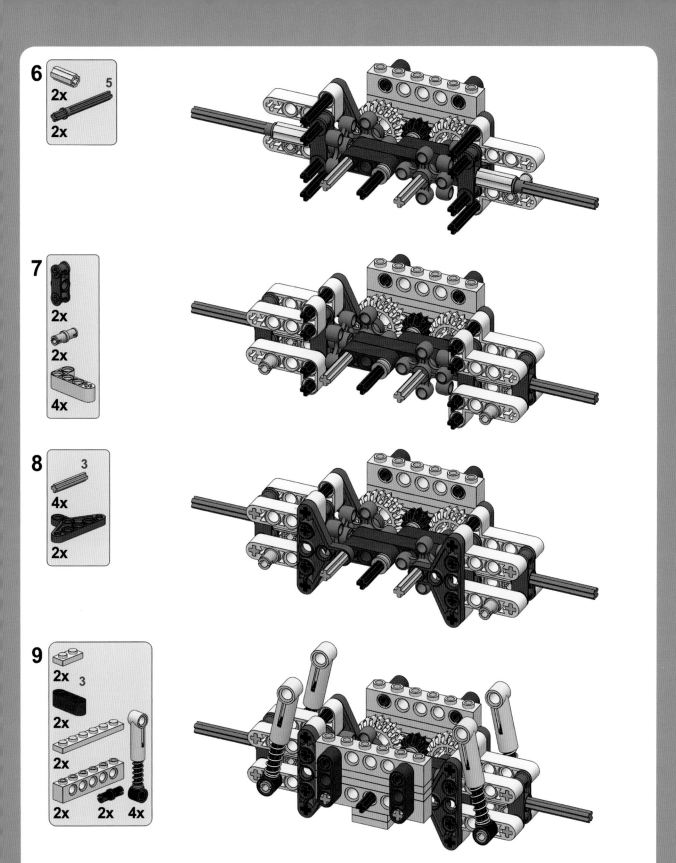

10

1x
2x
1x
2x

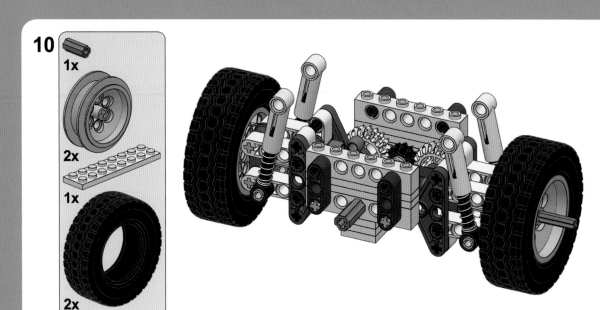

---

an independent suspension

This is a typical independent suspension. It's wide but provides good overall performance.

1

3x
4x
1x
1x 3
1x 3x

2

3
2x 8x
2x 2x

3

3

4x

2x   4x

4

3

4x

4x

5

12x

3   4x

4x   4x   2x

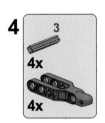

6

2x   2x   4x   4x

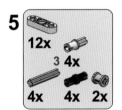

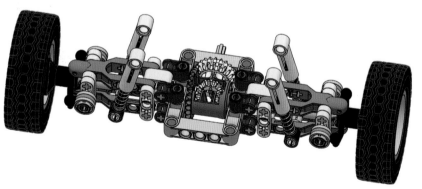

a floating axle with four links

This is a complex yet robust design with large travel. The instruction includes a partial body frame that can be easily extended to add another axle.

1

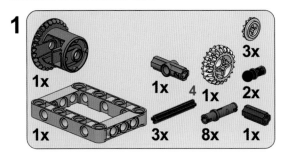

1x 1x 4 1x 3x
1x 3x 8x 1x

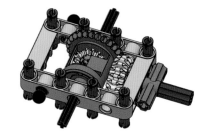

2

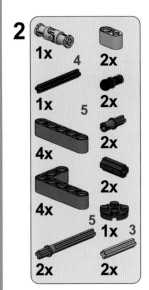

1x 4 2x
1x 5 2x
4x 2x
4x 2x
5 1x 3
2x 2x

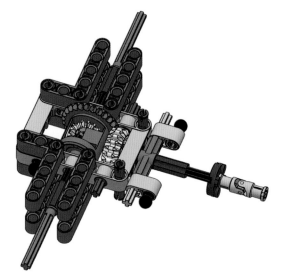

3

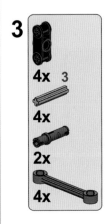

4x 3
4x
2x
4x

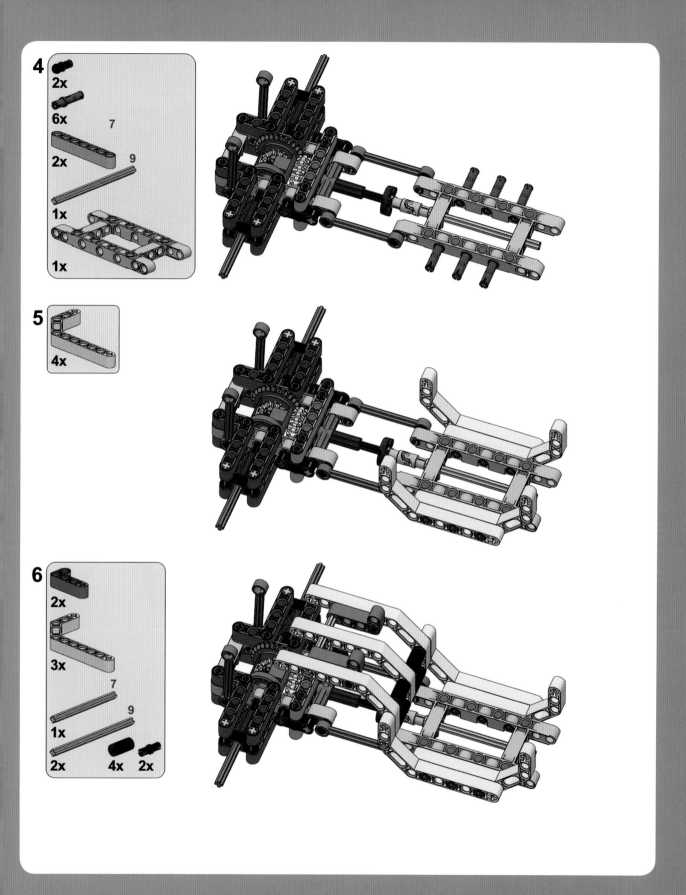

7

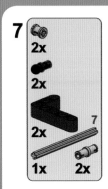

2x
2x
2x
1x 2x

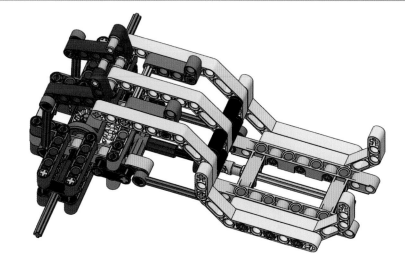

8

2x
5
1x
2x
2x 1x

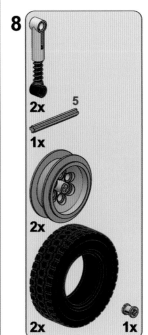

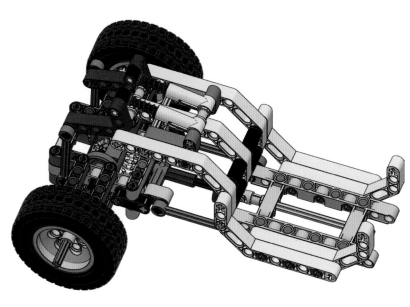

steered and suspended axles

a pendular steered axle

Here's a look at some building instructions for axles that are suspended but can also be steered. These are commonly used for the front axle of real-wheel-drive cars.

A simple design focused on small size. The red bricks simulate the chassis. Note that you can remove the shock absorbers if your vehicle's other axles make it stable enough.

1

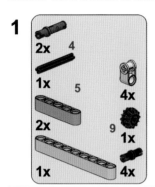
2x 4
1x 5
2x
1x 9
2x
1x
4x
4x

2

1x 3
2x
2x
2x 1x
4
2x 2
1x 2x

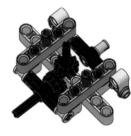

3

2x
2x
2x 3
2x

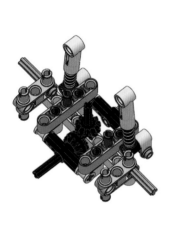

4

2x
1x
1x 9
1x 9
1x

5

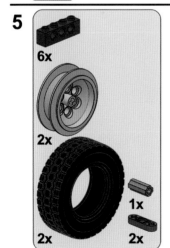
6x
2x
1x
2x 2x

an independent steered axle

This design uses a number of specialized pieces to create the narrowest independent suspension possible. It's well suited for small, light vehicles.

1

2

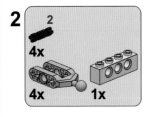

3

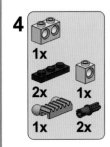

4

5

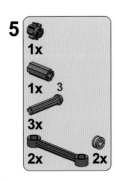

6

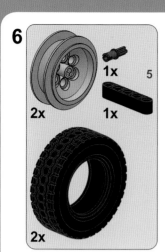

1x 5
2x 1x
2x

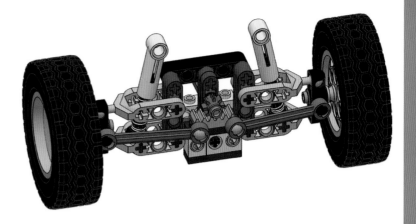

driven, steered, and suspended axles

Here are building instructions for the most complicated category of axles.

an independent axle

This axle is just slightly more complicated than the version without steering.

NOTE There is an older version of this suspension using different (older) pieces in the 8880 LEGO set.

1

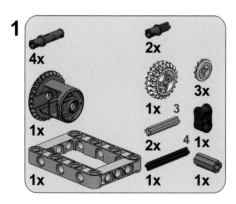

4x
1x
1x

2x
3x
1x 3
2x 4 1x
1x 1x

2

2x
2x 8x

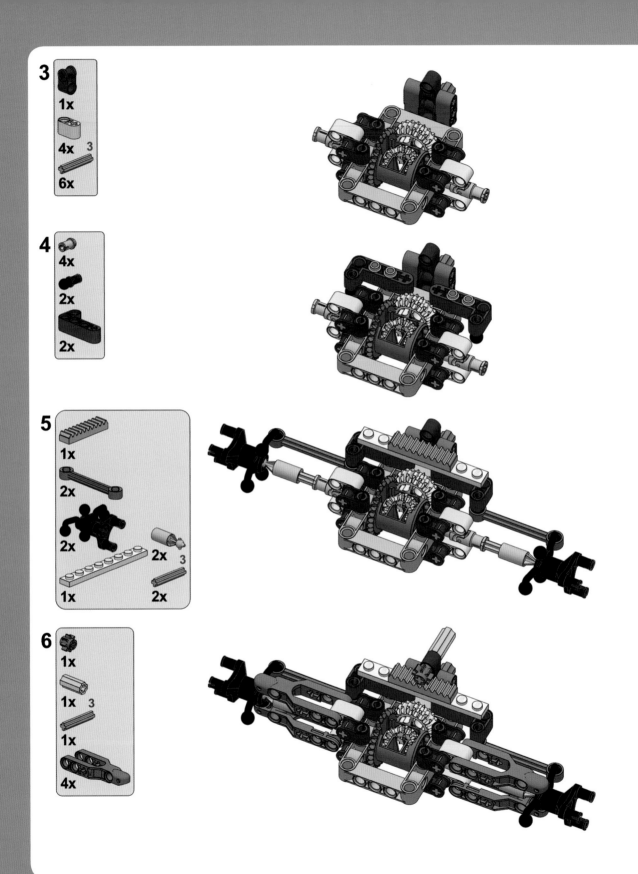

3
1x
4x 3
6x

4
4x
2x
2x

5
1x
2x
2x
2x 3
1x 2x

6
1x
1x 3
1x
4x

7

4x
3
4x
2x

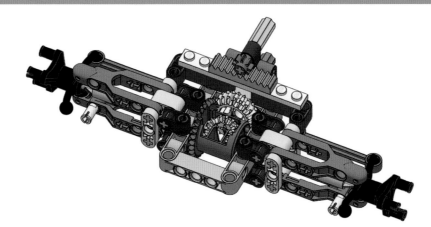

8

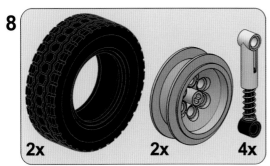

2x   2x   4x

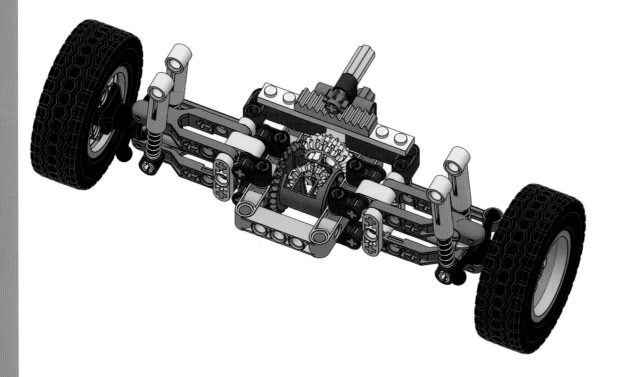

a heavy-duty pendular portal axle

This is a complex and extremely robust suspension designed for very rough terrain. It includes knob gears instead of a differential, and it consists mostly of basic studless pieces.

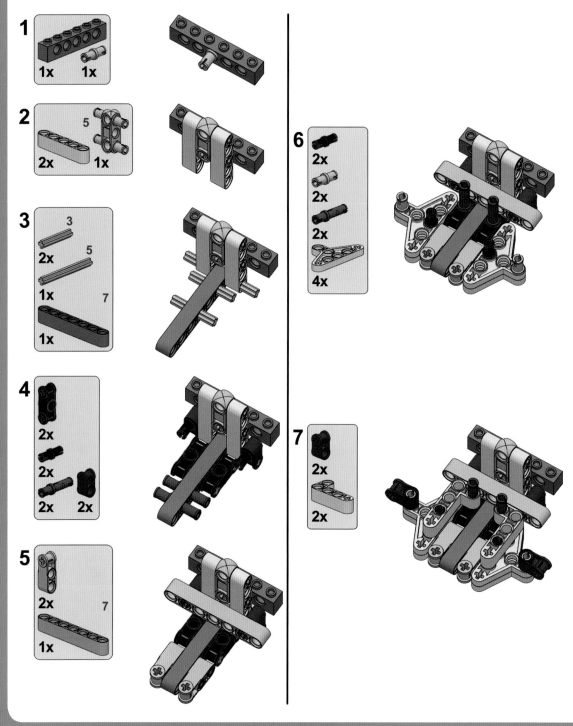

8

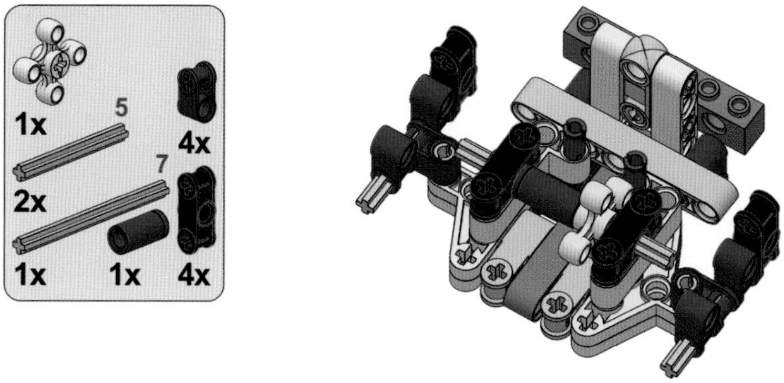

1x
5
2x
7
4x
1x 1x 4x

9

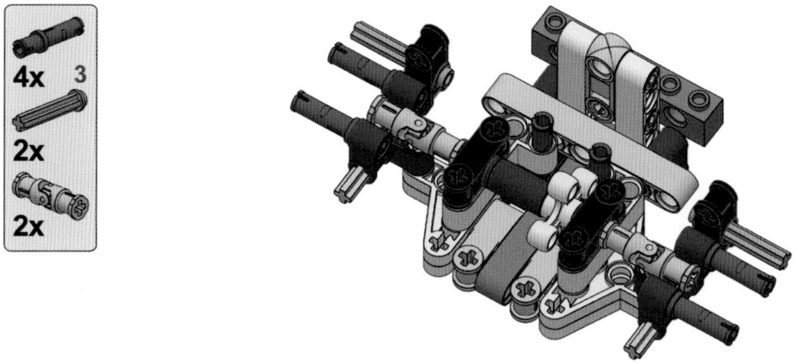

4x 3
2x
2x

10

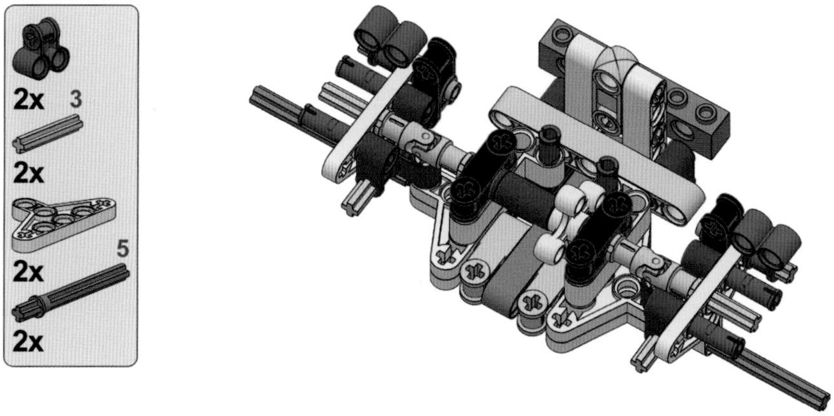

2x 3
2x
2x 5
2x

11

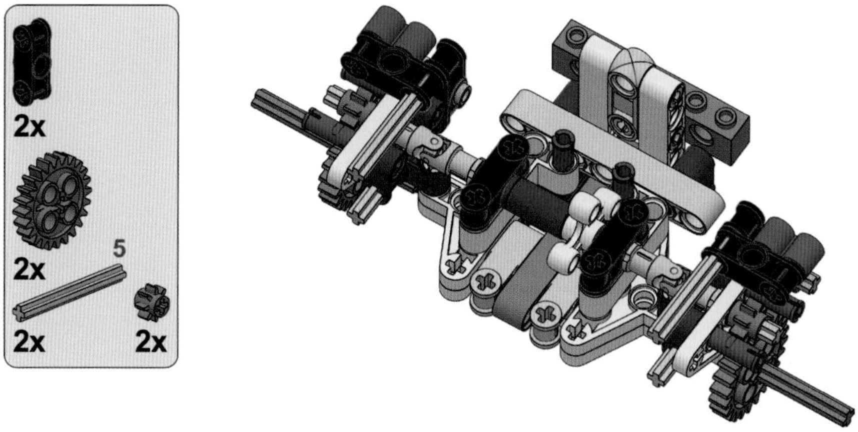

2x
2x 5
2x 2x

12

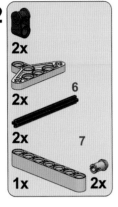

2x

2x 6

2x 7

1x 2x

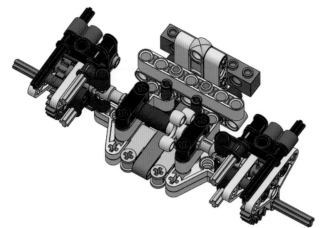

13

2x

4x 3

1x 5

1x

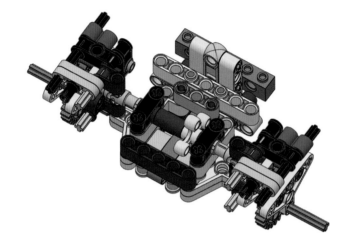

14

2x

1x

1x 6

1x 3x

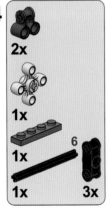

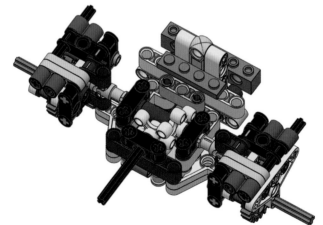

15

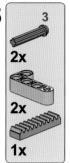

3
2x

2x

1x

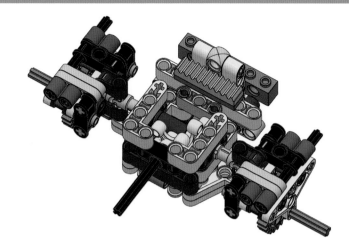

16

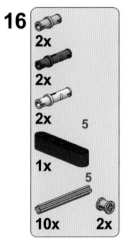

2x

2x

2x

5
1x

5
10x   2x

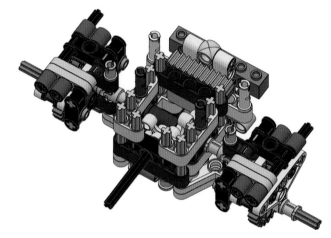

17

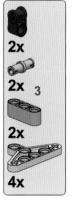

2x

3
2x

2x

4x

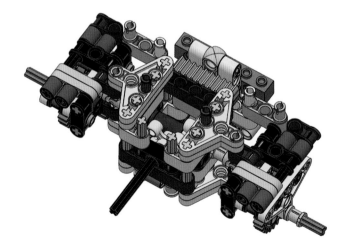

18

3x

4x

6x

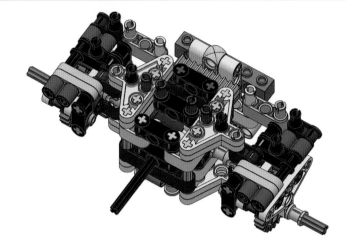

19

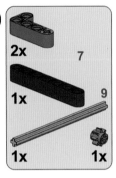

2x

7

1x

9

1x   1x

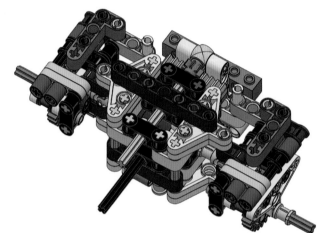

20

1x

2x

1x

4

1x

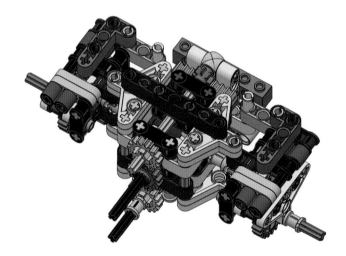

21

2x

2x

2x

22

3

2x

2x

2x   4x

23

2x   2x   1x

1x

a pendular axle with a worm gear

This is a compact suspension that uses the middle differential variant and a worm gear. This makes it well suited for use with motors that require substantial gear reduction. At the same time, it generates large backlash because of the two 8-tooth gears meshed with one another.

1

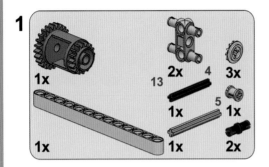

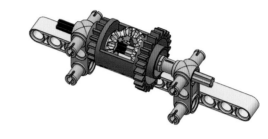

2

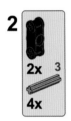

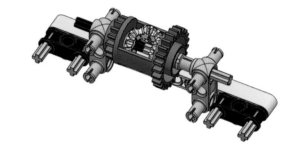

3

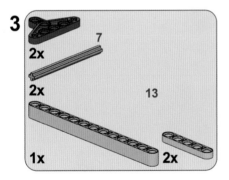

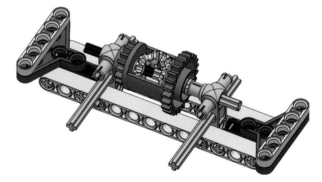

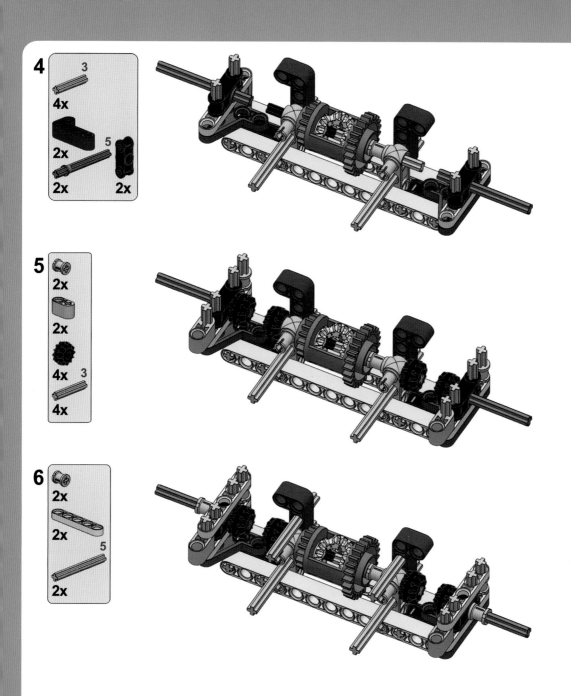

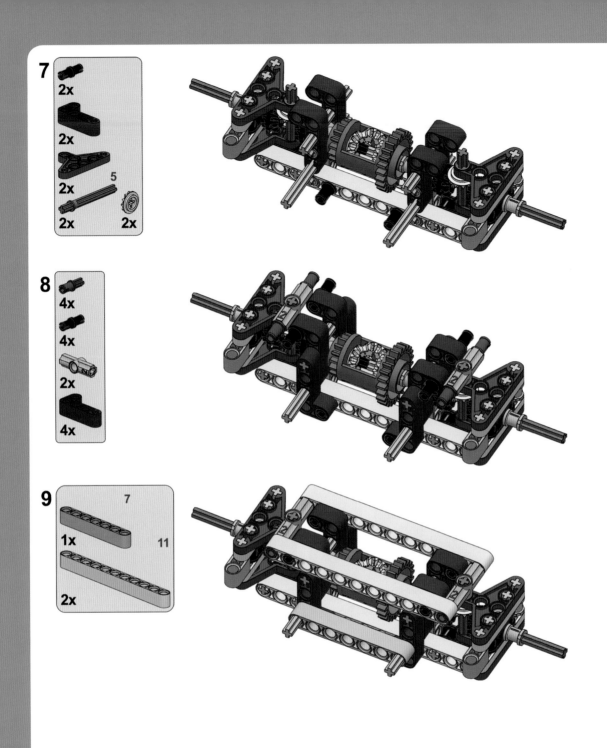

7

2x
2x
2x
5
2x
2x

8

4x
4x
2x
4x

9

7
1x
11
2x

10

2x

2x 7

1x 11 2x

11

2x

4x

1x

1x 5 1x

1x 2x

12

1x

1x 3

2x

2x 10

1x 1x 1x

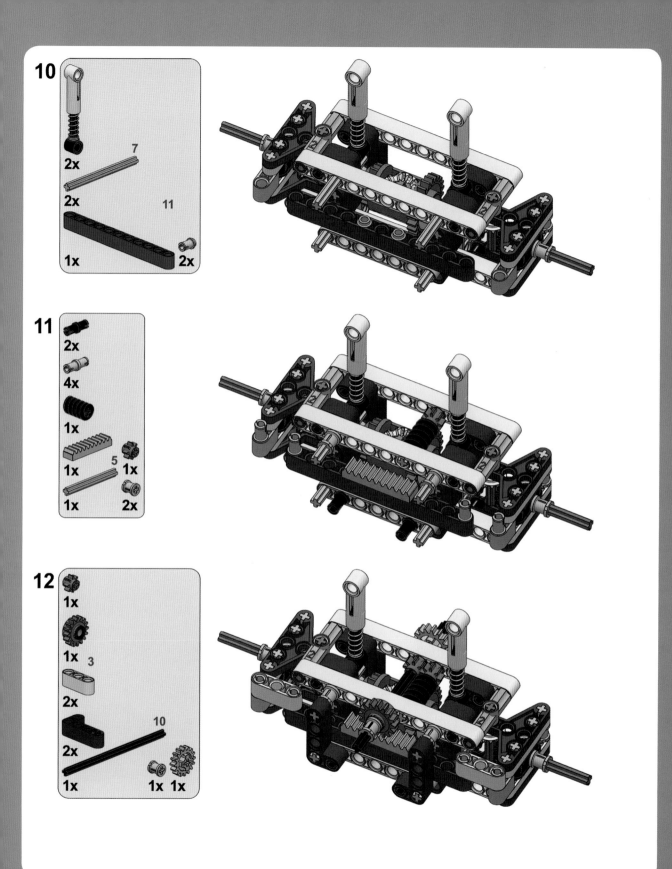

13

3

5x

4x

4x 10x

14

2x

1x

1x 3

1x 4

1x

15

2x

2x

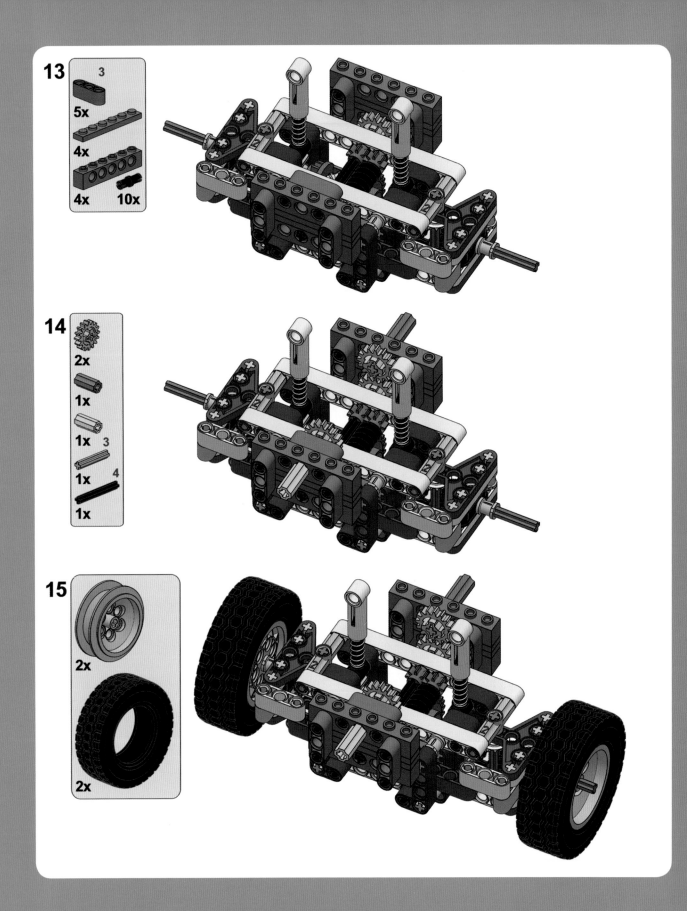

16

tracked vehicles and suspensions

Tracked vehicles are superior to wheeled vehicles for covering rough terrain. In a manner of speaking, tracks allow tanks and construction vehicles to "carry their own road" wherever they go. To create tracked LEGO vehicles, we have two options: rubber tracks and hard plastic tracks, each with a different set of advantages.

rubber tracks

LEGO's rubber tracks are made of a single, solid loop of rubber. LEGO produced seven rubber track variants, three of which are obsolete and difficult to find. The remaining four are quite similar to each other, and one variant dominates in terms of popularity (see Figure 16-1).

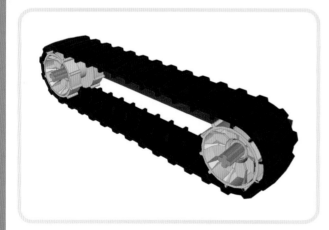

Figure 16-1: A large Technic tread and two Technic tread hubs

This track has 34 segments and is a little less than 3 studs wide. With its deep tread, the rubber provides excellent traction. The loop must be driven with a special type of sprocket wheel called a *tread hub*; the track requires two hubs 13 studs apart to be fully stretched, as shown in Figure 16-1. Tread hubs have a diameter of 3 studs, and their width is just a little bit less. They come in a variety of colors, and they use pin holes. In order to make your sprocket gears rotate with an axle, you must lock them with 16-tooth gears, as shown in Figure 16-2. You'll need two 16-tooth gears per hub—one on each side—or, to save space, you can use a single gear on one side and a bush on the other.

Figure 16-2: Two tread hubs: one empty (left) and one with a 16-tooth gear inserted (right). Since the hub is less than 3 studs wide, the gear sticks out slightly.

Advantages of rubber tracks:

* They are a single, unbreakable loop.
* They provide superb traction.
* They create minimal noise when driving.

Disadvantages of rubber tracks:

* Their length is limited and fixed.
* Their sprocket wheels are available in only one size.
* Rubber becomes less and less elastic over time.

hard plastic tracks

Hard plastic tracks (also known as *solid* tracks) are individual plastic links connected with one another. Their length can be easily adjusted, and they come in two versions: an older (and smaller) one and a newer (and bigger) one, both shown in Figure 16-3. Figure 16-4 shows a vehicle using the new plastic track type.

Neither type of hard plastic track measures a whole number of studs in width. Instead, the tracks are slightly narrower, which prevents them from abrading the structure around them as they rotate. The older tread type is slightly less than 3 studs wide, and the newer one is slightly less than 5 studs wide. The length of tracks is a little difficult to compare, as no link is an equal number of studs long either; however, a 15-link-long section of older track is equal to an 8-link-long section of new track, and those lengths are both equal to 13 studs, as shown in Figure 16-3. A single link of the newer type is thus equal to 1.875 links of the older type. A link of the new track is 1.625 studs long, while the older link is 0.867 studs long.

The older tracks come primarily in black, and they are similar in construction to LEGO chains, as you can see from their links in Figure 16-5. This means that any gear that works well with a chain can be our sprocket wheel for a tracked vehicle. As shown in Figure 16-6, a single link occupies two teeth on a gear.

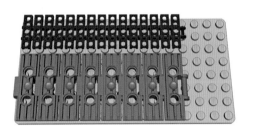

Figure 16-3: The older 15-link-long track and the newer 8-link-long track are both 13 studs long.

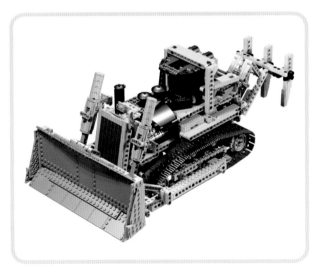

Figure 16-4: The newer type of solid track was introduced in the famous 8275 set.

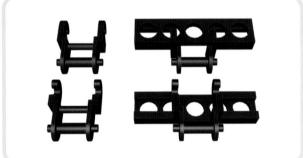

Figure 16-5: Regular LEGO chain links (left) and older-type track links (right). The older track links are just modified chain links.

Figure 16-6: A section of older track wrapped around a 16-tooth gear

Five types of gears can be used as sprocket wheels for the older tracks (see Figure 6-5 on page 58). Other gears just aren't suitable because of the shape of their teeth or simply because of their small diameter.

The small openings in the older tracks can hold a plate, a tile (as shown in Figure 16-7), or even a brick that is at least 4 studs long. While bricks aren't typically used because they fall off too easily, plates and tiles can make the tracks wider and improve their appearance.

Figure 16-7: A section of older track with tiles added. Note that only every other link can have a piece inserted into it.

Figure 16-8 shows my model of a Liebherr R944C excavator, which combined two types of gears to keep the tracks in place. I used 24-tooth gears at the ends of the tracks and 16-tooth gears to give shape to the tracks' upper sections.

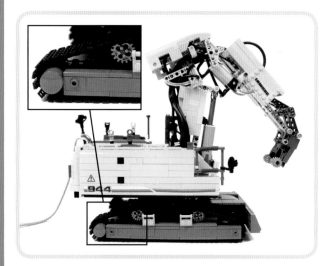

Figure 16-8: A model of a Liebherr R944C, using two types of gears

The newer tracks are made of massive links that come primarily in dark grey; black and metallic silver versions are available as well. Each link comes with two pin holes, which allow for modification (see Figure 16-9).

Figure 16-9: Adding a pin to a track allows us to attach bricks or tiles

The new solid tracks can't be driven by regular Technic gears; instead, they use special sprocket wheels. There are two options: a big wheel and a small one (both shown in Figure 16-10). The big sprocket wheel can have up to 10 links wrapped around it, is almost 2 studs thick, and comes primarily in yellow, with orange and black available, too. The small one can have up to 6 links wrapped around it, is 1 stud thick, and comes in black and pearl grey.

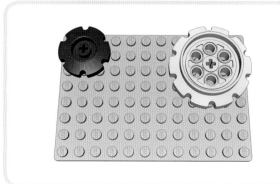

Figure 16-10: Sprocket wheels for the newer track type

The pin holes on top of the newer links can be used to attach Technic bricks (as shown in Figure 16-11) or beams (as shown in Figure 16-12) to them, making them wider and suitable for driving in snow. Both bricks and beams can be attached to every link using two half or three-quarter pins, with the latter ones being less likely to fall off. It is also possible to weave a regular rubber band into the pin holes, improving the traction of the tracks and reducing the noise they create while driving.

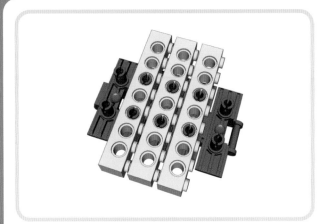

Figure 16-11: Section of the newer track with bricks attached

Figure 16-12: Section of the newer track with beams attached

The two solid track types differ in how much they can be stretched; the older type is more elastic but, at the same time, more fragile and prone to break. The newer type is much sturdier but very rigid, and as a result, it's difficult to obtain optimum tension with it. If your tread is too loose or too tight, it will affect how a vehicle drives. The rule of the thumb is to tighten it as much as possible and then give it at least half of a link of play.

Advantages of solid tracks:

* Their length is adjustable.
* They look more realistic than rubber tracks.
* They can be driven by a wider selection of sprocket wheels.

Disadvantages of solid tracks:

* They have poor traction.
* They're prone to coming apart (especially the older type).
* It's difficult to obtain optimum tension (especially with the newer type).
* They're noisy while driving (especially the newer type).

tracked wheel systems

Tracks greatly improve a vehicle's off-road performance, especially on mud, snow, or other unreliable surfaces. But how well a vehicle moves on its tracks depends largely on its wheels.

Strange as it may seem, wheels are no less important for tracked vehicles than they are for a car or truck. Firstly, they provide power to the tracks and keep them from falling off. Secondly, they can be suspended in order to improve the *flotation* of the vehicle, which describes how well the suspension handles obstacles. A suspension that adapts well to rough terrain provides good flotation, reducing the shock transferred to the vehicle as it moves.

NOTE The first tanks ever built provide a good example of just how important suspension is. Because these tanks lacked any kind of suspension, the crewmen of such tanks would often be knocked unconscious by shocks while traversing trenches.

Let's discuss the basic wheel systems. The simplest wheel system consists of two *sprocket wheels* per track, as shown in Figure 16-13. Usually about half of such a wheel comes in contact with the track, more than any other wheel in the system—which is why it's important that these wheels are those that drive the tracks. Usually only one sprocket

Figure 16-13: A track with two sprocket wheels: an idle one (grey) and a driven one (red)

wheel is actually driven, and it's often the rear one because it's convenient to have propulsion systems at the back of the vehicle. But it doesn't really matter which sprocket wheel is driven, as the track works like a chain and transfers the drive to the other wheel.

The second function of the sprocket wheels is to maintain the track's tension, which is particularly important as the vehicle moves over obstacles. Sprocket wheels can be suspended on an elastic element to maintain this tension. A loss of tension can cause the track to slip or even separate.

But with the basic two-wheel-per-track system, it would be difficult to add any suspension. We could suspend the nondriven sprocket relatively easily, but suspending the driven one would be much more challenging. This is why *road wheels* were invented.

A more advanced wheel system includes road wheels at the bottom of the vehicle (shown in blue in Figure 16-14). Road wheels can be used in any number, they are not driven, and they can be easily suspended. They are usually located closer to the ground than sprocket wheels, and they support the weight of the vehicle. Some vehicles come with sprocket and road wheels on the same level, making the road wheels difficult to suspend but increasing the total area of contact between the track and the terrain. Real tracked vehicles have been built both with many small road wheels (as shown in Figure 16-15) or with a few big ones. As a kind of compromise between the two extremes, modern tanks usually have six or seven road wheels per track that are just over half as big as the sprocket wheels.

The most complex wheel systems also include *return rollers* (shown in yellow in Figure 16-16). They are neither driven nor suspended, and their only function is to support the upper portion of the track. Return rollers can have minimal contact with the track and, in fact, don't even have to rotate—it's enough if the track can slide over them. As tracks are always more or less loose, vehicles with long tracks usually need at least two return rollers. It is also possible to use road wheels large enough to function as return rollers, as shown in Figure 16-17.

Figure 16-15: With 11 road wheels per track, the British Churchill tank is an extreme example of using a design that includes many small road wheels.

Figure 16-16: A track with two sprocket wheels, three road wheels, and two return rollers

Figure 16-17: Soviet tanks from the World War II era—such as this T34—used road wheels so big that they had contact with both the lower and upper portion of the track, thus eliminating the need for return rollers.

Figure 16-14: A track with two sprocket wheels and three road wheels

A good example of a modern wheel system is the one used on the classic Sherman tank. It includes two large sprocket wheels, six smaller road wheels, and two return rollers per track (see Figure 16-18). Note that the forward sprocket is driven and the rear one is idle.

Figure 16-18: The classic Sherman tank used a wheel system that included return rollers.

Now that you know what types of wheels are used in tracked vehicles, we can move on to the suspension systems.

suspension systems

The primary function of a suspension system is to increase stability and reduce the shock transferred to the vehicle. Its secondary function is to prevent the tracks from falling off. A suspension system achieves this function by keeping road wheels in close contact with the tracks regardless of the shape of the ground. The vast majority of tracked vehicles have suspension only on the road wheels, largely for simplicity's sake. All the suspension systems described below are designed for road wheels but can be used with sprocket wheels as well.

NOTE The type of LEGO track you use doesn't affect the suspension; it only determines the type of sprocket wheels you can use. The examples of suspensions in this chapter show variants for both LEGO track types to demonstrate how a given suspension works with various wheels.

bogies

A bogie is the simplest type of tracked suspension. It is simply a beam that has one road wheel on either end; this beam freely rotates around a central axle connected to the vehicle, as shown in Figure 16-19. As the road wheels on the bogie go up and down, only half of their travel is transferred to the bogie's central axle—for example, when a wheel moves upward by 2 studs, the axle will only move upward by 1, as shown in Figure 16-20. So bogies provide reasonably good flotation, but they don't reduce shock.

Figure 16-19: The yellow beam rotates around the central pin, creating a bogie with two road wheels.

Figure 16-20: In this example, one road wheel is raised by 2 studs, but the bogie's central axle (and thus the vehicle) is raised only by 1 stud.

NOTE The basic principle of bogies is that only 50 percent of the road wheels' vertical travel is transferred to the vehicle. But note that this principle is true only if the obstacle is shorter than the length of the entire bogie—that is, shorter than the span of two road wheels.

Figure 16-21 shows an example of a bogie for the newer LEGO track type. The newer tracks are larger and usually used with larger and heavier vehicles, which is why this bogie variant is reinforced on the front and back sides (and is therefore sturdier).

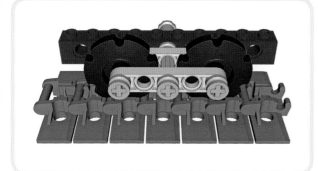

Figure 16-21: A reinforced bogie for the new LEGO track type

Figure 16-22: A simple trailing arm with a shock absorber

trailing arms suspension with shock absorbers

Trailing arms are used in more advanced suspension systems, where each road wheel is located on the end of an arm and supported against the weight of the vehicle by a shock absorber (or another elastic element), as shown in Figure 16-22. As most tracked vehicles usually have relatively low profiles, 6.5L shock absorbers are better suited to most tracked vehicles than their longer variants.

Trailing arm suspensions are sensitive to the direction of the tracks' rotation, and tracks always rotate more freely in one direction than the reverse. The arms are located *in front* of the road wheel.

There are a number of possible variants for this suspension system, depending on how much load each road wheel has to handle, how much space you can use, and what suspension travel and hardness you want to achieve. Figures 16-22 through 16-24 show some common variations.

NOTE The first and last road wheels in a track usually handle more load than the middle ones. It is therefore a good idea to use harder shock absorbers for these wheels than for the middle wheels. The weight distribution of the vehicle (front-heavy, center-heavy, or rear-heavy) should also be considered.

The setup in Figure 16-23 works only with 24-tooth gears and isn't that soft but takes little vertical space, which is helpful when you need the road wheels to be very close to each other.

Figure 16-24 shows another compact setup that works with all types of wheels, including those for the newer track system. It allows a lower overall profile, but it needs the road wheels to be spaced farther apart.

Figure 16-23: A more complex trailing arm system that works with 24-tooth gears

Figure 16-24: Another compact trailing-arm setup

trailing arm suspensions with torsion bars

Shock absorbers are efficient but large; their length can force us to build our vehicles taller than we would otherwise need to. Thankfully, there's a very attractive alternative when building a trailing arm suspension: torsion bars.

A torsion bar is a long, slightly elastic element, positioned perpendicular to a vehicle's hull. One end of the bar is locked to the chassis so that it can't rotate. The other end is attached to a trailing arm with a road wheel on the other end, and it rotates together with the arm. So as the road wheel goes up, the arm twists the bar around its axis, as shown in Figure 16-25. And the great news is that all LEGO axles (except for the very short ones) are elastic enough to function as torsion bars.

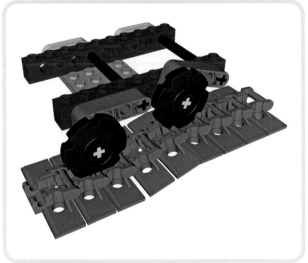

Figure 16-26: A more complex torsion-bar suspension

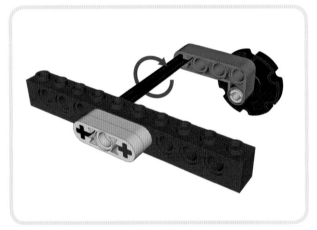

Figure 16-25: The basic scheme of a torsion bar

In the figure, the black 8L axle is functioning as a torsion bar; its one end is locked into the chassis (represented by the red brick), and its other end is locked into the trailing arm (represented by the dark grey beam). Now, if the road wheel at the end of the arm meets an obstacle that makes it go up, the trailing arm will oscillate around the axle, making it twist a little. Once the obstacle is passed, the axle will untwist, returning the arm and the wheel to the initial position. Of course, in a real vehicle the torsion bar needs to be supported.

Figure 16-26 shows a more complex example of the torsion-bar suspension in action, including such a support. Note that the 8L axles go through two bricks, but they are locked only with the one closer to the middle of the hull. They can freely rotate inside the outer brick, which is used only to support them.

The torsion-bar suspension requires only common pieces, and its hardness can be adjusted by using shorter or longer axles or by simply changing the point at which the axles are locked to the chassis (the closer to the trailing arm, the harder the suspension). Twisting LEGO axles may seem risky, but they are surprisingly resistant to damage. I have used 8L axles as torsion bars in a model with a total weight of around 3.5 kg, where each torsion bar handled an average load of almost 0.25 kg and a much greater load when negotiating obstacles. Even after the model went through a lot of tests on rough terrain, the axles were in pristine condition.

This kind of suspension, unlike shock absorbers, also has the advantage of using minimal space inside the tracks. Its disadvantages are that it takes 1 stud of vertical space at the bottom of the hull (as shown in Figure 16-27) and that this space is so densely filled with axles that it's usually impossible to use it for anything else. A torsion-bar suspension also doesn't work well for lightweight models. If the average load per road wheel is less than 100 grams, the effect of this suspension is barely noticeable.

In the example in Figure 16-27, only 1 stud of vertical space inside the hull is taken by the suspension system, but it is taken quite completely. Note that the bars on each side are separate axles—in this case, 7 studs long each. It is possible to use a single axle that traverses the whole hull as long as it's locked securely in the middle so that twisting one of its ends doesn't affect the other end.

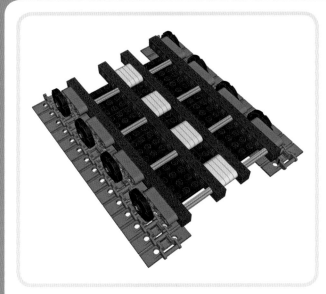

Figure 16-27: A hull floor of a vehicle with torsion-bar suspension

experimenting with road wheels

Early tracked vehicles were built with road wheels of solid metal. Later, engineers observed that vibrations between the tracks and the vehicles could be reduced by putting rubber rims over the road wheels. Today, rubber rims are considered standard for real-life tracked vehicles. Note that these rims are different from conventional tires: They are made of solid rubber, they're thin, and they have no tread.

There is an easy way to re-create a road wheel with a rubber rim using LEGO pieces so that it looks accurate: You can use a wedge belt wheel with a special solid tire (#70162), as shown in Figure 16-28.

Figure 16-28: A belt wheel with a tire. The tire is solid rubber and very easy to put on and take off.

We can use a pair of wedge belt wheels to create a single road wheel that braces the track from two sides, as shown in Figure 16-29. Wedge belt wheels look more accurate while modeling some tracked vehicles, and they also allow you to build compact suspensions, as shown in Figure 16-30. (LEGO models aren't heavy enough to effectively compress solid rubber, so the shock absorption effect achieved with these tires alone is minuscule.)

Figure 16-29: A pair of wedge belt wheels 1 stud apart can firmly secure the older type of track. If they are 2 studs apart, they can do the same with the newer type of track.

Figure 16-30: This suspension, which uses a trailing arm and a shock absorber, takes advantage of double road wheels to position the absorber as low as possible. With a central road wheel, the shock absorber would have to be moved to the outer side or be located much higher.

My model of a Soviet T-72M tank, shown in Figure 16-31, employed yet another approach: The wedge belt wheels with tires were simply inserted into the central portion of the track, and they held it in place surprisingly well. At the same time, they were all suspended on torsion bars.

Figure 16-31: A model tank using wedge belt wheels with tires, suspended on torsion bars

Another interesting thing about wedge belt wheels is that without the tire, they have a diameter that perfectly matches that of certain sprocket wheels. They can be used to conceal colorful sprocket wheels for aesthetic effect, as shown in Figures 16-32 through 16-34.

Figure 16-32: The diameter of a wedge belt wheel matches the diameter of a 24-tooth gear meshed with the central protrusion of the older track (left) or the diameter of a smaller sprocket wheel meshed with the central protrusion of the newer track (right). Thus, the wedge belt wheels can be used to conceal the real road wheels and improve aesthetics.

Figure 16-33: Concealing 16-tooth gears behind 18×8 mm wheels (#56902). As shown here, the two sides of these wheels look different and can be used together to create an interesting aesthetic effect.

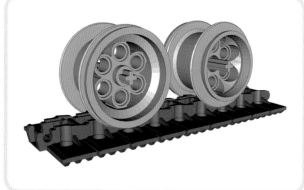

Figure 16-34: The newer type of track works fairly well with 49.6×28 VR wheels (#6595). These wheels also have two sides that look different, and their size and appearance make them very suitable for large models.

If you're curious about how we can power tracked vehicles like tanks and bulldozers, skip to "Subtractors" on page 280, where you'll learn the methods of steering tracked vehicles and independently driving each track.

Just like their real-life counterparts, LEGO transmissions are mechanisms capable of changing their internal gear ratio. They can increase gear reduction in the drivetrain when more torque is needed and decrease it when speed is of greater importance. It's the same principle at play when shifting gears in a car or in a bicycle, and it makes LEGO electric motors much more versatile.

A typical transmission has a number of fixed gear ratios, one of which can be selected at a time. Such a gear ratio is often simply called a speed or a gear: We can shift to lower gear (increasing the gear reduction) or to higher gear (decreasing the gear reduction). Therefore, a transmission must have at least 2 gears (as shown in Figure 17-1), while some of the most complex ones can have more than 10. Depending on their number of gear ratios, we call them 2-speed transmissions, 3-speed transmissions, and so on.

A transmission usually has a single input and a single output; the input is connected to the drive motor, and the output is connected to the final drive (wheels or tracks). A typical transmission also houses a number of gears, and each speed uses only a few of them. In other words, while some of the gears are used to transfer the drive and affect the current gear ratio, other ones just rotate unused. This makes them work like idler gears: driven but idle. In transmissions, they are called *dead* gears, and the fewer their number, the more efficient the transmission, as they add weight and thereby friction.

Lastly, we'll consider a special type of transmission called a *distribution* or *split transmission*. This type of transmission has one input but several outputs. Such a transmission allows several mechanisms to be driven by a single motor without interfering with each other, as only one mechanism is driven at a time. We will discuss this particular type of transmission at the end of this chapter; for now, let's focus on the simpler ones.

types of transmissions

When it comes to transmissions, we can organize our models into several disparate categories. Firstly and most importantly, a transmission can be *synchronized* or *nonsynchronized*. This refers to how easy it is to make gears mesh while shifting gears. Whenever a gear is shifted, one pair of gears has to *disengage*, and another pair has to *engage*. In synchronized transmissions, these gears can engage at any speed and any position; in nonsynchronized transmissions, engagement is a matter of making their teeth meet properly, which can succeed or fail, depending on the gears' positions and on the difference of their speeds. If gears fail to engage properly, they grind their teeth, and we have to try to shift the gear again. We can assume that gears will always engage in synchronized transmissions; in nonsynchronized ones, successful shifting is a matter of the shape of the gears' teeth, the speed of shifting, and a degree of luck. Some types of gears mesh more easily in nonsynchronized transmissions than others. For example, double-bevel gears, because they are beveled, engage more easily than typical

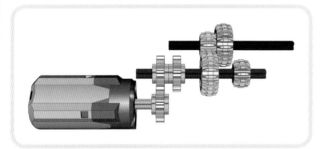

Figure 17-1: The inside of a simple 2-speed transmission. Consider what happens if we move the red axle 1 stud to the left and the green gears disengage and blue gears engage, changing the gear ratio between the motor and the output axle.

spur gears. Naturally, it's much easier to shift a nonsynchronized transmission while its input is stopped; in a synchronized transmission, it makes no difference.

Secondly, transmissions can be categorized as sequential or regular. *Sequential* (or *linear*) transmissions can only be shifted from one gear to the next closest one. That is, they can be shifted from 2nd to 3rd gear, but they can't be shifted from 2nd to 4th gear directly; instead, they have to shift from 2nd to 3rd and then to 4th. *Regular* (or *nonlinear*) transmissions, on the other hand, are not bound by this restriction, and they often use elaborate shift sticks, like the one in Figure 17-2. They can shift even from 10th to 1st gear directly, even though it may be dangerous to change the gear ratio so much so quickly. In real life, sequential transmissions are common in bicycles and motorbikes, while regular ones are found in cars.

Figure 17-2: The unique shift stick from the 8880 set, the first LEGO set with a nonlinear and synchronized transmission. The transmission has 4 speeds, and the stick can move in an H pattern, allowing it to shift from one gear to any other.

how LEGO transmission driving rings work

As building a synchronized transmission with regular pieces is quite difficult, LEGO has developed a special piece just for this task. It's called a *transmission driving ring*, and it's shown in Figure 17-3.

Figure 17-3: The transmission driving ring (red) has to be placed over a ribbed axle joiner (blue). The axle joiner connects two axles, with each of them going 1 stud deep inside it.

The transmission driving ring (red) has to be placed on an axle joiner (blue). This makes the transmission driving ring rotate together with the joiner; at the same time, the ring can slide forward or backward along the joiner. Figure 17-4 shows what happens when we put two 17-tooth gears with clutches on the axle next to the ring. The gears rotate freely on the axle, unless engaged by the driving ring that slides into them.

The easiest way to control the transmission driving ring is to use another special piece called the transmission changeover catch, shown in Figure 17-5. It was developed specifically to move the ring back and forth, engaging and disengaging it with the adjacent gears. It should be located above the ring, on a separate transverse axle.

Figure 17-4: There are three positions possible for a transmission driving ring: engaged with left gear, neutral (no gears engaged), and engaged with right gear. Note that only engaged gears rotate together with the axle.

Figure 17-5: The transmission driving ring and the transmission changeover catch. Note that the catch rotates together with the axle it sits on, but it can slide along it freely. Some transmissions make use of this property. To see an animation of this process, visit http://www.technicopedia.com/1994 .html#Parts.

Figure 17-6 shows a very simple 2-speed transmission that uses a driving ring controlled with a catch. If we engage the ring with the gear to its left (shown in the middle), the resulting gear ratio will be 3:1. If we engage the ring with the gear to its right (shown on the bottom), the resulting gear ratio will be 1:1. The key to understanding how this mechanism works is to remember that 17-tooth gears with clutches rotate freely on axles unless engaged with the driving ring. They can therefore be used to transmit drive *over* the axle they sit on, while not driving that axle or any other gears on it.

If you like the idea of using synchronized transmissions, you'll also want to know about a piece called an *extension driving ring*, shown in Figure 17-7. It works like an overlay for the regular transmission driving ring, allowing it to engage gears 1 stud farther away from it, as shown in Figure 17-8.

The main advantage of the transmission driving ring is that it can engage at any moment, at any speed, without the need to stop the input. The main disadvantage is that it works only with one particular type of gear, so additional gears are needed just to achieve various gear ratios, making plenty of dead gears unavoidable.

WARNING The transmission driving ring is also a torque-sensitive piece; it can disengage itself or even get physically damaged if a large torque is applied to it. This makes nonsynchronized transmissions a more common choice for high-torque applications.

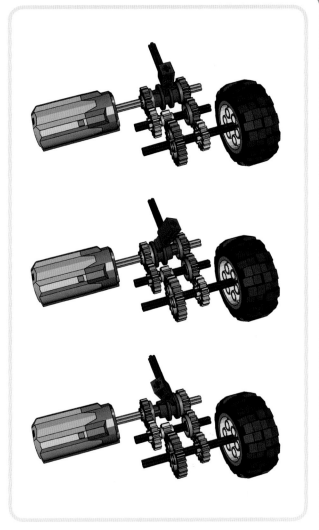

Figure 17-6: A simple 2-speed synchronized gearbox set on neutral gear (top), low gear (middle), and high gear (bottom)

Figure 17-7: The extension driving ring (light grey) can be put over the transmission driving ring (red), extending it by 1 stud. Note that there is a large backlash between the driving ring and the gear it engages through extension.

Figure 17-8: The extension driving ring fills the gap between the transmission driving ring and a gear 1 stud away from it, allowing the gear to be engaged.

transmission designs

This section lists a number of designs for complete transmissions. For each design, there is the type of transmission, a short description, and a scheme showing which gears are active at which speed. Building instructions for selected transmissions appear at the end of the chapter.

The following colors are used to mark pieces: green for the input axle, red for the output axle, and light blue for the active gears. The changeover catches are removed for clarity.

Keep in mind that it's also possible to combine two or more transmissions of any type by making one transmission's output another one's input. The number of speeds will be effectively multiplied: For example, a 2-speed transmission combined with a 4-speed one will produce 8 speeds.

Some builders like to include a reverse gear in their transmissions. This is accurate in relation to real transmission systems but redundant when used with an electric motor that can be reversed at any moment. I have omitted such designs on purpose because I think they waste a potentially useful speed for no real reason.

Many builders consider a sequential synchronized transmission the best variant of all because it can be easily shifted *remotely*. While beyond the scope of this book, such a transmission relies on a control mechanism that is independent of the actual transmission and that can be used with many of the designs shown below. For ideas on creating remote-controlled transmissions, check out the website of Sheepo, one of the best transmission builders: *http://www .sheepo.es/*.

2-speed synchronized transmission

Type: sequential, synchronized

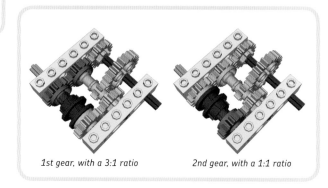

1st gear, with a 3:1 ratio   2nd gear, with a 1:1 ratio

This is the simplest synchronized transmission possible. (Building instructions are on page 261.)

2-speed linear heavy-duty transmission

Type: sequential, nonsynchronized

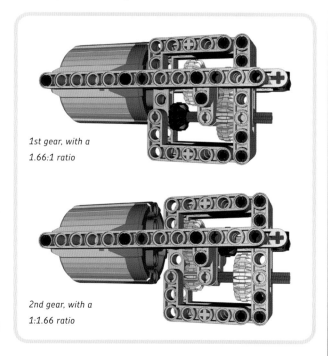

1st gear, with a 1.66:1 ratio

2nd gear, with a 1:1.66 ratio

A transmission designed specifically to handle high torque, shown here with the PF XL motor. Gears are shifted by sliding part of the transmission together with the motor attached to it. This makes the transmission simpler and reduces the number of gears. (Building instructions are on page 262.)

2-speed RC motor transmission

Type: sequential, synchronized

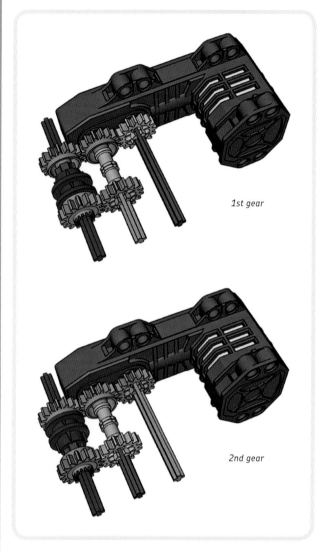

1st gear

2nd gear

2-speed orbital transmission

Type: sequential, synchronized

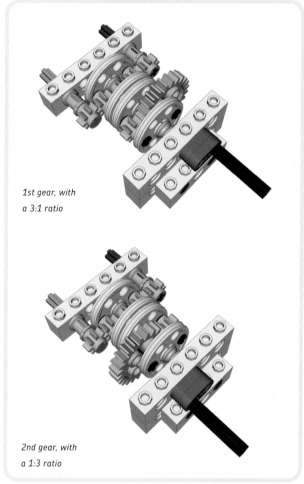

1st gear, with a 3:1 ratio

2nd gear, with a 1:3 ratio

This unusual transmission can be built with one or two RC motors. LEGO RC motors have two outputs instead of one, with the outer output having 26 percent more torque and less speed than the inner output. This transmission is connected to both of the motor's outputs at the same time, allowing us to select from which one it is driven. This allows us to make use of the difference in the outputs' properties, even though the gear ratio of the transmission itself is 1:1 at both speeds.

Building instructions are on page 264.

This transmission is placed between two gears and shifted by rotating it 180 degrees. In this example, rotation is done with a dark grey crank that should be blocked once rotated. You can use a worm gear to rotate and then block the transmission. The transmission is synchronized without using the transmission driving ring and provides a vast difference in gear ratios. Additionally, it has no dead gears.

Note the half bushes used to create a gap between the transmission and the bricks on its sides. The gap is intended to prevent the 4L axles on the sides of the transmission from getting into the holes in the bricks and blocking the transmission.

Building instructions are on page 266.

2-speed ratchet transmission

Type: sequential, synchronized

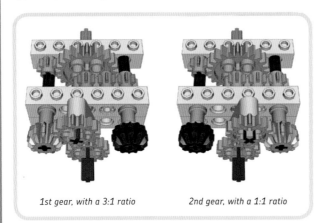

1st gear, with a 3:1 ratio   *2nd gear, with a 1:1 ratio*

This transmission uses a ratchet to shift gears. It shifts when the direction of the motor that drives it changes. It's small, simple, and synchronized without the use of the transmission driving ring. It can handle significant torque, but its output always rotates in the same direction, regardless of its input direction. So when it's used in a car, it makes the car drive only forward or only backward.

The transmission works like this: The direction of the input tilts the ratchet left or right. A 17-tooth gear on top of the transmission meshes with one of two 12-tooth double-bevel gears when the ratchet is tilted. The 17-tooth gear sits on an axle pin with friction, and the resistance created this way makes the ratchet press hard against the 12-tooth double-bevel gears. The greater torque is handled by the transmission. The greater the resistance on the ratchet, the harder it presses, meshing its top gear more effectively. There is, of course, a limit to how much torque can be handled.

Building instructions are on page 267.

3-speed linear transmission

Type: sequential, nonsynchronized

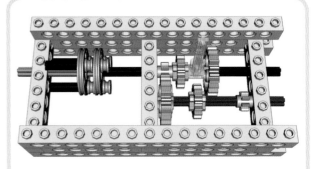

1st gear, with a 3:1 ratio

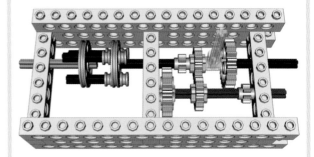

2nd gear, with a 1:1 ratio

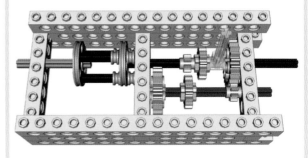

3rd gear, with a 1:3 ratio

This transmission is simple but large. It uses an extendable driveshaft to make the input driven and movable at the same time. The control lever is shown semitransparent for clarity.

Building instructions are on page 268.

4-speed double-lever transmission

Type: regular, nonsynchronized

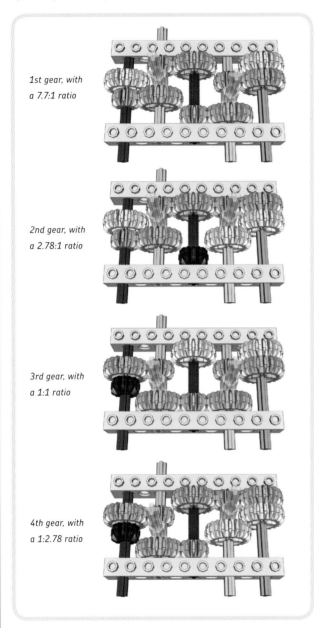

1st gear, with a 7.7:1 ratio

2nd gear, with a 2.78:1 ratio

3rd gear, with a 1:1 ratio

4th gear, with a 1:2.78 ratio

4-speed synchronized transmission

Type: regular, synchronized

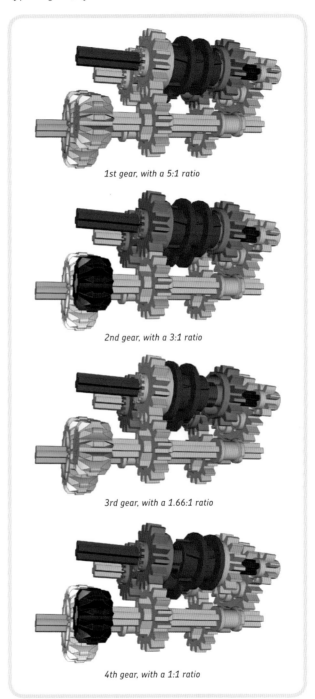

1st gear, with a 5:1 ratio

2nd gear, with a 3:1 ratio

3rd gear, with a 1.66:1 ratio

4th gear, with a 1:1 ratio

This regular transmission is strong and useful. It's very simple and relatively small, but it has two control levers, which is challenging when it comes to remote control. It consists of three shafts connecting input and output: one fixed and two that can slide by 1 stud. Due to its simplicity, no building instructions are provided, just the schemes of its speeds. The control levers are shown semitransparent for clarity.

NOTE The structural parts and the control levers have been removed for clarity.

This synchronized transmission, shown in Figures 17-9 to 17-11, has two transmission driving rings, only one of which should be engaged at a time. Relatively small and providing a large difference in gear ratios, it can be controlled by a single lever moving in an H pattern or by two levers, one for each driving ring. It has a lot of dead and idler gears.

Building instructions are on page 270.

Figure 17-9: The 4-speed synchronized transmission with a single control lever moving in an H pattern. Note the special so-called "changeover plates" (light grey) used to control the shifting lever's movement and to support the axle it moves along.

Figure 17-10: The 4-speed synchronized transmission with a single control lever moving in an H pattern. The lever is housed and supported by common LEGO pieces.

Figure 17-11: The 4-speed synchronized transmission with two control levers, each controlling a single transmission driving ring. Note that both rings can't be engaged at the same time: One has to be set in neutral position before the other one is engaged.

5-speed linear transmission

Type: sequential, nonsynchronized

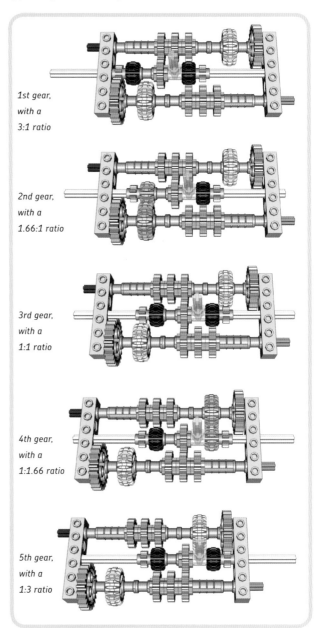

1st gear, with a 3:1 ratio

2nd gear, with a 1.66:1 ratio

3rd gear, with a 1:1 ratio

4th gear, with a 1:1.66 ratio

5th gear, with a 1:3 ratio

This transmission has one central shaft that can slide by 4 studs. Its disadvantage is that the central shaft makes use of a rare 16L axle, which can bend and disengage gears under high torque. Due to its simplicity, no building instructions are provided here, just the schemes of its speeds. The control lever is shown semitransparent for clarity.

10-speed synchronized transmission

Type: regular, synchronized

NOTE This is the bottom view with the structural parts and the control levers removed for clarity.

This transmission has a 4-speed design that's expanded further with the use of extension transmission driving rings.

If you study it closely, you'll notice that it can be expanded beyond 10 speeds by adding another pair of extensions and then four regular transmission driving rings. You can continue to expand it beyond this point by again adding two extension driving rings and so on. There's no limit to how many speeds can be added this way, except that the number of dead gears in the transmission increases quickly and a 14-speed version generates enough resistance to stall a PF XL motor. (Building instructions are on page 271.)

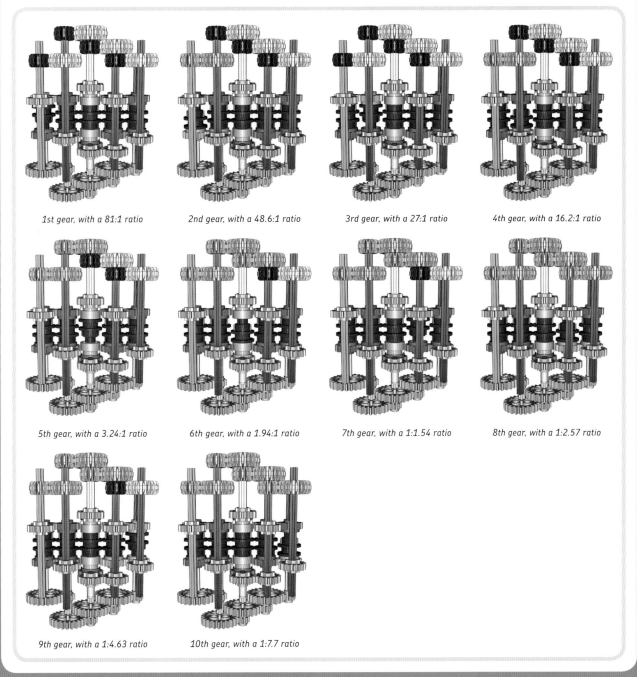

1st gear, with a 81:1 ratio   *2nd gear, with a 48.6:1 ratio*   *3rd gear, with a 27:1 ratio*   *4th gear, with a 16.2:1 ratio*

5th gear, with a 3.24:1 ratio   *6th gear, with a 1.94:1 ratio*   *7th gear, with a 1:1.54 ratio*   *8th gear, with a 1:2.57 ratio*

9th gear, with a 1:4.63 ratio   *10th gear, with a 1:7.7 ratio*

continuously variable transmission

Type: sequential, synchronized

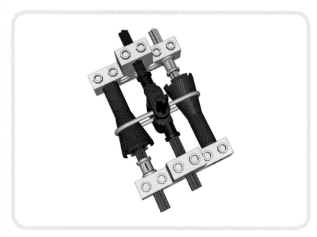

The continuously variable transmission (CVT) is a special type of a transmission. It doesn't have a definite number of speeds with fixed gear ratios. Instead, it has a minimum and maximum ratio, and it can be shifted continuously between them.

Real-life CVTs are very useful, but at the same time, they are very complex and often based on hydraulics or magnets. The easiest way to build a CVT with LEGO pieces is by using cones and a rubber band.

As you see, the transmission consists of input and output shafts with opposing cones connected by a rubber band. The band can be moved left or right so that it's wrapped around the broader portion of one cone and the narrower portion of the other. The circumference of the each cone is 22 mm at its narrowest and 50 mm at its broadest, which corresponds to a 1:2.27 ratio. This transmission can therefore be shifted smoothly between ratios 1:2.27 and 2.27:1.

The transmission can't handle much torque, and the tension of the rubber band has to be adjusted carefully in order for it to work properly. Too little tension will make the rubber band slip; too much tension can displace the cones. The original LEGO rubber bands work best as they are sticky and have a round profile; they come in many variants of different lengths that can work better or worse depending on the distance between the shafts in the transmission. Also note that the control lever module is mounted between two 1×2 bricks with axle holes. Axle holes not only keep the control lever straight. They also add some resistance so that it takes force to move the lever and thus the lever can't be moved by the rubber band's tension.

Building instructions are on page 276.

distribution transmissions

One type of transmission's primary function isn't to change gear ratios but to change which output is driven at the moment. This transmission, the distribution transmission, can be synchronized or not, depending on whether transmission driving rings are used. Distribution transmissions are very useful whenever there is a need for one motor to control one of many functions at a time, and they are quite popular in LEGO Technic sets.

In most cases, the distribution transmissions themselves are fairly simple; it's transferring the drive from them to several receiving mechanisms that can be tricky. Figures 17-12 to 17-16 present a few examples of such transmissions with various numbers of outputs, shown without housing for clarity. Note that the examples have a 1:1 ratio on all outputs for simplicity, but it's possible to create various ratios on various outputs.

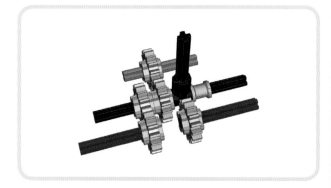

Figure 17-12: A nonsynchronized distribution transmission with two outputs

Figure 17-13: A synchronized distribution transmission with two outputs

Figure 17-14: A synchronized distribution transmission with four outputs

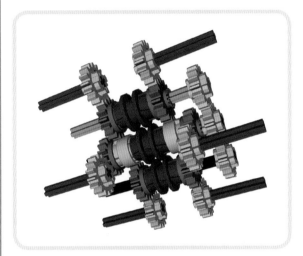

Figure 17-15: A synchronized distribution transmission with six outputs

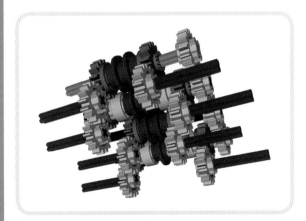

Figure 17-16: A synchronized distribution transmission with eight outputs

a 2-speed synchronized transmission

1

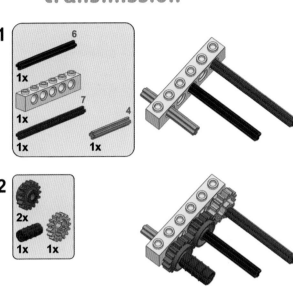

6
1x
1x
7
1x
4
1x

2

2x
1x
1x

3

1x
3
1x
1x
1x
1x

4

1x
1x
1x

a 2-speed linear heavy-duty transmission

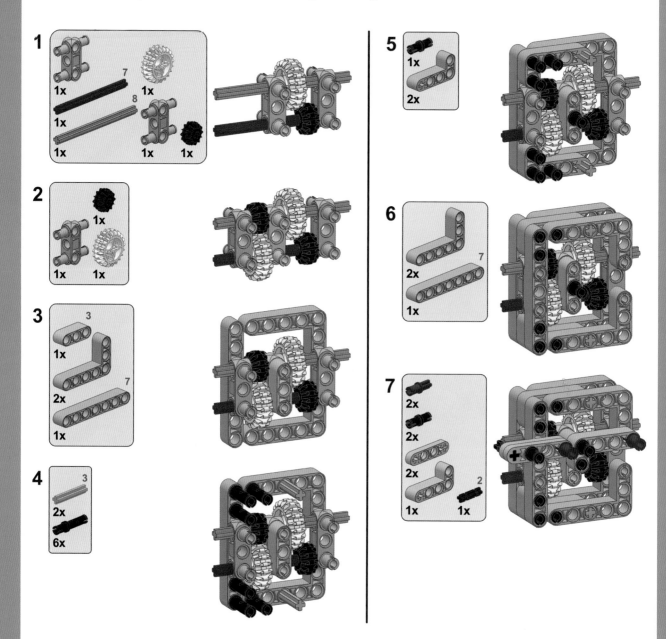

1
1x
7
1x
8
1x
1x
1x
1x

2
1x
1x
1x

3
3
1x
7
2x
1x

4
3
2x
6x

5
1x
2x

6
2x
7
1x

7
2x
2x
2x
2
1x
1x

8

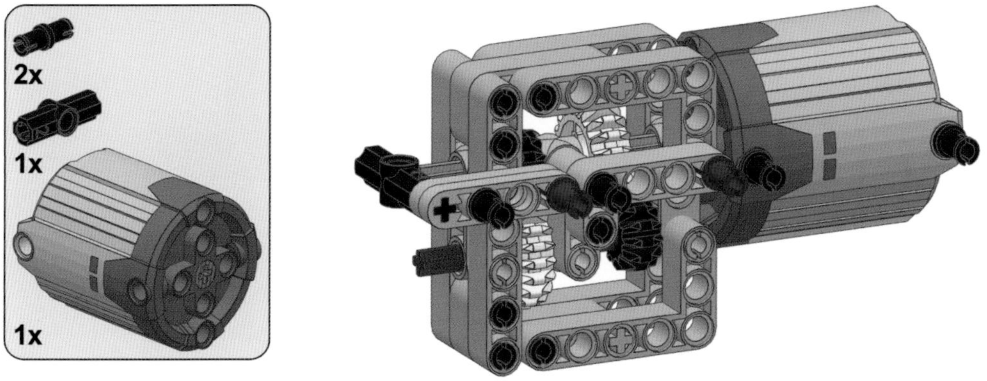

2x

1x

1x

9

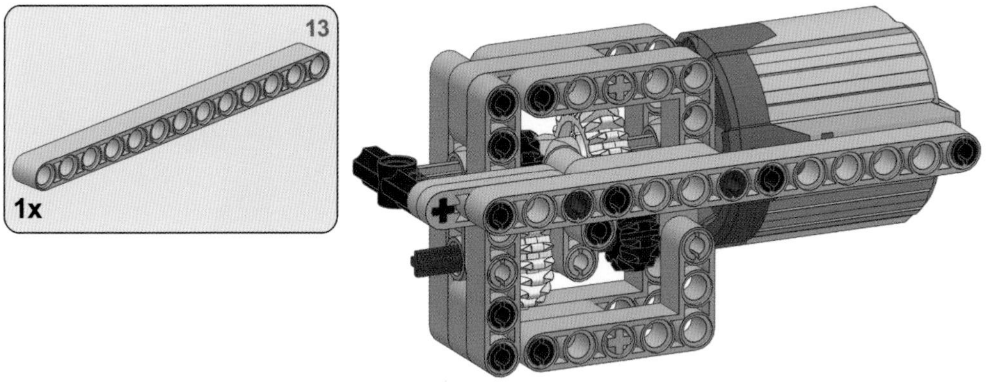

13

1x

10

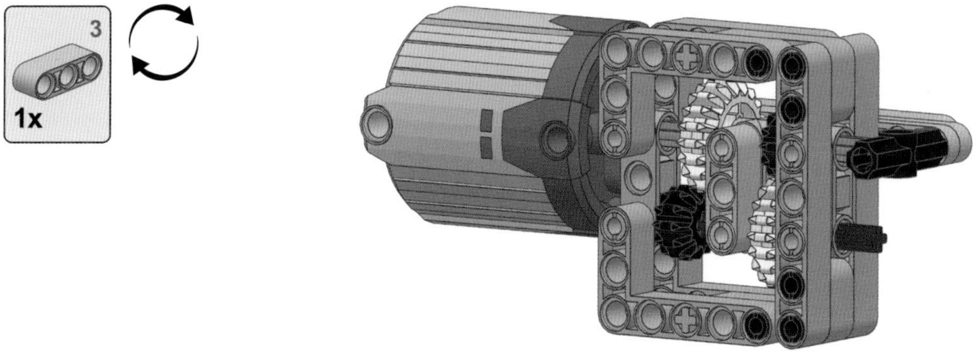

3

1x

11

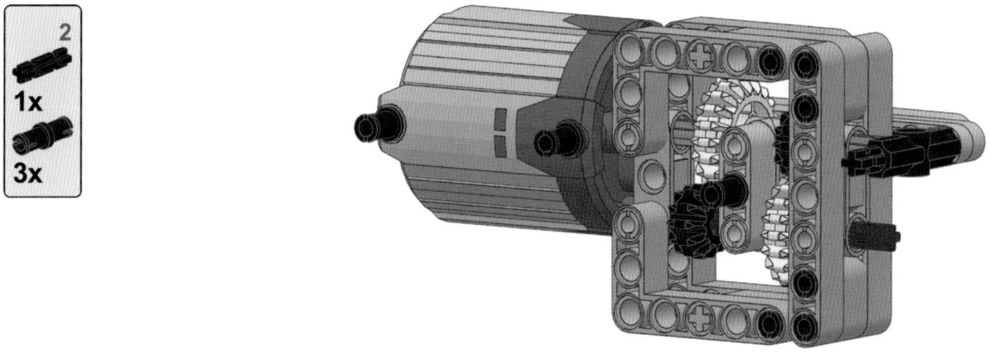

2

1x

3x

12

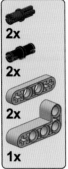

2x

2x

2x

1x

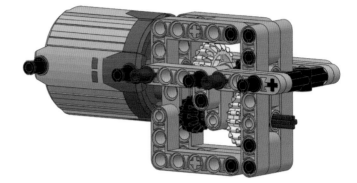

13

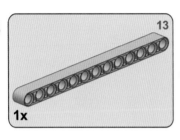

13

1x

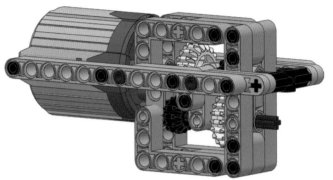

a 2-speed RC motor transmission

1

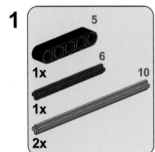

5

1x

6

1x

10

2x

2

1x

2x

1x   2x

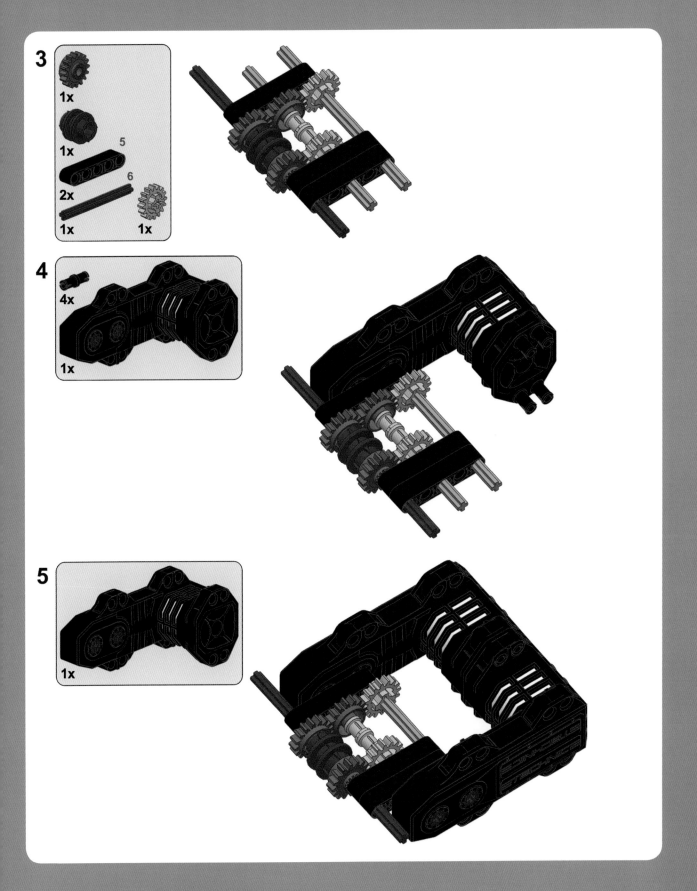

a 2-speed orbital transmission

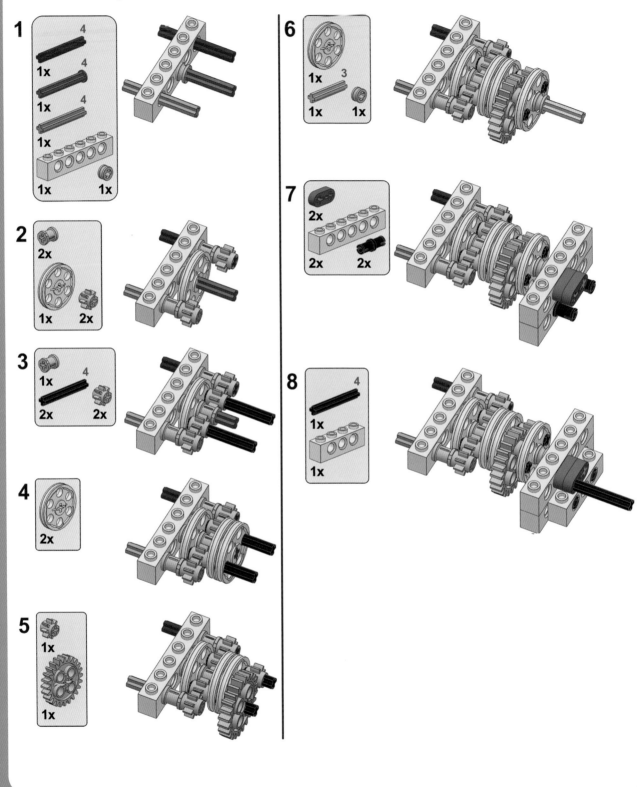

a 2-speed ratchet transmission

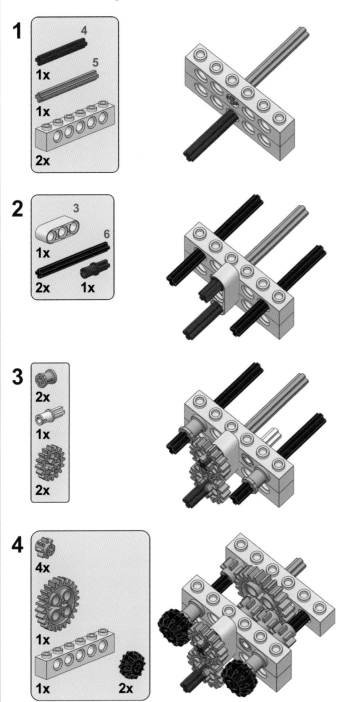

1

4
1x
5
1x
2x

2

3
1x
6
2x   1x

3

2x
1x
2x

4

4x
1x
1x   2x

a 3-speed linear transmission

1

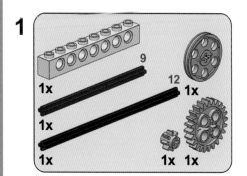

9

12

1x 1x

1x

1x

1x 1x

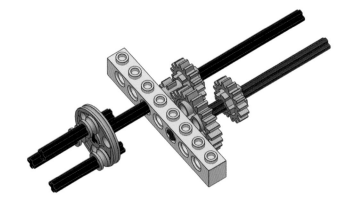

2

3x

2x

4

3x

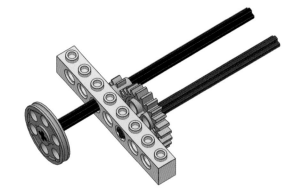

3

3x

1x

4

1x

5

1x 1x

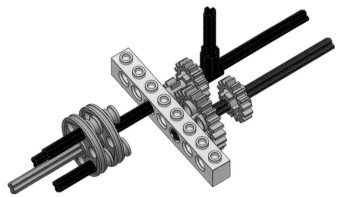

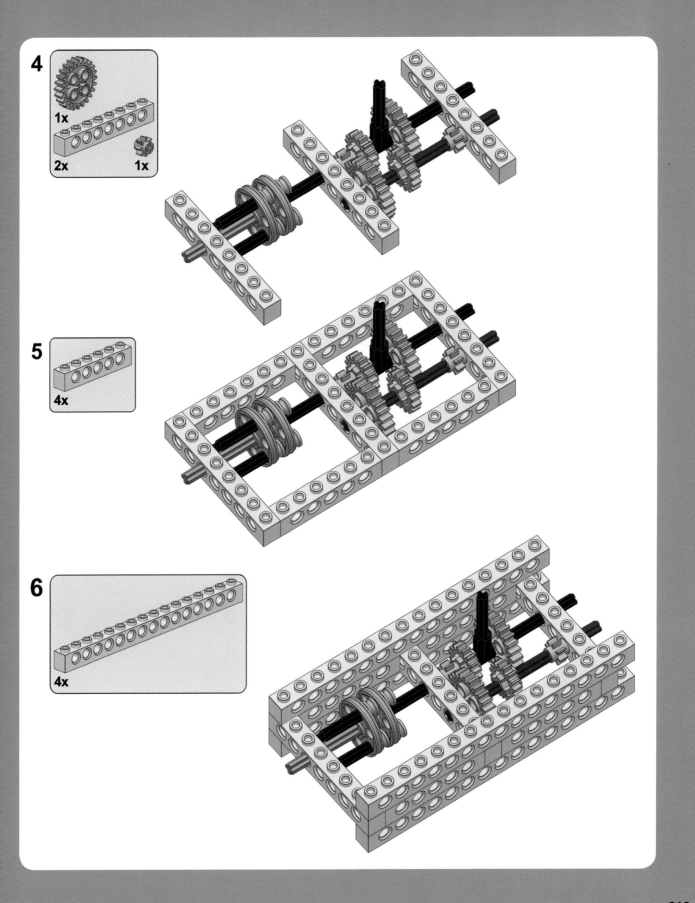

a 4-speed synchronized transmission

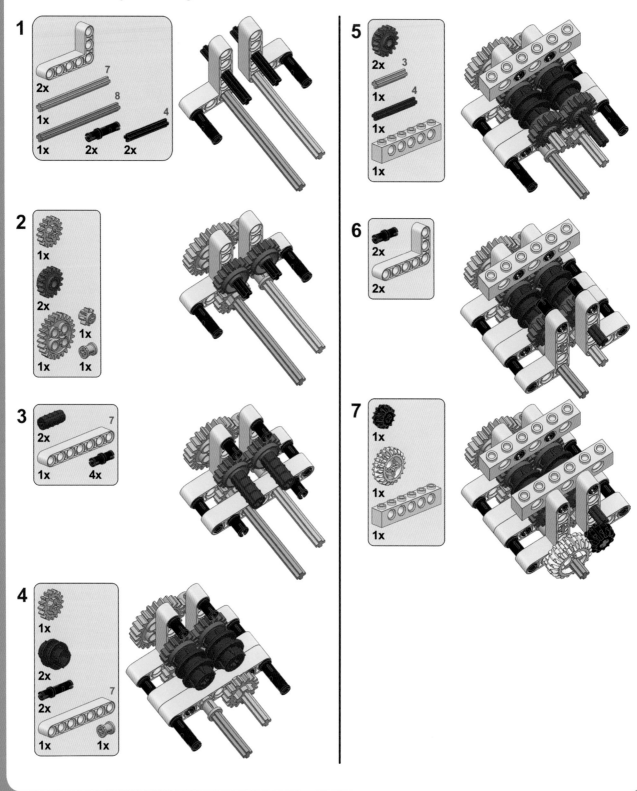

1
7
2x
8
1x
4
1x   2x   2x

2
1x
2x
1x   1x

3
2x   7
1x   4x

4
1x
2x
2x   7
1x   1x

5
2x   3
1x   4
1x
1x

6
2x
2x

7
1x
1x
1x

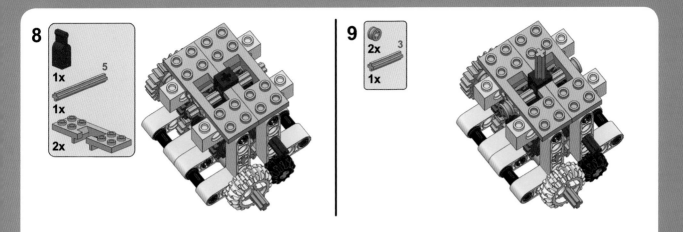

8
1x 5
1x
2x

9
2x 3
1x

a 10-speed synchronized transmission

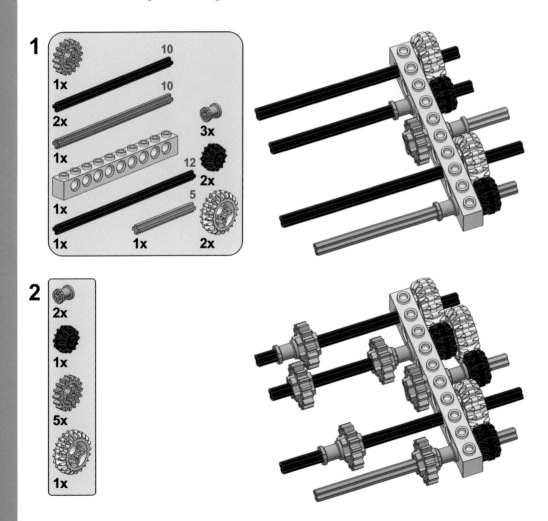

1
1x
10
2x
10
1x
3x
12
2x
1x
5
1x 1x 2x

2
2x
1x
5x
1x

3

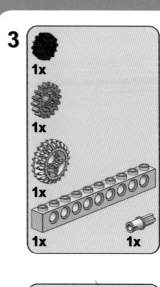

1x
1x
1x
1x 1x

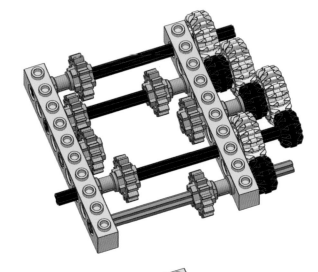

4

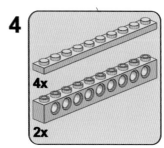

4x
2x

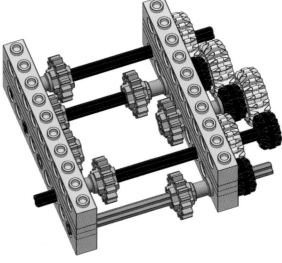

5

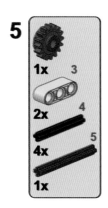

1x 3
2x 4
4x 5
1x

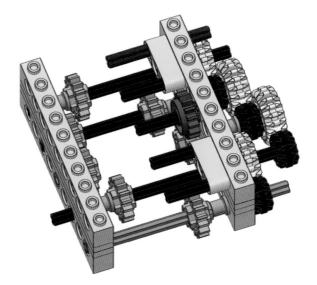

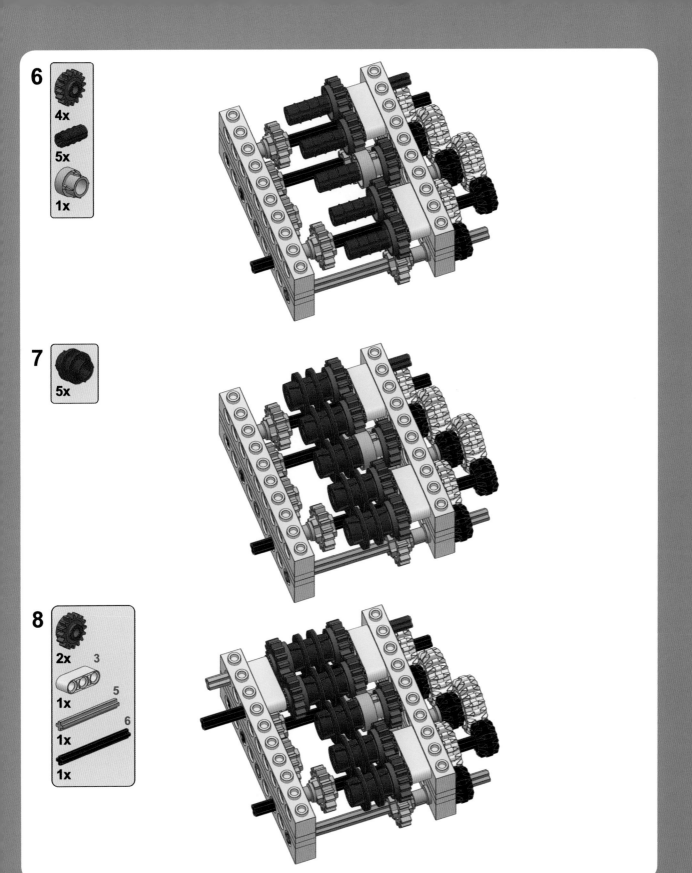

9

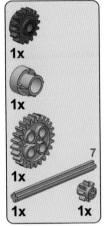

1x

1x

1x
7

1x   1x

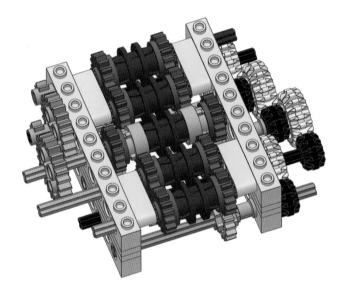

10

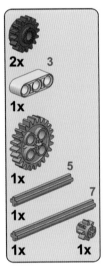

2x   3

1x

1x
5

1x
7

1x   1x

11

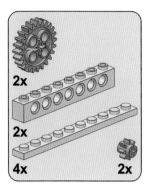

2x
2x
4x   2x

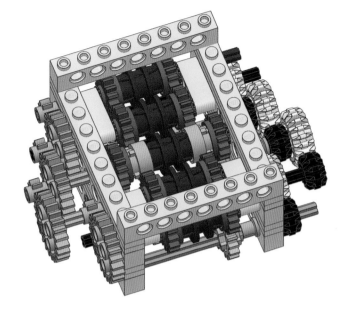

12

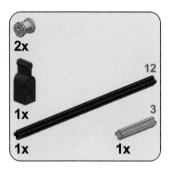

2x
12
1x   3
1x   1x

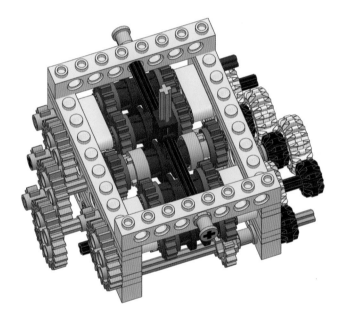

a continuously variable transmission

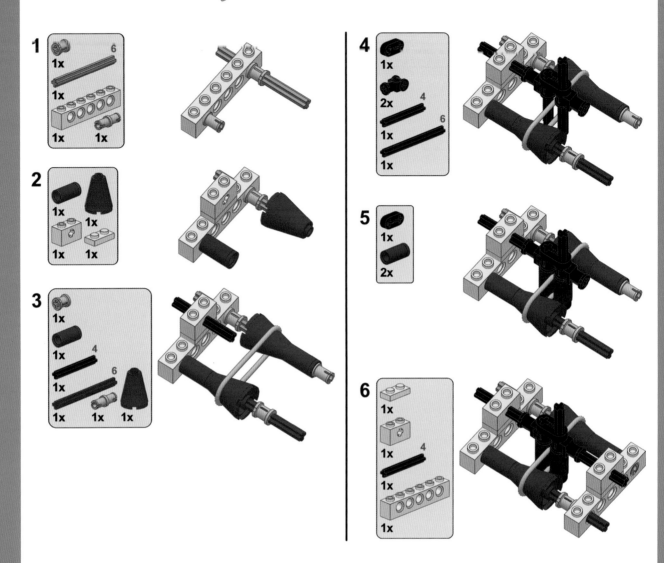

adders and subtractors

Adders and subtractors are mechanisms used to couple two or more motors together. Coupled motors are usually used to control a single function, most often the propulsion of a vehicle. They can work together (in an adder) or against each other (in a subtractor). Both mechanisms make use of differentials, and both are examples of advanced mechanics. The way subtractors work is particularly fascinating.

You'll find that using adders is a great way to give your motor even more power. Subtractors will be most useful when building tanks and construction vehicles, as these mechanisms have two outputs perfectly suited for controlling two treads.

hard-coupling

But first, let's consider a simpler solution to coupling motors, one that forces two motors to run at the same speed. Making such a connection is called *hard-coupling* (see Figure 18-1).

Figure 18-1: Two hard-coupled motors with a single output, shown in red

Forcibly slowing or speeding up a motor can be harmful and may permanently degrade its performance. Still, hard-coupling isn't that different from a LEGO motor's regular use, where motors are slowed down by a load or sped up by a vehicle rolling downhill. Hard-coupling two or more motors of the same type is a fairly low-risk solution for increasing your model's power. But what if we want to couple motors of different types or if we find hard-coupling too risky? This is where adders come in.

NOTE The performance of identical electric motors can vary, making their speeds differ by a few percent. This is because every motor includes moving parts that are prone to wear, and the precision of the motors' production process can vary between batches.

coupling motors with adders

Adders couple two motors to work as one; in doing so, adders sum the motors' individual torques. As a result of this coupling, the output will be the average of the two motors' rotational speeds. This means that we can use two coupled PF Medium motors in cases where one Medium motor is too weak and an XL motor is too large.

summing torque with an adder

An adder makes use of a differential in order to equalize the differences between two or more inputs and to drive a single output. A differential has three elements that can be used as inputs or outputs: the two axles that come out of it and the case of the differential itself, as shown in Figure 18-2.

Figure 18-2: A differential that includes two axles (green and blue) and the differential case (red)

A differential consists of a housing with three bevel gears inside, two of which are set on two axles that enter it from opposite sides. The third gear is connected to the housing only. The first two gears are called *spider gears* or *side gears*, and the gear fixed to the housing is called a *planet gear*.

When a differential is used to couple motors, any difference between inputs will be equalized by the system of the differential's inner gears. The output will be driven by the sum of the inputs' torques and the average of their speeds. Figures 18-3 through 18-6 show some examples of two motors coupled with an adder in various ways. The biggest distinction among these variations is the use of different differentials. The motors' inputs are blue and green, and the adder's output is red.

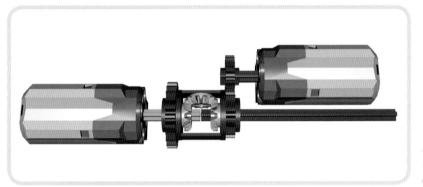

Figure 18-3: Two PF Medium motors are driving the differential case (blue) and one of the axles (green). The other axle (red) is the output.

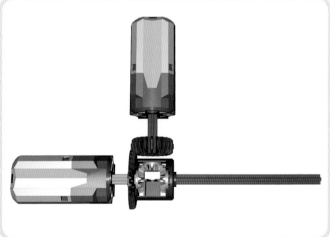

Figure 18-4: The same setup as in Figure 18-3 but with the motors placed side by side

Figure 18-5: An adder using the latest differential variant

Figure 18-6: An adder using the oldest differential variant

NOTE When using adders, always try to have similar gear ratios between the motors and the adder. Differences in gear ratios will make the motors share the load unevenly, with one motor working harder than the other. The gear ratio immediately after the adder (that is, between the adder and the mechanism it drives) does not affect the load distribution.

You already know that an adder sums the torques of its inputs and averages their speeds, but let's express these relationships mathematically. If we have one motor, $motor_1$, and another motor, $motor_2$, then the adder's *torque* is equal to

$$torque(motor_1) + torque(motor_2)$$

and if *n* is the total number of motors, the adder's *speed* is equal to

$$\frac{speed(motor_1) + speed(motor_2)... + speed(motor_n)}{n}$$

One important consideration when building adders is the direction each input rotates. Coupled motors are usually powered from the same source, resulting in an identical direction of rotation. But depending on whether the inputs' directions match, the two motors can work together or against each other. The latter case is obviously undesirable, as it results in decreased torque and speed.

All the examples shown above have motors running in the same direction; however, in some cases, it's convenient to have the motors oriented so that they run in opposite directions. For the adder to work properly in such a case,

we need to reverse the direction of one motor, either by powering it from a power source with the opposite polarity or by connecting it to a shared power source through a switch (shown in Figure 18-7). With older 9V motors, you can reverse the polarity of a motor by simply rotating its wire connector 90 degrees.

Figure 18-8 shows two examples of adders that need one of their motors reversed.

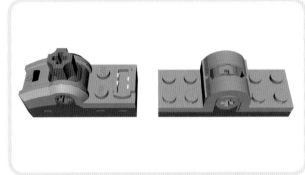

Figure 18-7: A Power Functions switch (left) and a 9V system switch (right)

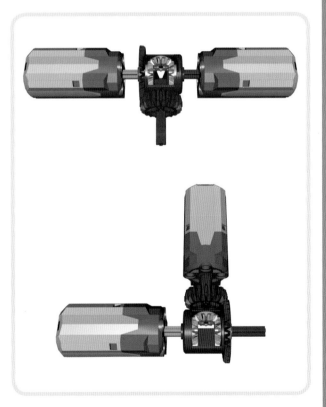

Figure 18-8: These two adders won't work properly unless we change one motor's rotational direction.

adding more than two motors

In most cases, coupling two motors will give us enough torque, but what if we want even more torque? We can use an adder to couple more than two motors, but unfortunately the mechanism's size and complexity will increase dramatically since every motor beyond two requires one more differential (see Figure 18-9).

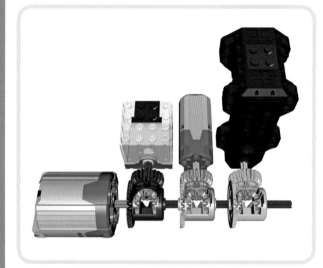

Figure 18-9: It takes three differentials to couple four motors in this chain of adders.

Each differential other than the first one has one input already taken, as it's connected to the previous differential (the second differential is connected to the first one, the third to the second one, and so on). Thus, we are left with only one free input, and we can add only one motor for each differential. Unfortunately, the resulting high torque makes chaining adders in this way fairly risky.

When more than two motors need to be coupled, it's usually a better choice to use motors of the same type and hard-couple them. This is true not only because it takes less space but also because with more motors, there is more torque to transfer, and differentials are not fit for handling high torque. Hard-coupling with knobs (shown in Figure 18-10) is a reasonable alternative.

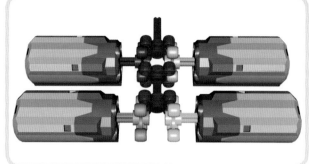

Figure 18-10: These four motors are hard-coupled with knobs, making them more torque resistant than differentials.

subtractors

Subtractors combine the power of two motors in a more complex way. Each subtractor has two inputs and two outputs and also uses two differentials. Rotating one input of a subtractor makes both outputs rotate in the same direction; rotating the other input makes the outputs rotate in opposite directions. Both inputs can be rotated at once, making the outputs rotate at different speeds.

It's easier to understand how a subtractor works when thinking of its most common use: driving tracked vehicles. A typical tracked vehicle has two tracks: left and right, as shown in Figure 18-11. When both tracks rotate in the same direction, the vehicle moves forward or backward along a straight line. When the tracks rotate in opposite directions, the vehicle turns in place. When the tracks rotate at different speeds, the vehicle makes a wide turn, as a car would, and the greater the difference between motor speeds, the tighter the turn.

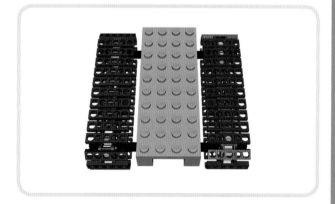

Figure 18-11: A simple tracked vehicle

With tracked vehicles, we can assume that one of the subtractor's input motors is for driving and the other is for turning. Let's call them *D* and *T*, respectively, and note that *D* is usually faster than *T*. If only *D* is running, both tracks (that is, both *outputs*) rotate in the same direction, making the vehicle drive straight. If only *T* is rotating, both tracks rotate in opposite directions, making the vehicle turn in place. Now, an interesting thing happens when both *D* and *T* are running at the same time: One track rotates at *D* + *T* speed, and the other at *D* – *T* speed. Depending on how much these speeds differ, each track can rotate very slowly (*D* > *T*), stop completely (*D* = *T*), or rotate in the opposite direction (*D* < *T*). Figure 18-12 shows how *D* and *T* affect the motion of a vehicle.

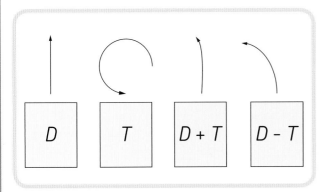

Figure 18-12: The path of a tracked vehicle with subtractors' inputs being driven. D represents the driving motor (faster), and T represents the turning motor (slower).

By adjusting our inputs' speeds, we can achieve any combination of the tracks' speeds: Each track can be stopped or can rotate forward or backward at a speed ranging from almost zero to the sum of the speeds of both inputs.

Note that the relationship between the motors' maximum speeds affects the way the subtractor works. As an example, let's imagine we have a vehicle driving straight at full speed and we start turning at full speed. There are three possibilities:

* If the speed of *D* is *greater* than that of *T*, neither track will be stopped or reversed; one track will slow down, and the other will accelerate. The vehicle will start turning along an arc while continuing to drive in the same direction.
* If the speed of *D* is *equal* to that of *T*, one track will stop, and the other will accelerate; the vehicle will start turning almost in place, with the stopped track being the center of the turn.

* If the speed of *D* is *less* than that of *T*, one track will be reversed, and the other will accelerate; the vehicle will start turning almost in place, with the center of the turn located between the tracks at a point proportional to their speeds (closer to the slower track, farther from the faster one).

The difference between the maximum speeds of *D* and *T* is a crucial consideration when selecting motors and gear ratios to drive the subtractor. Usually, the first of the three cases listed above (with the faster drive motor and the slower steering motor) is the most realistic and convenient case: A vehicle that goes straight faster than it turns is easy to control and behaves real tracked vehicles do.

Also, the turning input's speed is very important when a vehicle is turning in place. The tracks rotate in different directions, so the difference between the two tracks' speeds is equal to twice the turning input's speed. Applying too much turning speed will make our vehicle look like a carousel rather than, say, a tank. Additionally, turning in place involves significant friction, as the tracks scrub the ground over a large area. Therefore, it's a good idea to use gear reduction on the turning input, sacrificing speed for torque.

why use a subtractor?

As you might imagine, a tracked vehicle can be driven with two separate motors as well: one motor driving the left track and the other driving the right track. Using a subtractor takes two motors, too, but has several advantages:

better control   A vehicle with a subtractor can drive in a perfectly straight line, while a vehicle with two separate motors is sensitive to differences between the motors' speeds and to its own weight distribution, which can weigh down the motors unevenly.

lower power consumption   In a subtractor, one motor is for driving, and the other is for turning; therefore, we can use two different types of motors together. Driving, tracks separately, on the other hand, requires two identical motors, and two strong motors have a higher total power consumption than one strong motor and one weak one.

more mechanisms   Connecting another mechanism (a replica piston engine or a rotating fan in the engine bay, for example) to the drivetrain is easy with a subtractor, as it has one motor used specifically to drive. When two separate motors are used, connecting a mechanism to both of them is impossible, and connecting a second function to one motor can slow it down, resulting in a mismatch in speed.

better remote control Without a subtractor, you need the Power Functions remote with speed control dials to make the vehicle turn in an arc. The regular Power Functions remote will only be able to make the vehicle drive straight or turn in place.

The advantages of a subtractor are somewhat diminished if you have the Power Functions remote control with speed dials, which enables a driver to control the speed of each track independently. There are also some disadvantages to subtractors that should be taken into account at all times. First, a subtractor is relatively large and complex, requires plenty of parts, and adds to the vehicle's weight. Second, a subtractor relies on differentials, which can be damaged by high torque. My experience shows that using a subtractor to drive a vehicle heavier than 3 kg involves a serious risk of breaking the bevel gears inside the differentials, regardless of the gear ratio between the subtractor and the sprocket wheels. The other disadvantage to subtractors is that they don't give you the power benefit of having two drive motors.

longitudinal subtractor

A longitudinal subtractor's elongated, narrow shape makes it a good choice for tracked vehicles that have long, narrow hulls between their tracks. Figure 18-13 shows the driving input (D) in blue, the steering input (T) in green, the outputs in red, and the sprocket wheels driving the tracks in yellow.

Notice that each motor drives both differentials at once. The PF XL motor drives with a 1:1 gear ratio. The PF Medium motor turns with a 9:1 gear ratio. That ratio makes the turning input's speed slower than the driving input's speed, even though the Medium motor's rotational speed is faster than the XL's. The driving input rotates at 146 rpm (the normal speed of the XL motor), and the turning input rotates at 30.6 RPM (that is, the speed of the Medium motor reduced by a factor of 9).

Obviously, a subtractor can work with different combinations of motors and gear ratios; the one shown here exemplifies this and is the most efficient combination for most uses. If you use the right gear ratio at the sprocket

Figure 18-13: A longitudinal subtractor

wheel, you can easily use a single XL motor to drive a 2 kg vehicle. However, a vehicle's efficiency at heavier weights depends greatly on the type of surface the model is driving on. To achieve more power for heavier vehicles, you can connect more than a single motor to the driving input, for example, by using an adder.

The following are instructions for building this subtractor inside a studfull structure. Note that many details can be changed as needed, including the types and number of motors and the gear ratio of the inputs and outputs. You'll want to replace the bevel gears on the outputs with knobs if you're building a heavy vehicle.

a longitudinal subtractor

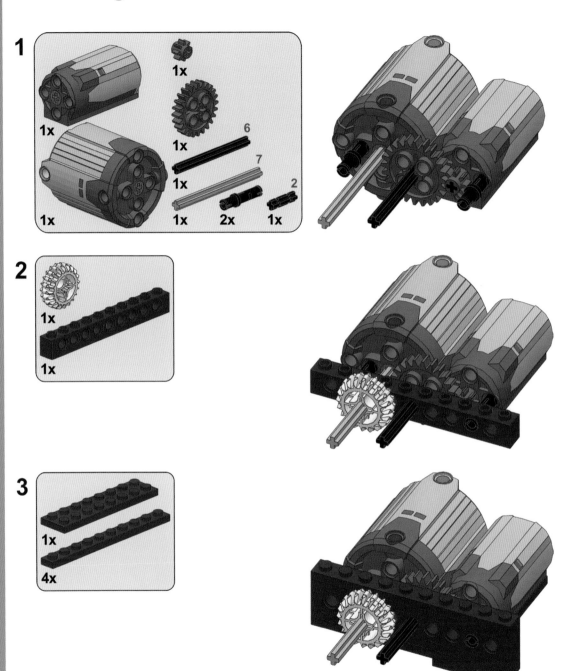

1

1x
1x
1x

1x
1x
1x   2x   1x

6
7
2

2

1x
1x

3

1x
4x

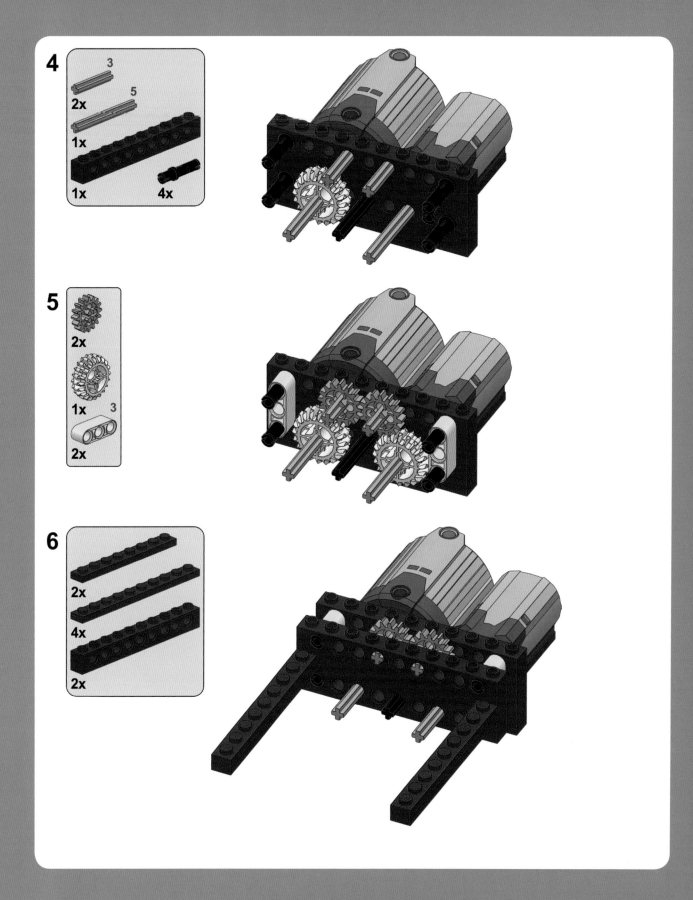

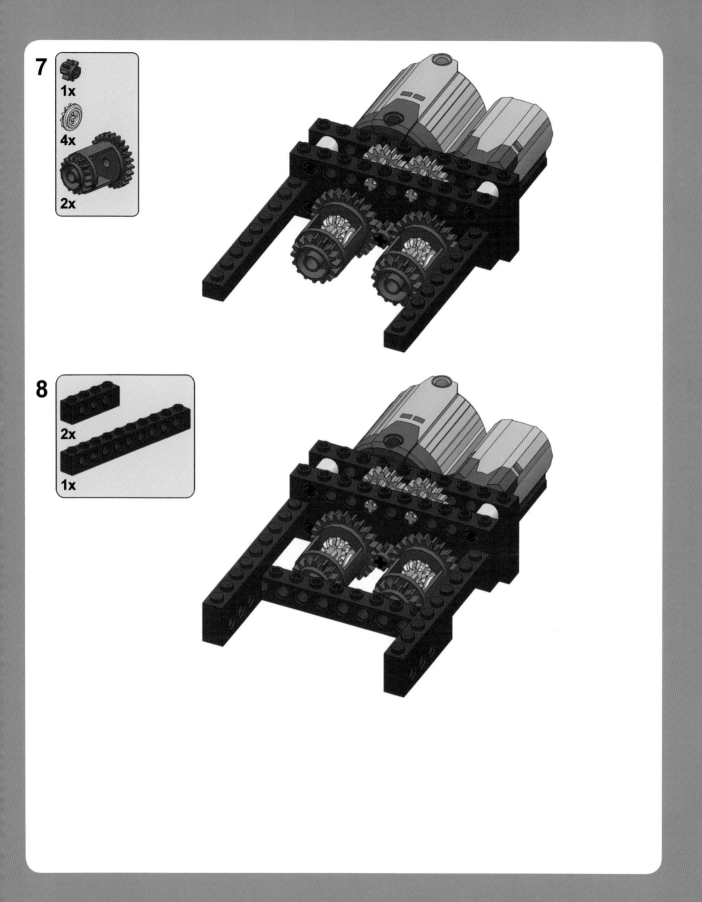

9

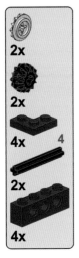

2x
2x
4x   4
2x
4x

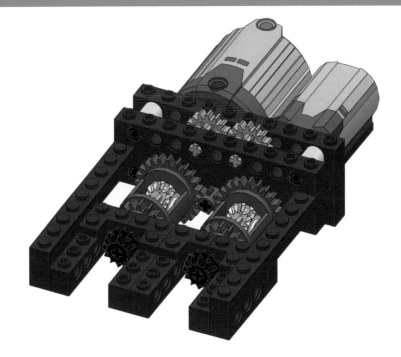

10

2x   7
2x
1x

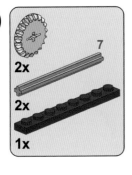

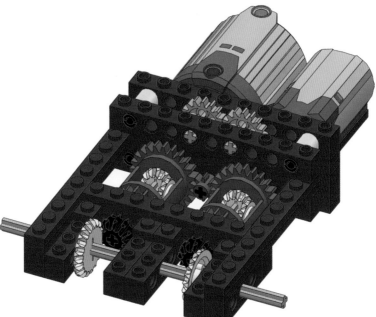

11

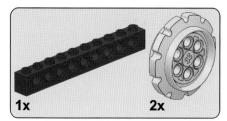

1x   2x

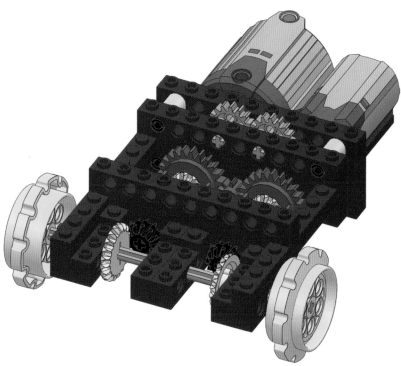

transverse subtractor

This subtractor is smaller and a little less complex than the longitudinal one. Figure 18-14 shows an example of this subtractor with two outputs (shown in red), the driving input (blue), and the turning input (green). Note that we can use the outputs coming from the other differential just as well, and it will work, but the inputs' roles will be swapped: The turning input will become the driving input, and the driving input will become the turning input.

The transverse subtractor differs from the longitudinal version in several ways. Each motor drives a single differential, and two sets of gears connect the two differentials. One set has an even number of gears, and the other an odd number. The important thing is that both sets have a 1:1 ratio. Therefore, when using this subtractor with two different motors, it's crucial to make sure that the stronger motor doesn't drive the weaker one—a gear reduction at the weaker motor should prevent this.

This configuration offers more room for experimentation than the longitudinal subtractor does. For instance, we can relocate the motors if we drive the differentials with worm gears, preventing the problem of one motor driving another, as shown in Figure 18-15.

Finally, it is possible to build a fully studless variant of this subtractor using the new 28-tooth differentials (see Figure 18-16). It looks very different, but it works just the same.

Figure 18-14: A transverse subtractor

Figure 18-15: A transverse subtractor with worm gears

Figure 18-16: A transverse subtractor with the latest differential variants

a transverse subtractor

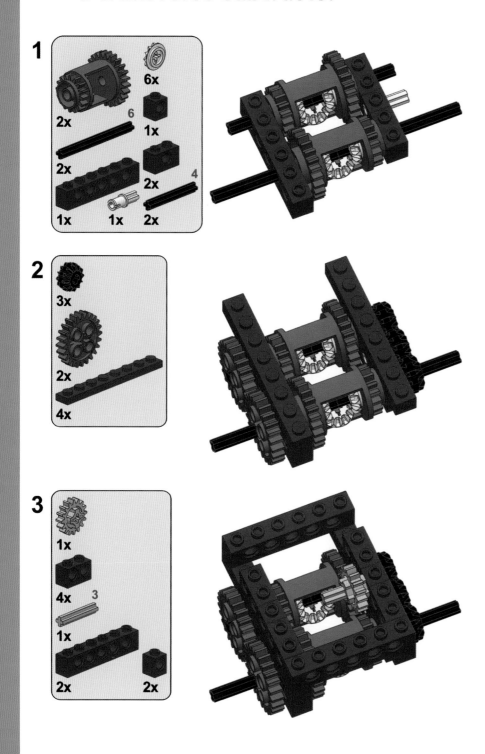

1
2x
6
2x
1x
2x
1x 1x
6x
1x
2x
4
2x

2
3x
2x
4x

3
1x
4x 3
1x
2x 2x

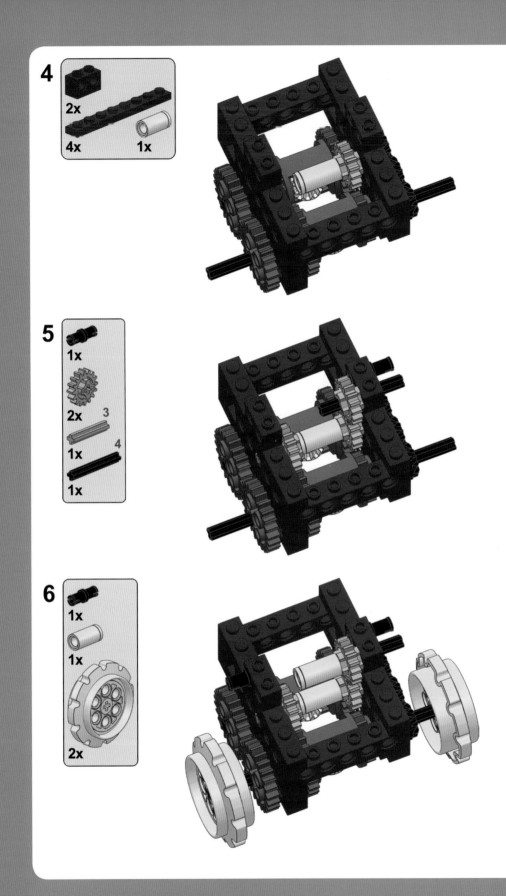

4

2x
4x
1x

5

1x
2x   3
1x   4
1x

6

1x
1x
2x

7

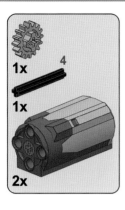

1x 4
1x
2x

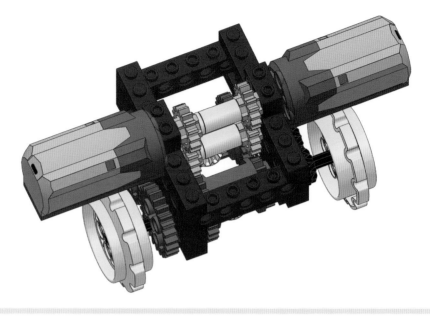

a studless transverse subtractor

1

8x
4x
2x

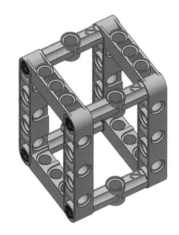

2

6x 4
2x
2x 6
2x

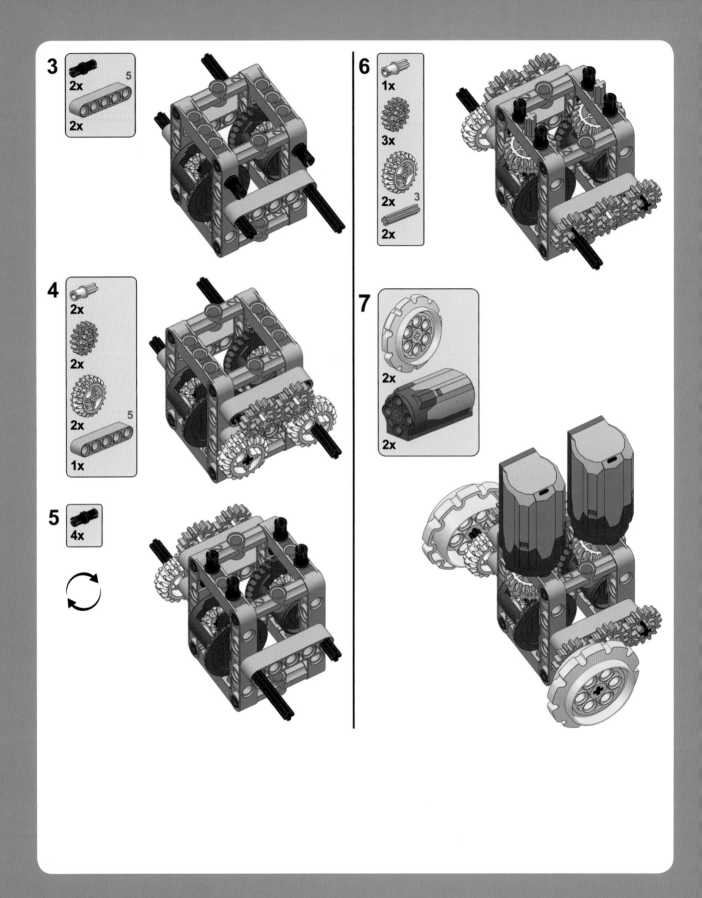

PART V

models

form vs. function

Builders are usually inspired to create their own models for two reasons: the desire to model a *real-life object* (like a favorite car or truck) or the desire to model a *real-life mechanism* or *function* (for example, a 4×4 drive or a pneumatic system). If you're inspired by mechanisms, just look for models that could include one. When you decide to build a model, you'll want to start by asking yourself three questions:

1. Can I make it work well?

2. Can I make it look good?

3. Can I find sufficient reference material to accurately model this object?

Finding a balance between the aesthetics and functionality of the model is an extremely sensitive task, and it often helps to decide which is more important to you before you start building. As you build and rebuild your models, you'll likely reexamine your priorities. It's best to accept one of two options before you even start building: *I can compromise the look in favor of functionality*, or *I can compromise functionality in favor of the look*.

Looking at the silhouette of the object you want to model may also help in the early stages. Bear in mind that most LEGO pieces fit well within straight lines, right angles, and rectangular shapes. This makes trucks much easier to build than motorbikes, for example. You can, of course, use flexible axles and Technic panels to model curved, flowing shapes, but the resulting aesthetic is generally poorly received outside the Technic community and sometimes within it, as well.

cars

Your typical car is challenging to model because of the limited space it provides for electric and mechanical components (see Figure 19-1). Big elements, such as power supplies, IR receivers, and motors, are difficult to incorporate into a car.

Figure 19-1: My 1969 Dodge Charger model appears to have a massive hood with plenty of space beneath it. However, since I decided to model the car's huge engine, almost none of this space was available for mechanical components, and I was barely able to fit a mechanism to lift the distinctive grille that reveals the car's headlamps. Most of the electric components ended up in the trunk.

In most cases, the only spaces available for those elements are the cabin floor, the central space between the seats, the trunk, and the space normally taken by the engine (if you choose not to include a replica of the engine in your MOC). You can also build a motor-free model, with all the functions activated manually, in the spirit of many LEGO sets.

Space constraints become even more challenging with sports cars, which are slung low to the ground and often have open tops, exposing any mechanism installed in the cabin. Cars of this type often use wide tires and independent suspensions, which can result in width issues if you decide to include both in your model. Finally, as sports cars' engines are particularly huge, choosing between a front-engine and central-engine car greatly affects the amount of space available in the front and in the rear, as well as the silhouette of the model. Figure 19-2 shows an extreme example of this, comparing a front-engine Dodge Viper and a rear-engine Pagani Zonda. Note how the silhouettes of the cars differ—the Viper's cabin is moved far back, adjacent to the rear wheels, while the Zonda's cabin starts just behind the front wheels. Both cars, although similar in many respects, offer different challenges and opportunities to a model builder.

Off-road cars, such as SUVs, have taller silhouettes and offer more space, especially in the chassis, but they also have more complex and space-consuming drivetrains and suspension systems. Their engines are usually under the hood, as in the Jeep Wrangler Rubicon shown in Figure 19-3. And many SUVs have hard-top bodies, making it possible to use some of the cabin's internal space (but also making the car more top-heavy).

Finally, there are cars such as buggies and truggies, whose bodies are built primarily with pipes and whose internal elements are exposed, as shown in Figure 19-4. There are many ways to install elements of the Power Functions system, such as motors and battery boxes, in these cars so as to mimic the original cars' fuel tanks and other parts.

trucks

Trucks have many qualities that make them easy to model, and they are one of the favorite themes of model builders. They are technically simple to build, and they offer plenty of space for internal components and many possibilities for experimenting with aesthetics. They are also often large enough to conceal even very complex mechanisms—for example, my tow truck model housed 17 motors.

Trucks can be divided into two categories with different appearances and different amounts of space available: longnose (or US) trucks and cab-over-engine (or European) trucks. Longnose trucks, which are designed to travel over longer distances, have a hood (or bonnet) with the engine in front of the cabin. They often have a sleeper module behind the cabin—that is, a simple structure adjacent to the cabin, where the driver can sleep or relax (see Figure 19-5). The cab-over-engine variant is generally smaller and more compact with, naturally, a simple cabin over the engine. European-style trucks have no hoods, and the optional resting space for the driver is located inside the rear part of the cabin rather than in a separate body module.

Note that trucks of both categories usually have *air deflectors* on top of the cabin. In longnose trucks, however,

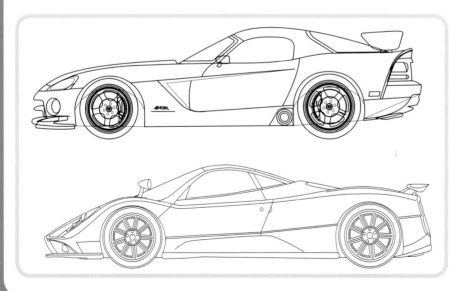

Figure 19-2: The Dodge Viper (top) and Pagani Zonda (bottom) are two sports cars with different engine locations.

Figure 19-3: My model of the Jeep Wrangler Rubicon, which is a small open-top car, had motors under the hood and the battery and IR receiver in the trunk. This way it had a good weight distribution and plenty of space left for some decorative elements in the cabin interior, including seats and the steering wheel.

Figure 19-4: LEGO 8296 set features a simple dune buggy with a typical pipebuilt body.

the sleeper modules may have their own extensive air deflectors that direct the air flow between the cabin and the trailer. With cab-over-engine trucks, the deflectors appear only on the cabin and may be quite tall to compensate for the difference in height between the cabin and the trailer, as shown in Figure 19-6.

Longnose trucks definitely have more advantages for model builders: They offer more internal space, especially with the addition of a sleeper module, and there are more ways to experiment with their aesthetics. Note that in the trucks with no hood—longnose and cab-over-engine alike—the engine is accessed by lifting up the cabin, which tilts

Figure 19-5: The longnose Peterbilt truck, shown without the sleeper module (top) and with sleeper module (bottom). The air deflector is marked with orange.

Figure 19-6: Three cabin variants of the same European MAN TGS truck (from left to right): with tall airfoil and resting space, with low airfoil and resting space, with low airfoil and no resting space

forward. This is difficult to include in a model, and engines are often omitted completely from the models of cab-over-engine trucks, especially since engines use space that is best suited for the steering system. Trucks with hoods, on the other hand, can have working hoods with replicas of the engine beneath, and this still leaves plenty of space below the cabin for steering mechanisms. As Figure 19-7 shows, the space under the hood can be used to create a fairly complex engine replica, as well as to house some electric components.

Figure 19-7: The hood of my tow truck model housed a replica of the original Caterpillar engine and a Power Functions battery, located between the engine and the front of the cabin. The red connector piece adjacent to the engine functioned as the model's master power switch.

Figure 19-8: The LEGO 8422 set features a typical motorcycle with a suspension system and a piston engine connected to the real wheel. Note that even though the model uses one of the largest LEGO wheels in existence, it's still rather small.

motorcycles

Motorcycles, like the one shown in Figure 19-8, are very challenging to model for a number of reasons—the most important one being the fact that they have only two wheels. In order to stand on its own, a model requires at least three wheels (or wide, flat tires). To enable a motorcycle model to stand on its own, we can add a small, unobtrusive wheel or a full sidecar. Sidecars have the advantage of offering plenty of internal space near the bike's rear wheel, so they can be used to house a propulsion motor. Another alternative is to build a trike or a quad, which is something like a four-wheeled bike.

Other difficulties you may encounter while building bikes include motorizing the steering system, the limited variety and size of matching LEGO wheels, and the overall small size and exposed body, which make it difficult to install any large electric components. All in all, motorcycles are aesthetically interesting models to build but difficult ones to motorize. Among the LEGO sets, as well as among MOCs, most motorcycles have only basic functions, such as a suspension system and drivetrain with a replica of an engine, while motorized models are a rarity. For an example of a motorized model, see Figure 19-9.

tracked vehicles

Tracked vehicles are a diverse group, but they are almost always fairly easy to model. First of all, the use of the tracks eliminates the need for any complex steering system (unless we decide to use a subtractor). Secondly, the suspension system is located either on the sides or on the bottom of the hull, taking little or no space inside the model, as shown in Figure 19-10. In fact, the hull of most tracked vehicles is a simple box with tracks on its sides and plenty of space inside, and it also functions as a body frame.

Tanks have large hulls whose space can be arranged in several ways. After building plenty of tank models, I have developed a reliable arrangement: The propulsion motors go in the lower-rear part of the hull, with IR receivers on top of them. For modern tanks with large turrets, the receivers have to be moved to the very rear end of the hull to avoid being blotted out. The central part of the hull can house the power supply with the turret rotation mechanism on top of it. The front part can be used for the power supply as well, but not for the IR receivers, as the models are typically controlled from behind. The turret itself can house the gun control

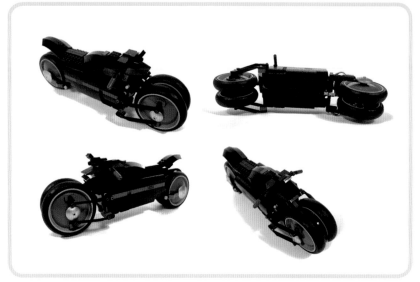

Figure 19-9: The Dodge Tomahawk concept motorcycle comes with double front and rear wheels, thus providing four fulcrums rather than two. I built a motorized model of this bike to prove that it could be motorized and drive stably; however, it couldn't turn because it was too small to house a steering system and a propulsion system at the same time.

Figure 19-10: The Swedish Hagglunds BV 206 personnel carrier consisted of two parts connected by an articulated joint. This very tiny model housed one steering and two propulsion motors, a battery and an IR receiver, while its simple suspension was located entirely within the tracks.

mechanism, but it's also a good, well-exposed place for the IR receivers if it's tall enough to house them. See examples of tanks I have modeled in Figures 19-11 and 19-12.

You might also want to model half-track vehicles, which have regular steered front wheels and tracks replacing the rear wheels, as shown in Figure 19-13. This rare combination is used almost exclusively in military vehicles, such as trucks and armored personnel carriers. Most of the vehicle, including the cabin, the front axle, and the engine bay, needs no alteration from a wheeled version, while the tracks need no steering system, as steering is provided by the front wheels. Some of the heaviest historical half-tracks, however, included a braking system that slowed one of the tracks while turning to improve handling of the vehicle.

Figure 19-11: My T-72M tank model was small and low, with an angled glacis plate that left very little space in the front of the hull. The very front of the hull housed only some wires, and the glacis plate was removed to access the battery.

Figure 19-12: My model of the Leopard 2A4 tank was large and heavy. I used four XL motors for propulsion, powered from two battery boxes located in the middle of the hull. It wasn't fast, but it had plenty of torque and handled obstacles extremely well for its weight.

Figure 19-13: My model of a half-track truck. Vehicles of this type are driven by tracks and steered by front wheels.

aircraft

Modeling aircraft offers plenty of intriguing possibilities and challenges. Such vehicles can be motorized to have rotating propellers or turbines. They can also have working ailerons, elevators, and rudders, as well as retractable gears and flashing position lights. But LEGO aircraft can't fly.

NOTE Building a 100 percent LEGO plane or helicopter capable of flying is physically impossible because of the weight of LEGO pieces and the limited power of LEGO motors. Additionally, an aircraft built exclusively with LEGO pieces would have difficulties with balance and with achieving an aerodynamic profile.

Any aircraft you model can be made even more impressive when installed on a boom that can lift it up and move it around, imitating free flight. The LEGO 8485 set includes such a model, shown in Figure 19-14.

planes

One of the main challenges involved in building a model of a plane is the shape of its hull. A plane hull's cross section is more or less circular. You can model it with studfull pieces using curved slopes, or you can just mark some edges of the hull with flexible axles. The wings and tail can be modeled with slopes, plates, and tiles, or with axles or even bricks and beams if you mark only the edges, as Figure 19-15 shows.

Minifigure-scale planes can use the ready-made tails, noses, and hull sections that can be found in regular LEGO sets.

Your model can also take advantage of one of the large number of ready-made LEGO propellers, shown in Figure 19-16. These propellers can work in air as well as in water, and when motorized, some of them can generate thrust that is noticeable, though still insufficient for flying.

With jet engines, it's relatively easy to create mock-ups of turbines that can rotate. Figure 19-17 shows a simple example of a mock-up built around a 4-stud-long bar. You can also use LEGO LEDs with translucent red or translucent orange pieces to illuminate the engine's nozzle. Installing a small LEGO propeller inside a duct with a round cross section can generate more thrust than when the same propeller works outside the duct.

helicopters

Helicopters are generally easier to model than planes. They have dense hulls, tiny wings or no wings at all, and a single boom with a tail rotor. They offer plenty of internal space and often include more functions than planes do: Some helicopters come with winches to lift loads off the ground, some come with retractable gear, and even the simplest helicopters have large rotating blades that look impressive when motorized.

When it comes to modeling a helicopter, the primary challenges are the windscreen, which has a complex shape in some machines, and the rotors. A typical helicopter comes with a single main rotor with two to six blades and a single

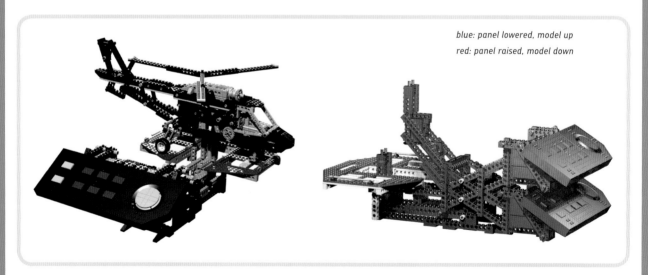

blue: panel lowered, model up
red: panel raised, model down

Figure 19-14: The LEGO 8485 Control Center II set features a large helicopter on a simple boom (left). By manually lowering the control panel (right), which acts as the helicopter's counterbalance on the boom, we can lift the model up and simulate the movement of free flight—for example, the tilting of the hull.

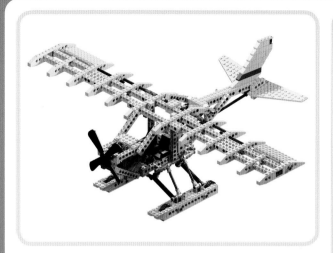

Figure 19-15: The LEGO 8855 Prop Plane set is a fairly typical example of a Technic plane. It has no motors and just basic functions, with parts such as ailerons and elevators controlled by a single yoke.

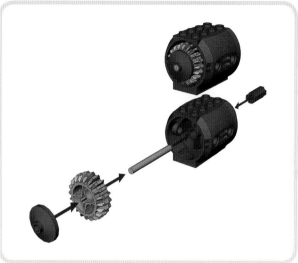

Figure 19-17: One of many ways to build a small mock-up of a turbine engine with just a few LEGO pieces. The axle joiner (blue) allows us to connect the central bar to a regular axle and thus motorize the "turbine."

Figure 19-16: The LEGO ready-made propellers with pin holes (red) and axle holes (yellow), along with the #2952 propeller (blue), which can be used in pairs to create a 1-stud-thick, four-bladed propeller.

tail rotor with two to four blades. Figure 19-18 provides an example of a helicopter with a six-bladed main rotor, which helps the aircraft handle its weight. Some helicopters, such as the Kamov Ka-50 Hokum, come with two main rotors and no tail rotor. The two rotors rotate in opposite directions, and if they are coaxial—which is not always the case, as Figure 19-19 shows—modeling them can be an interesting technical challenge.

The tail rotor is usually located on one side of the tail fin. In some helicopters, however, it is mounted inside an opening in the fin. Such a design, shown in Figure 19-20, is called a *fantail*, and rotors used in it are smaller and have

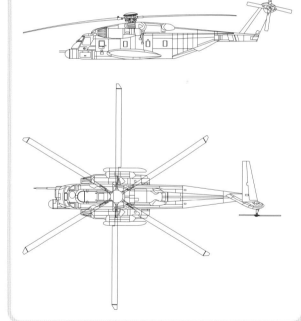

Figure 19-18: The Sikorsky MH-53 Pave Low is a massive military transport helicopter. Its six-bladed main rotor helps to handle its weight, which can reach 21 tons when the chopper fully loaded.

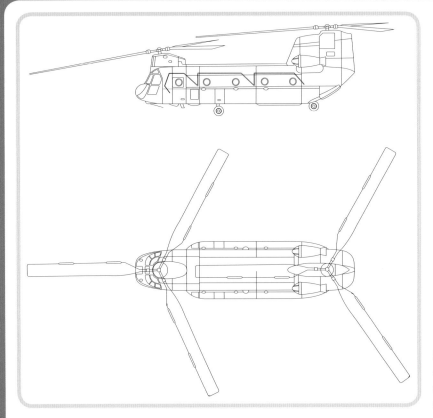

Figure 19-19: The Boeing CH-47 Chinook also comes with two main rotors, located at opposite ends of the hull and at different heights. Such an arrangement is called a tandem.

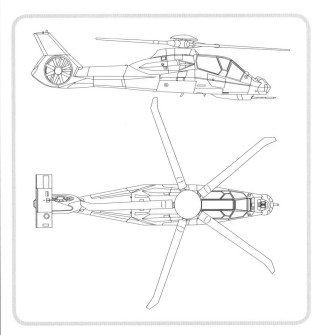

Figure 19-20: The Boeing Sikorsky RAH-66 Comanche was designed to be an advanced reconnaissance and attack helicopter. It used a fantail instead of a typical rear rotor, and the complex shape of its hull resulted from incorporating stealth technologies.

between 8 and 18 blades. It's very difficult to properly model a fantail because there is no easy way to mount and drive a LEGO rotor inside it.

The real main rotor head of any helicopter is an advanced mechanism, allowing adjustments to the pitch of its individual blades or all blades together to weather conditions. This enables the vehicle to perform complex movements, such as flying backward or sideways. A simple mechanical solution allowing the rotor to tilt forward and backward or left and right is shown in Figure 19-21. Tilting the rotor in multiple planes is also possible with the use of towballs and links, as shown in Figure 19-22.

The rotor itself consists of a rotor hub with blades attached around it. The blades can easily be built with plates and tiles or with ready-made pieces from the 9396 Helicopter set, though building the rotor hub to connect these blades can be more difficult. Figures 19-23 to 19-25 show example hubs, with short red plates noting blade placement.

Now that you've seen the possibilities and challenges of different vehicle types, it's up to you to choose what to model. Assuming that you have a model in mind ready to scale, proceed to the next chapter, which explains how to model it accurately.

Figure 19-21: An example of a simple rotor-tilting mechanism. The black axles with a universal joint are the driveshaft, connecting the rotor on the top with a motor on the bottom. Retracting and extending the linear actuator changes the angle of the axle above the joint and thus of the whole rotor.

Figure 19-23: Simple hubs with two to four blades

Figure 19-22: A mechanism for tilting a rotor in two planes. Rotating the green axle tilts the rotor in one plane—for example, forward and backward—while rotating the blue axle tilts the rotor in another plane—for example, left and right. Thanks to the use of links and towballs, both angles of the rotor can be changed simultaneously without interference.

Figure 19-24: A six-bladed hub can be built by doubling the three-bladed version or by simply attaching the blades to a wedge belt wheel with pins so that the centrifugal force of the rotating rotor aligns them.

Figure 19-25: Finally, a hub with any number of blades can be built by attaching 1×1 plates with clips to the edge of a wedge belt wheel. This solution, invented by Polish builder Marcin "Mrutek" Rutkowski, results in a surprisingly robust setup, which can be made even stronger if you attach blades using two wedge belt wheels and two clips. You will, however, need to align the blades by hand, so a protractor may be useful.

20

scaling a model

Scaling is a fairly straightforward process requiring simple multiplication and division. To begin, we need two things: a *blueprint* of the original object and a *point of reference* that will determine the resulting size of our model.

blueprints

A blueprint is a technical drawing that typically includes a front, side, rear, and top view, as Figure 20-1 shows. We'll want to find blueprints whose views show the object at the same scale.

A proper blueprint shows only the important edges of the object, without any filling, shading, colors, or textures. Figure 20-2 shows the same object with and without the central perspective—that is, a "vanishing point." As you can see, perspective can distort the image and thus affect the measurements we take from it.

Where do you find blueprints? The best free source is *http://www.the-blueprints.com/*. If you can't find the blueprint you need there, you can check LEGO MOCs websites, like *http://www.brickshelf.com/* and *http://mocpages.com/*, as some builders publish their MOCs along with the blueprints they used. If you plan to model construction equipment, such as

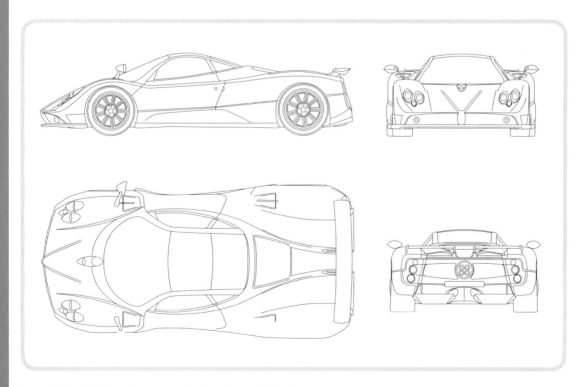

Figure 20-1: A typical blueprint showing the Pagani Zonda C12 F sports car

excavators, dump trucks, and so on, you can check the website of the original machine's manufacturer. Many major manufacturers, such as Caterpillar, JCB, Komatsu, Liebherr, and Volvo, publish product brochures, usually as PDF files, that include a blueprint showing a machine's dimensions in at least two views. Alternatively, you can look for 3-D models—some vehicles are popular with 3-D artists, who often present their work on the Internet in a blueprint-like form. Model-building kits can also be a source of high-quality blueprints, as their instructions often include painting diagrams that look exactly like blueprints. For example, Revell offers many instructions for free (*http://www.revell.com/support/instructions.html*).

As a last resort, you can use photographs in place of a blueprint. The ideal set of photos shows the entire unobstructed vehicle from direct angles, preferably from a distance. The photos should obviously be as large, clean, and bright as possible, and they should be scaled to show the object at the same size from various angles. Figures 20-3 and 20-4 provide examples of unusable and usable photos, respectively.

Figure 20-2: Side view of the same model with central perspective (top) and without central perspective (bottom)

Figure 20-3: These photos can't be used in place of a blueprint. They show the object from mixed angles (for example, rear/side), and they are highly distorted by perspective, as a result of having been taken from a short distance.

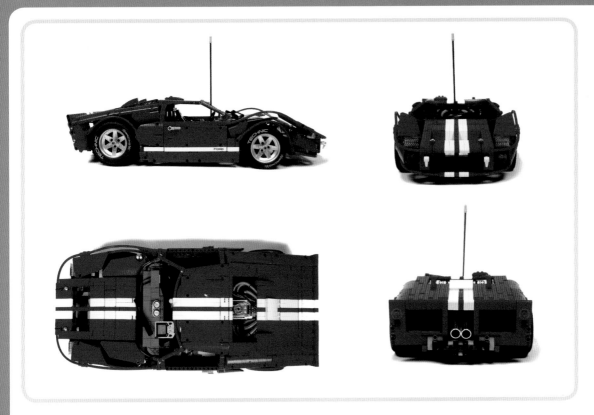

Figure 20-4: These photos are perfectly usable in place of a blueprint. They present the object from direct angles, and they are taken from far enough away that the images are not distorted.

points of reference

A *point of reference* is a constituent part that determines the size of a model. We use it to calculate how much smaller (or larger) than the original object the model has to be. Basically, we need some part in our model whose size can be compared with the size of its real counterpart. For wheeled vehicles, comparing wheels—or, more specifically, the diameter of tires—works best. Because LEGO wheels have a fixed size, we can easily scale the rest of our model to be the appropriate size.

The general rule of thumb for any build is to select the vehicle's most specialized part. Since we can't adjust the size of LEGO wheels, tracks, or propellers, we have to start with them as a reference point and then scale accordingly. Bear in mind other space constraints, like a vehicle's hull dimensions and your model's target functionality, as you work from your point of reference.

For tracked vehicles, we can use the width of the tracks as a reference point. This is an optimal reference point because a poor fit is usually more noticeable when it comes to track width than, for instance, the diameter of the sprocket wheels.

A helicopter model can be scaled using the ready-made LEGO propeller that will be used as the tail rotor. A jet plane model can be scaled using the cylindrical LEGO piece that will be used as the jet engine housing. And a boat can be scaled using a ready-made LEGO hull (these come in many variants, including watertight ones).

scaling

Let's assume we have a good blueprint of the vehicle we want to scale and we have chosen a LEGO wheel as our point of reference. Now we can begin the actual scaling. (Note that the following process works the same way regardless of the part we use as our reference point.)

We will be taking various measurements off the blueprint. We can do that directly in the blueprint file, measuring distances with a program such as GIMP or Windows Paint. When you open the file in Paint, for example, and draw a line, the dimensions of the line (in pixels) will be shown in the lower-right corner of the program window. By holding down the SHIFT key while drawing, you can make sure the line is perfectly horizontal or vertical. The other way to measure the blueprint is to print it out and simply use a ruler. Personally, I prefer this method, as it allows me to add notes to the printout, and it doesn't require using a computer every time I need to measure something. The notes on such a blueprint can become quite elaborate and include a great deal of information, as Figure 20-5 shows.

First, we have to determine the *scaling ratio*—the difference in dimensions between the blueprint and our model—which will allow us to calculate all of our model's target dimensions. We can do this by comparing the size of our point of reference—in this case, a LEGO wheel—with its counterpart on the blueprint.

Let's assume that we want to scale a Dodge Viper using a wheel from the 8448 Super Street Sensation set, which has a diameter of 10 studs. We begin by measuring the diameter of the wheel on a blueprint (indicated by the blue line in Figure 20-6), and the result is 28 mm. Now we divide the diameter of our LEGO wheel by the diameter of the wheel on the blueprint:

$$\frac{10 \text{ studs}}{28 \text{ mm}} = 0.357 \text{ studs/mm}$$

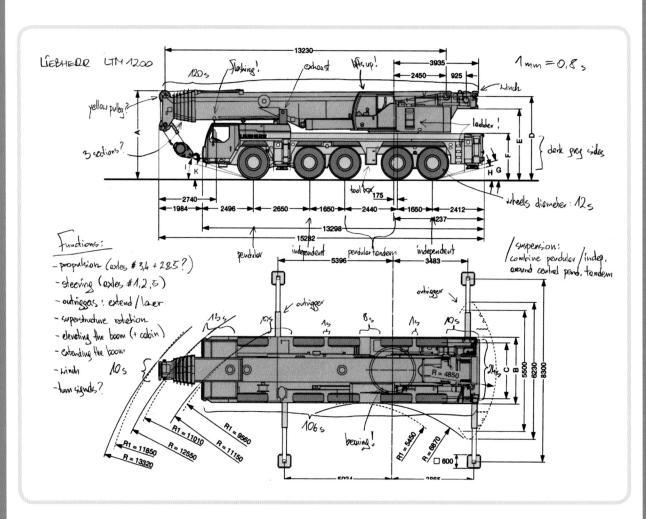

Figure 20-5: A printout of a Liebherr LTM1200 mobile telescopic crane blueprint. All basic dimensions and functions are marked, and the scaling ratio is noted in the upper-right corner. The blueprint comes from the manufacturer's product brochure.

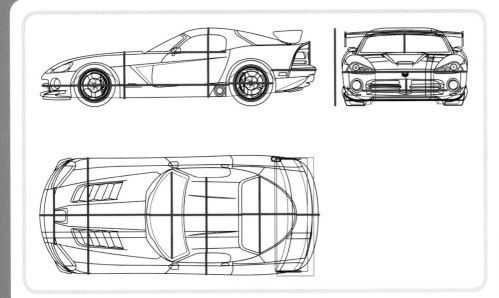

Figure 20-6: A Dodge Viper's blueprint with three views. Colored lines mark various dimensions that can be easily measured.

We can round this value to 0.36 studs/mm. This is our scaling ratio—it shows how many studs are equal to 1 mm on the blueprint:

$$1 \text{ mm} = 0.36 \text{ studs}$$

Now we can calculate any dimension of our LEGO model by measuring the corresponding dimension on the blueprint and multiplying it by the scaling ratio. For example, we can start with the width of the vehicle, which is 81 mm on the blueprint.

$$81 \text{ mm} \times 0.36 \text{ studs/mm} = 29.2 \text{ studs}$$

The width of my model should be 29 studs.

We can summarize the calculations we have done with the following formulas:

$$\text{Scaling Ratio} = \frac{\text{Dimension}_{\text{reference}}}{\text{Dimension}_{\text{blueprint}}}$$

$$\text{Dimension}_{\text{model}} = \text{Dimension}_{\text{blueprint}} \times \text{Scaling Ratio}$$

Putting it all together, we get this:

$$\text{Dimension}_{\text{model}} = \text{Dimension}_{\text{blueprint}} \times \left(\frac{\text{Dimension}_{\text{reference}}}{\text{Dimension}_{\text{blueprint}}} \right)$$

Let's put the formula to work to see how wide the same model would have to be if I scaled it for smaller LEGO wheels:

$$\text{Dimension}_{\text{reference}} = 8 \text{ studs}$$

$$\text{Dimension}_{\text{model}} = 81 \text{ mm} \times \left(\frac{8 \text{ studs}}{28 \text{ mm}} \right)$$
$$\approx 81 \text{ mm} \times 0.29 \text{ studs/mm}$$
$$\approx 23.49 \text{ studs}$$
$$\approx 23 \text{ studs}$$

And if I scaled for slightly bigger LEGO wheels:

$$\text{Dimension}_{\text{reference}} = 12 \text{ studs}$$

$$\text{Dimension}_{\text{model}} = 81 \text{ mm} \times \left(\frac{12 \text{ studs}}{28 \text{ mm}} \right)$$
$$\approx 81 \text{ mm} \times 0.43 \text{ studs/mm}$$
$$\approx 34.83 \text{ studs}$$
$$\approx 35 \text{ studs}$$

With the scaling ratio determined, we can proceed to take all the measurements we need from the blueprint. As Figure 20-6 shows, practically any object can be broken into a number of lines marking distances along the three basic dimensions: length, width, and depth.

For our Dodge Viper, the most important dimensions to calculate are the following:

* Total length, width, and height
* Height from the bottom of the body to the top of the cabin
* Height from the bottom of the side window to the top of the cabin
* Height from the bottom of the body to the top of the hood
* Length of the body behind the rear wheels
* Length of the body in front of the front wheels
* Distance between the front and rear wheels
* Length, width, and height of the windshield and all windows
* Length of the trunk and hood
* Length and width of the cabin roof
* Distance between the headlights
* Distance between the side window and the edge of the body
* Length and width of the front grille
* Height of the body's rear end above the bumper

Figures 20-7 to 20-9 show the most important dimensions of other types of vehicles.

Once you have your dimensions, it is possible to determine the *scale* of your model. To do this, we need to compare certain dimensions of the model with the dimensions of the original object using the same units. It's a good idea to check body width—it's one of the most important dimensions of any vehicle. Let's assume that I have built my Dodge Viper model 29 studs wide, as originally planned. Because 1 stud equals 8 mm, 29 studs equal 232 mm. According to Dodge, the body width of the real car is 1,920 mm. Now, 1,920 / 232 equals 8.276. We can round this number to 8, which makes 1:8 the scale of my Viper. In other words, my model is 8 times smaller than the real vehicle.

NOTE Before dividing, make sure you're using the same units for both dimensions.

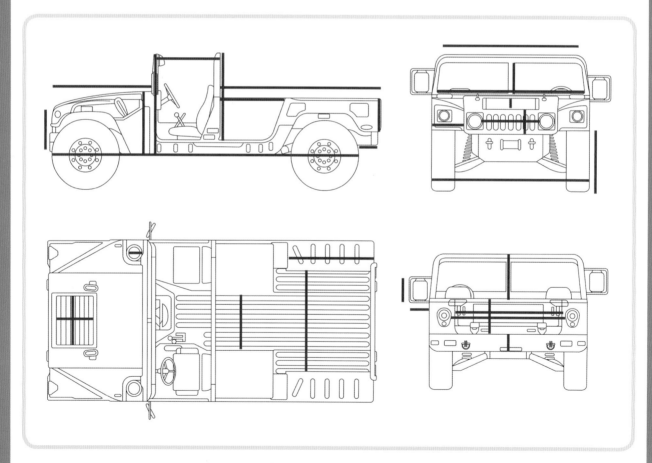

Figure 20-7: A blueprint of the Humvee with the core dimensions marked. The angular silhouette of this car is convenient for both measuring and modeling.

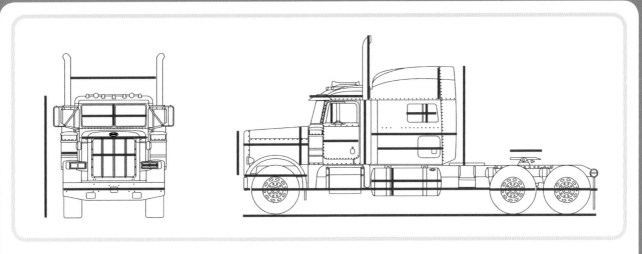

Figure 20-8: A blueprint of the Peterbilt 379 truck with the core dimensions marked. These include the dimensions of the airfoil, fifth wheel, hood, and side fuel tanks.

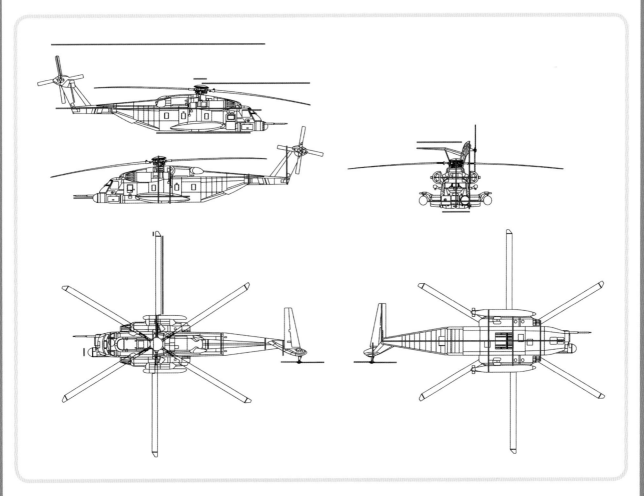

Figure 20-9: A blueprint of the Sikorsky MH-53 Pave Low helicopter with the core dimensions marked. These include the dimensions of the hull, tail boom, tail fin, both rotors, and main rotor hub.

Here is the formula:

$$\text{Scale} = \frac{\text{Dimension}_{\text{model}}}{\text{Dimension}_{\text{real}}}$$

where

$\text{Dimension}_{\text{model}}$ = the dimension on the model

$\text{Dimension}_{\text{real}}$ = the same dimension on the real object

Sometimes you may want to build a model in an already determined scale. For example, you might want to build a model that matches the size of someone else's construction. Building a model in an already determined scale makes calculating the dimensions slightly more complicated. First, you need to know at least one dimension of the original object and compare it to the same dimension on the blueprint. Let's assume I want to build the 1,920 mm wide Dodge Viper in a 1:12 scale. The width on the blueprint is 81 mm. We need to calculate the *blueprint ratio*, that is, the difference between the dimensions of the real car and those of the car on the blueprint. In this case, the ratio is 1,920 / 81, which equals 23.7. We can round the result to 24 to get our blueprint ratio. The formula is as follows:

$$\text{Blueprint Ratio} = \frac{\text{Dimension}_{\text{real}}}{\text{Dimension}_{\text{blueprint}}}$$

Now we can proceed to calculate any dimension by measuring the part on the blueprint, multiplying it by the blueprint ratio, and then dividing it by the scale. For example, let's check to see what size wheels I'm going to need for my 1:12 model. The wheel's diameter on the blueprint is 28 mm. Therefore, we perform the following calculation:

$$\frac{28 \text{ mm} \times 24}{12} = 56 \text{ mm}$$

This means the diameter of the model's wheels should be 56 mm, which equals exactly 7 studs.

Given this information, we can calculate any dimension for a predetermined scale using the following formula:

$$\text{Dimension}_{\text{model}} = \text{Dimension}_{\text{blueprint}} \times \text{Blueprint Ratio} \times \text{Scale} \times \left(\frac{1 \text{ stud}}{8 \text{ mm}}\right)$$

Of course, the actual vehicle consists of more complex shapes than just those created by perpendicular lines, and these shapes need to be approximated with LEGO pieces. But by keeping our approximation within the core dimensions, we make sure the model has the right size, right angles, and right proportions. A model that has few details awry but accurate proportions always looks better than a model with plenty of intricate details but wrong proportions. Details can impress, of course, but they can't hide errors in the proportions of the model.

Now that we can calculate the important dimensions, the next chapter will focus on modeling and other details.

21

the modeling process

Now that you have your ideal model in mind and you've learned how to scale all dimensions of the object accurately, it's time to start building. This is where you start putting your plans to the test, figuring out all those little forgotten details.

size matters

While many builders are tempted to build big, and while size can indeed be an impressive feature of any LEGO construction, Technic models don't necessarily benefit from large size. Going big creates a number of problems that increase rapidly with size, including significant stress on many sensitive pieces and problems with the mobility, balance, and structural integrity of a model. One of my models was tall and very heavy, with a tracked chassis that I thought was strongly reinforced. When it reached a weight of 7 kg, the chassis was bending so much that it couldn't keep the body stable while moving. Even sturdy Technic bricks become quite elastic if the load exerted on them is large enough.

A good rule of thumb, especially for less experienced builders, is to *build as big as needed rather than as big as possible*. In other words, you should aim to make your model as small as possible. To estimate how small it can be, you have to consider the largest single-piece elements it's going to house, such as battery boxes, motors, and IR receivers. Tracked vehicles are a good example here—their box-shaped hulls need to be wide enough for two motors set either side by side (see Figure 21-1) or back to back (see Figure 21-2). If a narrower hull is used, wider elements—such as the power supply—must be set above the tracks.

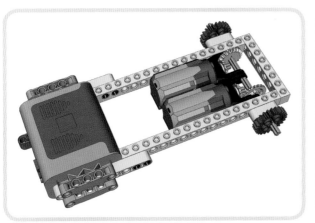

Figure 21-1: An 8-stud-wide hull with a 6-stud-wide internal space, large enough to house two PF Medium motors side by side, one driving the left sprocket wheel and the other driving the right sprocket wheel. A Power Functions battery box can also be housed inside if you make holes for it in the sides of the hull. The protruding parts of the battery box can be concealed inside the tracks.

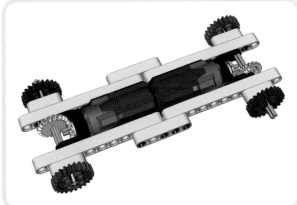

Figure 21-2: A 5-stud-wide hull with a 3-stud-wide internal space, large enough to house two PF Medium motors back to back. As the red and blue colors indicate, one motor drives the front right sprocket wheel, while the other drives the rear left one. The remaining two sprockets are idlers. Wider elements, such as the power supply, must be moved above the tracks where the hull is wider.

There are many creative ways in which you can fit large elements into a small model. For example, when building an excavator, you can try to fit small motors, such as PF Mediums, in the arm if it's massive enough, or you can install them between the tracks if the ground clearance allows (see Figure 21-3). You can also try to disguise the motors. One of the trucks I built could house motors only in its cargo hold. When I covered the motors up with plates, it looked like the cargo hold was gone. When I left the motors exposed, they looked like a load carried by the truck. Try to experiment—the more solutions you attempt, the closer you are to finding the best one.

Figure 21-4: My tow truck model housed 17 motors and nearly 19 meters of electrical wires, requiring ducts inside the body. Note that the mechanical and electrical parts are all enclosed within the body, with a few minor exceptions, such as the PF Medium motor, which is partially visible by the boom's winch, and the gears of the steering system, which are visible next to the front mudguard.

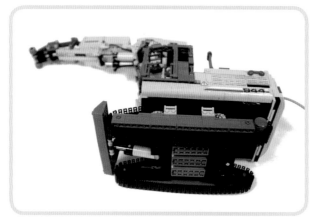

Figure 21-3: My model of the Liebherr R944C tunneling excavator housed more motors in the chassis than it did in the superstructure, at the cost of nearly zero ground clearance. With more space available inside the superstructure, I was able to take better care of its aesthetics.

The complexity of a model is another issue. Very complex models are always impressive, but they are also very difficult to build. My most complex model so far, the tow truck shown in Figure 21-4, housed 17 motors and nearly 19 m of electrical wires. To make it possible, I had to provide special isolated ducts inside its body specifically for wires. It's always a good idea to keep in mind that *complexity should be a result, not a goal in itself.*

Regardless of how confident you feel, it's good to gather some experience building reasonably small and simple models before trying something big and complex. With enough experience, you will notice that big and complex vehicles are often basically a sum of what you've done with smaller ones. For example, you might combine one model's suspension with another's gearbox. Bigger and more complex projects feel more rewarding when completed, but they are also more likely to fail.

wheels

Most LEGO wheels have different proportions than wheels used in real vehicles—they are significantly wider. While this may not be a big problem for many types of models, it can become an issue for vehicles that have more than two wheels on a single axle, trucks being the primary example.

The vast majority of trucks use double wheels on all rear axles. Models with single wheels, no matter how wide, just don't look accurate. For example, the 62.4×20 wheels, a favorite of LEGO truck builders, are 5 studs wide when doubled. That means that an axle with four wheels of this type needs a 10-stud-wide space just for the wheels alone. As Figure 21-5 shows, such an axle can't possibly get narrower than 16 studs, unless you abandon the differential.

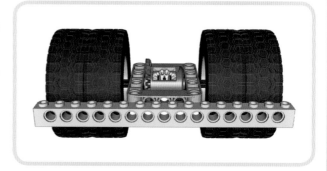

Figure 21-5: It's possible to build a driven axle with four 62.4×20 wheels that fits within a 16-stud width—but just barely.

As you can see in Figure 21-6, the width of the driven axle is one of the major factors affecting the size of the model. And things get even more difficult when there is a suspension system, especially an independent suspension that takes plenty of space between the chassis and the wheels.

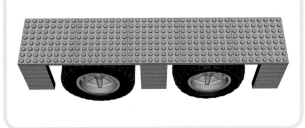

Figure 21-8: The Technic Racing wheel with a regular tire (left) and a balloon tire (right), viewed from the side and under a mudguard. The regular tire appears bigger because of its larger side surface, even though its diameter is actually slightly smaller than that of the balloon tire.

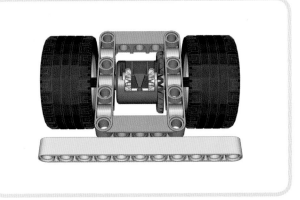

Figure 21-6: Small wheels are often wide, so it's difficult to use more than two per axle. These wheels, often used in small trucks, are 3 studs wide with just a 5.5-stud diameter. An axle with two of these is 11 studs wide, while an axle with four would be 17 studs wide.

Another important issue is the profile of the tire, which can be rectangular (as with regular tires) or round (as with so-called balloon tires). Figure 21-7 shows the same wheel with a regular and a balloon tire. The balloon tire is bigger, with a slightly larger diameter, but its side surface is smaller because of its profile. Balloon tires look good fully exposed, but when viewed from the side, especially when enclosed within the body, they can actually appear smaller than regular tires, as Figure 21-8 demonstrates.

The final issue involving wheels is steering geometry. In most real cars, when the wheels are steered, they rotate around a pivot point—that is, a vertical axle that goes nearly through their center. As the wheel is turned left or right, its center stays in place, as shown in Figure 21-9. The only LEGO wheels that follow this behavior are from the 8448 Super Street Sensation set, shown in Figure 21-10. The other wheels rotate around a pivot point that is near their side but far from their center. This means that their centers actually move around when they are turned, as shown in Figure 21-11. LEGO portal axles are most problematic when it comes to steering geometry due to the distance between the wheel and the pivot point (see Figure 21-12).

The crucial difference between the two behaviors is the amount of free space required around the wheel in order for it to turn. Wheels with "real" steering geometry require very little space, and they fit within very tight mudguards. Wheels with the LEGO steering geometry require much more space, as they move back and forth relative to the body when being turned. This means that *steered wheels in LEGO models need bigger mudguards than real steered wheels.*

The difference in the size of the mudguards can also affect the look of the LEGO model. LEGO mudguards are larger than those of the original vehicle, and the wheels appear smaller inside them. Figure 21-13 shows the difference.

As you can see, wheels require careful consideration during the modeling process. It's a common mistake to make them too small, which is more evident in a finished model than when they are too big. Many inexperienced builders produce otherwise well-designed models on wheels that are clearly too small. When in doubt, try to make your wheels too big rather than too small.

Figure 21-7: The so-called Technic Racing wheel with a regular tire (left) and a balloon tire (right). The tires are very similar in size, but the balloon variant is softer, has deeper tread, and usually works better on rough terrain.

Figure 21-9: The steering geometry of a real vehicle's wheel: As the wheel is steered, it rotates around a pivot point going through its center, marked in this series of images by an "imaginary" red axle.

Figure 21-10: Of all existing LEGO wheels, only the 8448 set's wheels rotate around their centers when steered—and they are still a little off.

Figure 21-11: When steered, a typical LEGO wheel rotates around a pivot point that is often well outside it. It requires more free space around the wheel, and it also makes the front of the vehicle move while steering in place.

Figure 21-12: LEGO portal axles are worst in terms of steering geometry. Their pivot point is located between the chassis and the gear hub, quite far from the actual wheel.

Figure 21-13: Because of their unrealistic steering geometry, LEGO wheels need more spacious mudguards than real wheels do. If the mudguards of my tow truck weren't sized up relative to the real ones, the wheels would collide with them.

other circular elements

Circular parts are quite tricky to model. You either have to use ready-made pieces, whose variety and availability are limited, or create complex structures of many small pieces, which are fragile and can disintegrate in an instant if sufficient stress is applied. Figures 21-14 and 21-15 show examples of such structures.

colors

Colors are a tricky issue when it comes to LEGO pieces. Typical Technic sets use a fairly limited palette, with yellow and red being dominant. When choosing a color, you are always limited by the availability of LEGO pieces in a particular color, and it only gets worse with bigger, more complex models that require more pieces to be visible from the outside.

Over the years, more than 150 LEGO colors have been developed, including speckle colors, glitter colors, semitransparent colors, chrome colors, and even a glow-in-the-dark color. Some of the colors have been discontinued, while new ones are added every now and then. Some colors are actually very difficult to tell apart, such as the very light bluish-grey color that dominates the Mindstorms NXT sets and regular white. In terms of the number of pieces they're used for, the top five LEGO colors are white, black, red, yellow, and blue.

Figure 21-14: The 53983 turbine is an example of a singular circular piece that builders may find disappointing. Not only does it come with a pin hole instead an axle hole, which makes it difficult to drive, but also its inner and outer blades are set in opposite directions, making it useless as a propeller. Finally, the mixed colors appeal to few.

Figure 21-15: Two circular structures built with small basic pieces. One is built around bricks with studs on the side, and the second is built with hinge plates embracing a tire. Both are prone to disintegration if sufficient stress is applied.

When making use of colors in your models, remember that dividing a model into a few unicolored areas almost always produces a better effect than mixing colors. Due to the rectangular shape of most LEGO pieces, mixtures of variously colored pieces just don't look good and make details difficult to spot.

Building the inside of your model in black conceals gaps in your model's body. Dark colors also make your model appear larger. Keep in mind that it's quite common for LEGO builders to substitute certain colors for others when they can't match the actual vehicle exactly. The most common example is LEGO dark bluish grey, which builders often use in military models instead of khaki and olive, which have no LEGO counterparts.

Sometimes it's impossible to find a given LEGO piece in the color you desire, but few builders paint their pieces to remedy this issue. This is because painting rarely produces an effect even remotely close to a stock-colored LEGO piece and is often considered cheating in the community. But this isn't true when it comes to chrome; any LEGO piece looks excellent when chromed, yet there are fewer than 100 types of originally chromed pieces. Consequently, many builders try *custom-chroming* regular LEGO pieces. The resulting size of the piece is slightly increased by the thin chrome film, so chromed pieces are best used for purely decorative purposes rather than as mechanical elements. During custom-chroming, one part of the piece is usually attached to another piece and remains free of the film; this is the only visible difference between original and custom-chromed LEGO pieces (see Figure 21-16). The two largest sources of custom-chromed LEGO pieces include the ChromeBricks shop, at *http://chromebricks.com/*, and Chrome Block City, at *http://www.bricklink.com/store.asp?p=Aurimax*.

Figure 21-16: The 62.4×20 wheel in stock metallic silver (left) and custom chromed by Chrome Block City (right). Note that the inside of the custom-chromed piece's axle hole lacks chrome film and shows that the wheel was originally white.

devil in the details

When building LEGO models, we regularly have to build things smaller than our scale would indicate. It's very difficult to model details smaller than a single stud, and that means that a lot of approximation is involved. Approximating means that some elements of your model will only vaguely resemble the real ones. You have to make some of them bigger or smaller than they should be and discard some elements entirely. Some builders also resort to custom-made stickers to reproduce the tiniest details.

The barrels of tanks are a particularly good example of approximate building. They almost always consist of a number of sections with slightly different diameters, and it's difficult to find circular LEGO pieces whose differences in diameter are proportionally the same. Because of this, some parts of the barrel need to be built thinner or thicker, as shown in Figure 21-17. It's important to consider the impression each of these deviations will create. People expect a tank to look threatening, which it does with a thick barrel. I have built many tanks with barrels too thick, and not a single person noticed it. But when I built one with a barrel too thin, I received plenty of complaints about it.

Figure 21-17: Two sections of my T-72M tank's barrel. They are made of slightly different pieces, but they have identical dimensions and a clearly visible notch between them. The resulting barrel, over 20 studs long, is surprisingly sturdy.

A good way to plan a model is to decide which of its features are most important and to try to retain or even exaggerate those features. If the original object you chose has distinctive big wheels, high ground clearance, or an elongated silhouette, exaggerating those features (within reason) can ensure that your model will be easily recognized. Bear in mind that it's easy to go over the top, as Figure 21-18 shows.

Figure 21-18: Exceptionally high ground clearance is one of the distinctive features of the real T-72M tank. This feature, however, has been exaggerated in my model.

When looking for distinctive features, always try to think in three dimensions. For example, I have built two models of the Scania trucks, whose distinctive feature is a massive front grille with large horizontal openings. The first model simply used black plates to mimic the openings, and it looked very flat when compared to the real truck. So in the second model, shown in Figures 21-19 and 21-20, I created 1-stud-deep openings closed with black plates, and this turned out much better.

Figure 21-20: I created the openings in my Scania truck's grille using a mixture of plates and tiles. It was crucial to make the ledges between the openings as thin as possible; they are only 1 tile thick here.

building at odd angles

Both Technic and non-Technic connector pieces can be used to re-create complex angles. Certain vehicles, such as the armored personnel carrier shown in Figure 21-21, have bodies with almost no right angles. By building such models with plates and tiles joined by hinged connectors, shown in Figure 21-22, you can make them look good and weigh little. Some particularly challenging angles can be retained by using Technic connectors with ball joints; Figure 21-23 shows an example of this. Bionicle sets are a good source for these kinds of connectors.

Figure 21-19: The cabin of my second model of the Scania truck with 1-stud-deep openings in its distinctive massive grille.

Figure 21-21: The Spanish BMR-2 is a typical armored personnel carrier, with a body made of surfaces connected at complex angles. My model had a body made of plates and tiles kept in place by a system of hinge plates.

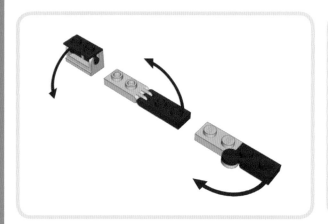

Figure 21-22: Various non-Technic connector pieces, in this case hinge bricks and plates, can keep other pieces oriented at unusual angles.

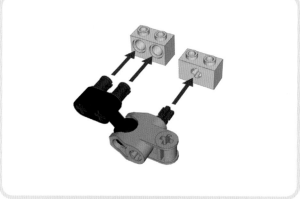

Figure 21-23: To re-create very complex angles, you may resort to joining certain Technic connectors by a ball joint. The connectors shown here can be combined with regular bricks and keep them at almost any angle.

building cleverly

When working on details, the crucial rule is to *match the pieces to the details, not the details to the pieces*. In other words, you should focus on how a detail looks and how to reproduce that look with LEGO pieces. Some builders make the mistake of focusing on some piece they want to use and then looking for a detail that looks vaguely similar.

Many objects have little details that are so distinctive that it's best to include them. For example, when building a Land Rover S2 model, I tried to re-create its distinctive tilted fuel cap. As Figure 21-24 shows, I eventually succeeded using a variant of the 1×1 brick held at an angle between two regular 1×2 Technic bricks.

minifigure chainsaw, with a hatchet attached in back and a telescope and a fire hose's nozzle in front. The gun's distinctive, large box magazine was made from a few plates with a tile on top, and it was attached to the gun with a 1×1 plate with a clip. The gun was a total of nine simple pieces, and the result prompted some viewers to ask for instructions to build it or for the address to buy the gun.

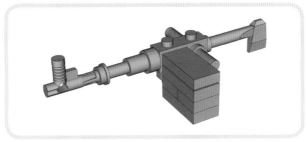

Figure 21-25: The commander's gun from my Leopard 2A4 tank model was built with nine pieces total, including minifigures' utensils, a few plates, and a tile.

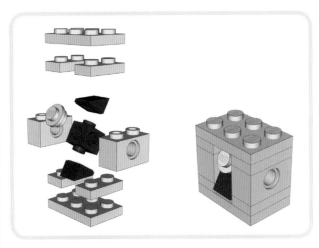

Figure 21-24: An exploded view and a complete assembly of my Land Rover S2 model's tilted fuel cap. The key was using a variant of a 1×1 brick and setting it at an angle.

A number of tiny pieces, especially LEGO minifigures' utensils, can be combined to great effect. For example, many tanks come with a commander's gun on top of the turret. In large-scale models, these guns have plenty of details, and their look is often unique for a given type of tank. When building a model of the Leopard 2A4 tank, I had the choice to use some simple piece that looked like a gun to me or to use one of the few ready-made LEGO guns. Neither of these options produced an accurate-looking result, so I eventually combined a few minifigures' utensils, creating the gun shown in Figure 21-25. The gun was built around the body of a

the next step: controlling your models

Finally, remember that the fun doesn't have to end with building your model. Building a controller for complex models can be a challenge of its own, as exemplified by a model of the Demag H135 excavator built by Emil "Emilus" Okliński (see Figure 21-26). The model uses two NXT bricks in conjunction with another two bricks in the remote to enable realistic remote control. The remote includes complex joysticks built around NXT motors with internal rotation counters, and it takes advantage of the Bluetooth link to connect with the model. Some functions of the model, such as its internal pneumatic compressor, are controlled automatically, and some of its working parameters can be read from the remote. An extensive description of Emil's model is available at *http://www.eurobricks.com/forum/index.php?showtopic= 64131*.

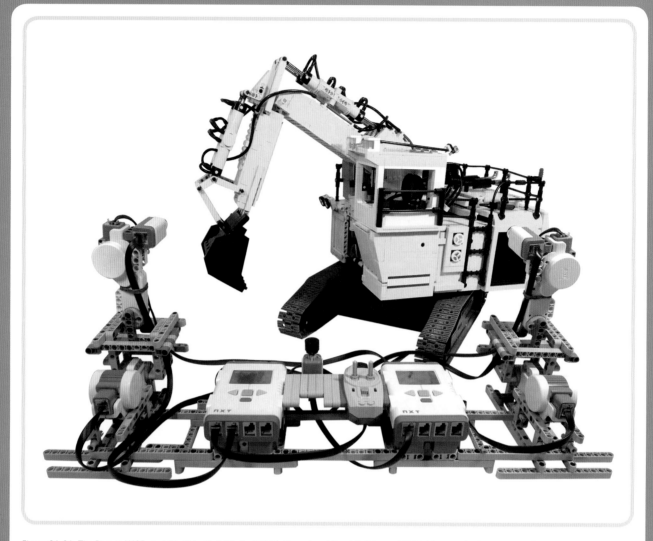

Figure 21-26: The Demag H135 model built by Emil "Emilus" Okliński employed four Mindstorms NXT bricks—two in the remote and another two in the model—to achieve realistic remote control. The complex joysticks based on NXT motors and the use of a Bluetooth link between the remote and the model provided the "driver" with an unparalleled experience.

afterword

I hope that by now you've gained a good understanding of the LEGO Technic system and how to build your own models. If you're looking for more avenues to explore, I can recommend other interesting pieces no longer in production, such as elements of the radio control system (8366 set) and the barcode IR system (8479 set), an entire discontinued building system (8369 set), and some very rare modern pieces, like the Power Functions solar panel and energy display (9688 set).

And of course the LEGO Group also keeps introducing new parts, making new solutions possible or simplifying existing designs. Even if you're a fan of the old school "all studfull" style of building, it pays to keep track of these novelties. For more inspiration, there is the worldwide community of LEGO builders who keep inventing and perfecting designs and sharing their ideas freely for others to try.

Having built well over 120 MOCs in the last few years, I can say that the trial and error of building your own constructions is not the bad part of building—it's actually the most enjoyable part. Getting to play with your finished working construction is a nice touch, but the real pleasure comes from successfully tackling problems, big and small, which always crop up when you choose to create rather than to build from instructions. With enough trial and error, the only real limit to what you can build is your own imagination.

It is my wish that this book helps you to experience plenty of that pleasure as you play with LEGO pieces.

index

hockey spring, 195
Hoeken's linkage, 73
holes in bricks, 10
hoses
    connecting, 110
    non-LEGO, 112
    pneumatic, 108–109
    splitting, 110
    use of term, 109
hubs, *305*
Humvee, *26, 312*
hydraulic system, turning pneumatic
    system into, 113

I

idler gears, 44–45, 59
independent axle, 226–229
independent suspension, 220–221
    defined, 204
    double-wishbone, 206–207
input axle, 44
interacting gears, 45
intermittent rotary motion, 89
inverse tangent (arctangent), 202
inversely proportional, speed and
    torque as, 44

J

Jeep Wrangler Rubicon, *297*
jib, 158–159
joints, universal. *See* universal joints
jumper plates, 15

K

Kenworth Road Train model, *18*
knob wheels, 55, *203*
knobs
    hard-coupling with, *280*
    wear of, *160*

L

L motor, Power Functions, 168
large cylinder, 107
LEDs, 91–92, 187–188
LEGO pneumatic engine (LPE), 124–134
Leopard 2A4 tank, *301*, 323
levers, 67–71
    classes of, 68–69
    effort of, 67

fulcrums of, 67–69
law of the lever, 67
and linkages, 69–71
load of, 67, 70
mechanical advantage of, 72
parallel, 70, 71
remotes with, *179–180*
Liebherr LTM1200 mobile telescopic
    crane, *310*
Liebherr R944C, *243*
liftarms, 12
lights
    flashing, 91–92
    reverse, 90–91
    turn signals, 92–95
linear (sequential) transmissions, 252
linear actuators, 183–186
    flawed, 184–185
    large, 183–185
    vs. pneumatics, 185–186
    production code on, 184–185
    small, 185
    transferring drive to, *184, 185*
linear clutches, 83–84
linear motion, converting rotary motion to,
    71–72
linear speed, defined, 3
linkages, 71–76
    Chebyshev linkage, 73
    Hoeken's linkage, 73
    and levers, 69–71
    pantograph, 73
    Peaucellier–Lipkin cell, 74
    rocking motion of, 71, 74
    Sarrus linkage, 74–75
    scissor linkage, 75–76
    Scott-Russell linkage, 75
    Watt's linkage, 76
live axle. *See* floating axle suspension
load
    of levers, 67, 70
    rotating under large loads, 55
load-bearing structures, 151–159
    rails, chassis, and body frames, 151–153
    trusses, 154–159
        Brown truss, 155–156
        choosing, 157–159
        triangular Warren truss, 156–157
        Warren truss, 156
locking mechanisms, 82–83

long pins, 11, 12
longitudinal subtractor, 282–287
longnose trucks, 296–298
LPE (LEGO pneumatic engine), 124–134
L-shaped beams, *143*
luff tackle, 63

M

M (Medium) motor, Power Functions,
    28, 168
Maltese cross mechanisms. *See* Geneva
    mechanisms
MAN TGS truck, *298*
manometer, 112
maximum steering angle, 6
mechanical advantage, 61–62
    levers, 67, 72
    pulley systems
        differential pulley system, 64–65
        power pulley system, 65–66
        simple pulley system, 62–63
mechanical power, defined, 3
mechanical solutions, custom, 77–101
    differential, 77–78
    differential locks, 78–82
    double-axle turntable transmission,
        96–100
    eccentric mechanisms, 84–85
    flashing lights, 91–92
    Geneva mechanisms, 89–90
    linear clutches, 83–84
    Oldham couplings, 87–88
    ratchets, 82–83
    reverse lights, 90–91
    Schmidt couplings, 88
    Scotch yokes, 85–86
    stepper motors, 88–89
    turn signals, 92–95
    universal joint, 101
mechanics, vs. pneumatics, 47
Medium (M) motor, Power Functions,
    28, 168
microleaks, 103
Micromotor, 166–167
Micromotor pulley, 59, 65
mineral oil, 113
misaligned pieces, 27
MOCs (My Own Creations), 17
Model Team approach, 26

motors, 163–164
  controlling, 171–174
  E motor, 167
  L motor, 168
  Medium (M) motor, 168
  Servo motor, 169
  XL motor, 169
power supplies, 172–175
receiver, 175–176
remotes, 176–177
  controlling, 172–174
  modifying, 177–182
switches, 28, 90, 92
power pulley system, 65–66
power supply, 173
power take-off (PTO), 110
powertrain, 6
pressure generator, 103
pressure switch, automated, 123–124
production code, on linear actuators,
    184–185
propellers, 302, *303*
PTO (power take-off), 110
pulleys, 59–61
  vs. chains, 60
  in Micromotor, 167
  ratios between, 59–60
  rubber bands used with, 60
  slippage, 60
  string and pulley systems, 61–66
    differential pulley system, 63–65
    power pulley system, 65–66
    simple pulley system, 62–63
pumps, pneumatic, 105–106
  in motorized compressors, 115–116
  in New system, 104
  in Old system, 103
pushrods, 84

R

rack gear, 193
rack-and-pinion gearset, 191
racks, driving with worm gear, 49
radius, turning, 6–7, 199
rails, 151–153
ratchets, 82–83
RC motor, 170
reach stacker, 7
rear-wheel drive (RWD), 7

receivers, 172–176
receiving mechanism, 6
rechargeable battery, 175
red pieces, strength of, 160
regular (nonlinear) transmissions, 252
regular LEGO bricks, 18
reinforcement, 137–160. *See also* load-
    bearing structures
  choosing strongest pieces, 159–160
  defined, 19
  of differential casings, 144–148
  right way to reinforce, 140–144
  where to reinforce, 138–140
  why things fall apart, 137–140
  of worm gear casings, 149–150
remotes, 176–177
  with central steering wheel, 181–183
  modifying, 177–182
  multiple, using simultaneously, 174
  with sideways lever, *179*
  with steering wheel, *178*
  using many receivers with single
    remote, 173
resistance, and surfaces, 4–5
return rollers, 245
return-to-center steering, 194–195
reverse gear, in transmissions, 254
reverse lights, 90–91
RG-35 4×4 MRAP vehicle, *26, 26, 214*
ride height, 8
rigid connections
  vs. nonrigid connection, 21
  between perpendicular beams, 22
  using single axle, 21
ripple, of motorized compressors, 115
road wheels, 245, 249–250
rocking compressor, 116–117, *118*
rocking motion
  converting rotary motion to, 84–85
  converting to linear motion, 71
  of linkages, 71, 74
rolling resistance, 4–5
rotary motion
  continuous, converting into
    intermittent, 89
  converting to linear motion, 71–72
  converting to rocking motion, 84–85
rotational direction of gears, controlling,
    47–48
rotational speed, defined, 3

rotors, 303–305
RPM (rotations per minute), 3
rubber bands
  used for self-centering steering, 195
  used with CVTs, 260
  used with pulleys, 60
rubber tracks, 241
RWD (rear-wheel drive), 7

S

Sarrus linkage, 74–75
scaling, 307–314
  and blueprints, 307–309
  and points of reference, 309
Schmidt couplings, 88
scissor linkage, 75–76
Scotch yokes, 85–86
Scott-Russell linkage, 75
seams, weak, 138
sequential (linear) transmissions, 252
Servo motor, Power Functions, 169
sets, Technic, 24–26
shock absorbers, *209, 211*
  alternative to, 248–249
  flexible axles as, 34
  for road wheels in a track, 247
  Tatra-type suspension stabilized with,
    217–220
  trailing arms suspension with, 247
  used with chains, 58
side gears (spider gears), 278
sidecars, 299
sideways lever, remotes with, *179–180*
Sikorsky MH-53 Pave Low helicopter,
    303, 313
single-bevel gears, 50, 51
single-cylinder pneumatic engines, 125–127
size considerations, 315–316
size of parts, and efficiency, 5
sliders, 130
sliding worm gear, 120
slippage
  of 24-tooth gear with clutch, 52
  and differentials, 78, 80
  in pulley system, 60
small cylinder, 108
smooth half bush, with cutout, 37
snow groomer, *25*
soft axles. *See* flexible axles

updates and additional resources

For updates, errata, and other information about the book, visit *http://nostarch.com/technicbuilder*.

While you're there, check out the online resources for this book, including gearing tools, a tire reference sheet, parts datasheets, a list of LEGO fan communities, and much more. To follow Sariel's work, visit him at *http://sariel.pl*.

More no-nonsense books from **no starch press**

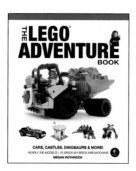

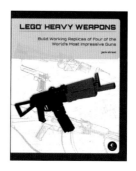

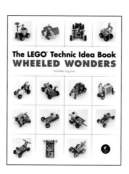

Visit *nostarch.com/ catalog/lego* for a full list of titles.

phone 800.420.7240 or 415.863.9900 | fax 415.863.9950 | sales@nostarch.com | www.nostarch.com